Greece

Greece

A Short History of a Long Story, 7,000 BCE to the Present

Carol G. Thomas

WILEY Blackwell

This edition first published 2014
© 2014 John Wiley & Sons, Inc.

Registered Office
John Wiley & Sons, Ltd, The Atrium, Southern Gate, Chichester, West Sussex, PO19 8SQ, UK

Editorial Offices
350 Main Street, Malden, MA 02148-5020, USA
9600 Garsington Road, Oxford, OX4 2DQ, UK
The Atrium, Southern Gate, Chichester, West Sussex, PO19 8SQ, UK

For details of our global editorial offices, for customer services, and for information about how
to apply for permission to reuse the copyright material in this book please see our website at
www.wiley.com/wiley-blackwell.

The right of Carol G. Thomas to be identified as the author of this work has been asserted in accordance
with the UK Copyright, Designs and Patents Act 1988.

Library of Congress Cataloging-in-Publication Data

Thomas, Carol G., 1938–
Greece : a short history of a long story, 7,000 BCE to the present / Carol G. Thomas.
    pages   cm
  Includes bibliographical references and index.
  ISBN 978-1-118-63190-4 (cloth) – ISBN 978-1-118-63175-1 (paper)   1. Greece–History.
2. Greece–Civilization. I. Title.
  DF757.T46 2014
  949.5–dc23
                                              2014015660

A catalogue record for this book is available from the British Library.

Cover image: Banana Pancake/Alamy

Set in 9/11pt Sabon by SPi Publisher Services, Pondicherry, India

Printed in Singapore by C.O.S. Printers Pte Ltd

1   2014

Contents

Preface

The history of Greece is the story of one of the world's most durable cultures. Even omitting the earliest wanderers into the Greek mainland who began to arrive about 70,000 years ago, the story reaches back to nearly 7,000 BCE[1] with the first settled villages of farmers and herders. No written evidence exists to identify these peasants as Greek speakers. However, one view is that agriculture and domestication spread from what is now Turkey to Greece and then further west and that the carriers were people who spoke an Indo-European language. Greek is an Indo-European language. Thus, if not in the form that Thucydides and Socrates spoke, the language of these early farmers would have been the ancestral version of Classical Greek. Inasmuch as an abiding characteristic of Greek identity is the Greek language, the account of people living in the peninsula jutting into the Aegean Sea and on the islands of that same sea reaches deep into prehistory.

This view that agriculture and Indo-European languages spread together is not universally accepted but, even so, it is certain that the language of the second millennium Bronze Age civilization in Greece was an early form of Greek. Tablets discovered in the remains of citadel centers like Mycenae, Pylos, and Thebes were inscribed in a syllabic mode of writing that has been deciphered as an archaic form of later Greek. Thus the heroic age associated with the Homeric epics can be associated with the latter-day heroes of the Persian Wars. While the Bronze Age centers in the Aegean underwent the same time of troubles that disrupted life in the entire eastern Mediterranean, shrunken relics of the past glorious world persisted through a 400 year period often known as the Dark Age, although as we will see it was not completely dark. After the widespread destruction and depopulation at the end of the second millennium, inhabitants of tiny hamlets survived, then slowly but steadily they began to grow in numbers and skills. By the end of the eighth century BCE, an age of revolution marked the end of darkness. The product was the Classical Age, the age of the *polis* (the type of community that formed the basis of this period of Greek history) and the brilliant institutional and intellectual life it produced. Its language attested in texts and inscriptions was Greek.

When the Macedonian kings Philip II and his son Alexander III harnessed Greek hoplite strength to the Macedonian army and proceeded to conquer the east as far distant as the Indus River Valley, the Greeks found themselves in a larger, different world. Nonetheless, this world did not lose its Hellenic base and the three centuries from 323 to 30 BCE are known as Hellenistic, or Greek-like, due to the strong continuing Greek elements that helped to secure its foundations. The language of the Hellenistic kingdoms was Greek, albeit influenced by languages in the territories brought under Greco/Macedonian control.

Much the same situation prevailed when the Romans replaced the Hellenistic kings: Greece became a province to be sure but some of the best of the Romans agreed with the Roman poet Horace that "Conquered Greece took its captor captive."[2] One concrete example is the important *polis* of Corinth which had been destroyed in the mid-second century BCE and was re-founded as a Roman city; its inhabitants were Latin-speaking Romans. Within two generations, however, the dominant language had become Greek. In fact, the eastern portion of the once-unified empire was spared the collapse of the western half, surviving after 476 CE to become a new empire centered on the city of Constantinople, which had been founded a millennium earlier as a Greek colonial *polis*. Changes in institutions, beliefs, and values were numerous, certainly. However, the official imperial language reverted to Greek and treasures from the past – both physical and intellectual – were deliberately preserved.

Constantinople could not withstand either the Crusaders from the west or the Ottoman Turks from the east; the Byzantine Empire officially disappeared in 1453 CE. Nonetheless, Ottoman rule left much of the governance of its Greek appendage to local authority. Consequently, Orthodox Christianity, the Greek language, and basic patterns of daily existence persisted through the more than 350 years of Ottoman control. In the last decades of that control, support for Greek freedom was fueled by a philhellenism that was grounded as much in the glory of the Greek past as in the present-day nature of the land and its people.

Knowledge of the link between the past and the present increased with the recognition of the new, independent Greek state. It is valuable to note the concurrence of three events in the year 1834: a king of Greece (Otho) made his official entry into the new capital, Athens; restoration of the Parthenon was begun; and the Governmental Archaeological department was established. The success of the Modern Greek state was an incentive to learn more about the past history of the country as it emerged from subject status to become a fledging independent state under the tutelage of major powers and, finally, became an active partner in international affairs.

Thus, evidence to connect Greek-language speakers with the eastern-most peninsula of Europe exists but, even if the story is connected, how can the wealth of information of 9,000 years be packed into a short history? The father of history, Herodotus, crafted an account of the war between the Greeks and the Persians which dates to roughly a decade from 492 to 479 BCE. His history covers 400 pages in the Oxford Greek edition!

Two helpful aids exist. First, life in Greece has produced clear divisions between major periods of time. At some points an existing way of life was almost completely destroyed. The Age of Heroes, identified now with the Bronze Age, is a powerful example: some, but not many, people were spared from events yet unknown and they managed to reconstruct a stable life from the existing elements over five centuries. At other points in its long history, Greece was taken captive by non-Greeks – the

Romans and later the Ottoman Turks. Greece survived the fall of Rome and recreated the Greek Byzantine Age. With the initial defeat of the Ottomans in 1821, Greeks began to reshape their Modern Greek culture. These changes create manageable periods of the nature of Greek life over time.

The existence of neatly defined periods is extremely useful but there are nine of them. How is it possible that the complete story of each of them be told in a short history? The standards of Herodotus would require about 3,600 pages of printed text! A second tool of archaeologists and anthropologists offers a solution. It is termed Systems Theory and focuses on the two elements in a "system" – people and the natural environment in which they live. The interplay of humans with the environment produces the six basic features of a culture:

1. means of subsistence: how the environment can maintain human life;
2. material goods and technology: how the environment can provide tools;
3. social structure and intrapersonal relations;
4. political organization;
5. communication and trade beyond the immediate community;
6. symbolic attributes: ways of expressing knowledge, beliefs, and feelings about the world.

As is often the case with theoretical analysis, the Systems Theory approach is not universally admired or employed although appreciation of its value has increased from the time of its introduction in the mid-twentieth century. It is extremely useful in providing a picture of the six aspects of a given culture and, when joined with the pattern of life in the several periods of the long story, it offers a tool for comparison. Has the life of inhabitants of Greece over 9,000 years demonstrated a persistent similarity in the interaction between people and their environment or rather does that way of life reveal fundamental differences?

The use of this approach has the additional merit of allowing us to consider both positive and negative change in the larger picture of the culture as the result of specific developments in one or more of the aspects of interaction between people and their environment. The six basic features of this interaction are liable to damage or even collapse the existing structure if changed conditions cannot be absorbed. As mentioned above, the story of Greece has fragile as well as strong ages. An important question, consequently, is whether a rebuilding after collapse will retain earlier features or whether the new structure will be entirely different.

These tools, then, facilitate a coherent short history of the long story of Greece: a focus on the phases of that narrative will concentrate on the six aspects of culture produced by the interaction of people with their environment. However, a history of a way of life based on features created between people and their environment may be boring as well as incomplete since history is the story of people, many of whom shaped the events and products of their own times. For each chapter, specific individuals will personalize the nature of Greece during that period of time. The choices reflect that variety of participants in the long story: women *and* men; the common members of society as well as the elite; farmers, philosophers, *and* political leaders, and even non-Greeks, are all excellent windows to a culture.

The first chapter examines the location in which it originated and which has remained essentially the same to the present. This location fashioned a way of life that suited the often unfriendly conditions of the Aegean region. The emergence of the first complex civilization in that location is the subject of the second chapter – "The Age of Heroes" – which examines Bronze Age Greece. After the collapse of this civilization, the struggle to survive the difficult Dark Age over more than four centuries produced a reconstruction of Greek society that would become the Classical civilization of Greece. This process is the subject of the third chapter while the "second age of heroes," from the late eighth century to the fourth BCE, is the story of the fourth chapter.

Chapter 5 surveys the history of Greece as an appendage to Macedonian power. After the successful expansion of Philip II into the Greek world followed by Alexander's campaigns reaching to India, Greece was subservient to the new kingdoms of the Hellenistic monarchs of the east into the first century BCE. Subsequently, the Hellenistic kingdoms fell to the empire forged by the Roman legions, the subject of Chapter 6. When the Roman emperors were superceded by Germanic kings in the west, the Byzantine Empire took root in the east. Its history is the subject of Chapter 7. Ottoman rule from 1453 to 1821, treated in Chapter 8, ended with the creation of a modern nation state of Greece. The final two chapters continue the story from the early nineteenth century into the present century. A brief conclusion draws together the major forces of these 9,000 years.

Four major themes intertwine from the start of the story to its end: environment, location, outreach, and the impact of other cultures. Geography is essential to a proper understanding of any people's history but it is a critical factor in Greek development. Nearly 80 percent of the mainland and islands that constitute the land is mountainous; navigable rivers are virtually absent and annual rainfall is limited. Consequently, obtaining even bare subsistence is often extremely difficult. Inasmuch as such difficult conditions have remained largely unchanged from the Neolithic Age to the present, efforts to maintain life consume much of the collective energy of the inhabitants of Greece.

These same conditions have fostered regionalism throughout Greek history from the time of the first small villages to the late twentieth century. Evidence from the Neolithic Age indicates that villages were independent of one another. As recently as 1980, Greece could count approximately 2,000 separate villages but only three urban centers. This physical division will encourage particularism and it has worked against centralization until just recently. On its entrance into the European Union, the Hellenic Marine Consortium recognized the need to consolidate the efforts of Greek ship owners but a founding member of that Consortium rued, "For 20 Greeks to agree is difficult. For 1,000, it would be impossible." Greeks of the Classical Age living in more than 1,000 independent *polis* communities would surely agree.

The significance of the location of the Greek world is another abiding influence in the story. It stands at the crossroads of three continents: Asia is eastward across the Aegean, Africa on the southern coast of the Mediterranean, and Europe northward in the Balkans. Communication is not difficult once sea travel has been mastered. And since the sea offered the easiest means of travel, Greeks became skilled in

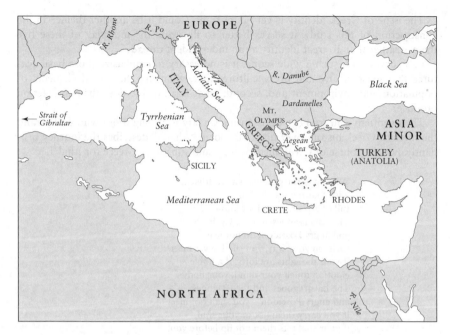

Figure 0.1   The Mediterranean Sea. Source: Jason Shattuck

navigation from very early times. Greeks would constantly learn from and teach others in the Mediterranean region. And others would be attracted to Greece for various reasons, some cordial, others militantly unfriendly. The direction and nature of these contacts will explain much in the history of Greece.

Such interaction is the root of another theme, namely the balance between indigenous and external features of culture in Greece. Many newcomers have been drawn to Greece to become permanent inhabitants since 7,000 BCE. Also, for more than 1,150 years of its story, Greece was controlled by outside powers – Hellenistic kings, Romans, and Ottoman Turks. How much of the Hellenic way of life survived these long periods of dependence? Is Modern Greek culture a true descendant of its earlier manifestations? The question of continuity and discontinuity should be asked not only of the newest phase of the story of Greece but throughout its long history.

The long history of Greece has produced tensions linked with the question of how Greeks of one age identify with Greeks living in an earlier age. What is their identity and how is that identity defined by language, culture, and political form? The Ancient Greek language – both spoken and written – is not identical with Modern Greek language. Culture has obviously changed significantly, as a comparison between Modern Greek Orthodox religion and faith in the Olympian deities clearly demonstrates. Greece is now an independent nation-state rather than a bevy of individual city-states.

The issue of Greek identity is very important. Could it be another theme? In the construction of this study, it serves better to illustrate the interplay of these five themes rather than to treat identity as an independent thread.

In a survey with such a wide scope, it is necessary to emphasize those basic features that exist in any and every culture: first, what are the linked elements of population and environment and, second, what form of life does their interaction produce?

The twentieth-century poet Constantine Cavafy is among those who understand the force of Greek history over time. His poem "Ithaka" describes the journey brilliantly. For the course of Greek history, we could substitute Greece for Ithaka.

> When you start on the way to Ithaca,
> wish that the way be long,
> full of adventure, full of knowledge.
> The Laistrygones and the Cyclopes,
> and angry Poseidon, do not fear:
> such, on your way, you shall never meet
> if your thoughts are lofty, if a noble
> emotion touch your mind, your body.
> The Laistrygones and the Cyclopes,
> and angry Poseidon – you shall not meet
> if you carry them not in your soul,
> if your soul sets them not up before you.
>
> Wish that the way be long,
> That on many summer mornings,
> with great pleasure, great delight,
> you enter harbours for the first time seen;
> that you stop at Phoenician marts,
> and procure the goodly merchandise,
> mother-of-pearl and coral, amber and ebony,
> and sensual perfume of all kinds,
> plenty of sensual perfumes especially;
> to wend your way to many Egyptian cities,
> to learn and yet to learn from the wise.
>
> Ever keep Ithaca in your mind.
> Your return thither is your goal.
> But do not hasten at all your voyage,
> better that it last for many years;
> and full of year at length you anchor at your isle,
> rich with all that you gained on the way;
> do not expect Ithaca to give you riches.
> Ithaca gave you your fair voyage.
> Without her you would not have ventured on the way.
> But she has no more to give you.
>
> And if you find Ithaca a poor place
> she has not mocked you.
> You have become so wise, so full of experience,
> that you should understand already what
> these Ithacas mean.[3]

Notes

1. The dates range over the two major phases of the human story. In this book, they are denoted by BCE and CE, namely before the common era and the common era.
2. Horace, *Epistles* II, 1, 156–157.
3. Constantine P. Cavafy, "Ithaca," translated by George Valassopoulo, *The Criterion* 2/8, July 1924.

Acknowledgments

This short history of the long story of Greece has a long history of its own and represents the contributions of many people over numerous years. My own sphere of teaching and scholarship focusing on Ancient Greece expanded as I realized that the on-going history of Greece demanded attention. The Hellenic Studies Program at the University of Washington (which I directed for eight years) was designed to include the longue durée. With essential aid from my colleagues, I developed a gradually expanding course that culminated in Greek History from the Neolithic Age to the present. I am deeply indebted to those colleagues who were my "mentors" and to the students who took that course and were willing to offer their advice for additions and improvements.

Several years ago, a book seemed a possibility. The award of the Vidalakis Professorship in Hellenic Studies provided funds for me to secure the necessary resources and the aid of assistants. The professorship was endowed by Drs Nick and Nancy Vidalakis whose support of Hellenic studies is widespread and generous. To hold the professorship that they established at the University of Washington is a great honor.

The efforts of several graduate students in the department of history have been critical in the later stages of creating the book. Amy Absher helped to organize a first draft, vetted chapters, created illustrations, and carefully organized the results. These tasks were assumed by Arna Elezovic (currently a graduate student) when Dr Absher took an appointment at Case Western University. Arna has continued all of the above tasks as well as writing essays on some of the individuals who illustrate the nature of life in each period. Her technological capabilities are akin to those of Jason Shattuck (now Dr Shattuck) who created the maps and many of the illustrations. Another former graduate student and co-author of two books (Craig Conant) has compiled the index. Anne Lou Robkin (PhD, friend, scholar, and artist) produced two of the images. In a word, students have been essential partners in mutually interactive scholarship.

Publishing with Wiley Blackwell has been a joy on several occasions. In fact, it was a goal since I first visited the Blackwell store in Oxford as a recent PhD: "Perhaps one day," I thought, "I might be a Blackwell author." The editors with whom I have worked are extraordinary. For this book I thank Haze Humbert and Allison Kostka and, at an earlier stage, Ben Thatcher. Included in the process have been the comments of readers who are anonymous to me but I am thankful for their helpful, encouraging comments. The assistance of Joanna Pyke in the final copy-editing was flawless.

Such support was supplemented by the engagement of numerous Greek friends. I am especially beholden to Dr Theo Antikas and Laura Wynn-Antikas in Greece; Dr George Stamatoyannopoulos at the University of Washington; and the Rakus family of Seattle.

The most crucial role was that of Richard Rigby Johnson, my English-American husband and Professor of Early American History. I have a photo on my desk showing him as an Oxford University student standing by the wall at Tiryns. We have travelled often to Greece together; those visits, his advice, and his steadfast importance to my life are embedded in these pages.

1

Mountains and Sea

As Poseidon explains in the *Iliad*, three brothers born to Rhea and Cronus divided the universe into equal shares among themselves on the death of their father. Poseidon got the sea as his eternal domain, while Zeus was allotted the broad sky with clouds and bright air and Hades received the underworld. Earth and Mount Olympus were common realms to all. The gods, too, understand the importance of the mountains and the sea.[1]

The division also describes the two physical features that have shaped life throughout the region bounded by the Aegean and Adriatic seas from deep antiquity to the present: mountains that are the predominant feature of the Greek landscape and the omnipresence of the sea. Comprising 75 percent of the landmass, the mountainous terrain prescribed a way of life in both economic and political respects while the surrounding seas provided access to outsiders and enabled inhabitants to expand beyond their core.

A history of a culture should begin with its physical environment for two reasons. First, of the two major elements that shape the nature of a culture – namely the nature of its environment and the humans that do the shaping of the environment – the environment was earliest in place. Thus the essential nature of the environment had been formed millennia before the human element entered the picture. A second reason is that for the prehistoric past, it is difficult – sometimes impossible – to identify the human element. Bones, when they have been found, do not speak a language and, consequently, identification with a specific people is impossible. In the case of Greece, the setting also deserves priority inasmuch as the entire history of Greece is grounded in virtually the same place and environment. Thus, many of the same climatic conditions and natural resources as well as the configuration of the land and proximity to the sea have presented both assets and difficulties to the people who must deal with them. The physical situation of people bounded primarily by the Aegean and Adriatic/Ionian seas brought contact with other groups over the millennia of the human story. Contact may occasion hostility or it may produce borrowings of features of other cultures. The interplay is an on-going theme of this book.

Greece: A Short History of a Long Story, 7,000 BCE to the Present, First Edition.
Carol G. Thomas.
© 2014 John Wiley & Sons, Inc. Published 2014 by John Wiley & Sons, Inc.

Figure 1.1   Greece: "Mountains and Seas." Source: Jason Shattuck

Greek culture is not unique in being shaped by its physical environment but it is important to appreciate the enormous role that its physical setting has played in the 9,000 years of Greek history. Positioned mid-way between the prevailing environmental conditions of the European continent and those of North Africa, Greece must be understood in terms of its location within the sea that combines the conditions of Europe with those of Africa. The relation shaped its earliest way of life and remains fundamental today as each period of Greek history demonstrates.

Although it was identifiable as a body of water 150 million years ago, the final shaping of the Mediterranean occurred more recently, some 15 million years ago. In size, the sea is 2,965,500 square kilometers. It extends 3,733 kilometers from west to east and its width varies considerably due to the configuration of the surrounding land: the southern coast is generally smooth while the northern coast is defined by jutting peninsulas and deep bays that are seas in their own right. The configuration draws continents together at several points, but separates them in other regions. In the west, the Iberian peninsula is separated from northern Africa by the Strait of Gibraltar which, at its narrowest point, is a little more than 24 kilometers. Moving eastward, the islands of Corsica and Sardinia are separated from the mainland by the Ligurian Sea to the north and the Tyrrhenian Sea to the east that extends to the 1,046 kilometer long peninsula of Italy. The toe of Italy is narrowly separated from the island of Sicily which, in turn, is roughly 160 kilometers from the north coast of Africa. The Adriatic Sea divides the Italian peninsula from the Greek peninsula while the Aegean stands between the Greek peninsula and Anatolia. A voyage of more than 885 kilometers, as the crow flies, must be undertaken to reach the coast of Africa from the northern Aegean. However, even in the more expansive eastern waters, a sailor is rarely out of sight of land, either a portion of the coastal ring of land encompassing the sea or one of the numerous islands that dot the waters of the sea. Knowledge of distances between landmasses coupled with an understanding of seafaring on the part of peoples in the Mediterranean sphere make contact between them likely.

The Mediterranean is connected with other bodies of water by straits to both the west and the east: the Strait of Gibraltar leads to the Atlantic Ocean and the Dardanelles provide an entrance to the Propontis and ultimately to the Black Sea. Inflow of water from these two points provides much of the replenishment of an otherwise essentially static body of water. This contained nature of the water produces a high salinity due to a greater rate of evaporation than of precipitation of new water. The seafloor is deep; in most parts of the Mediterranean the water's depth is at least 10,620 meters; in the Ionian Sea soundings have indicated a depth of twice that amount. Water temperature remains quite constant at 13 °C throughout the year. The consistency of these conditions throughout the Mediterranean stimulates common environmental conditions, with both positive and negative results.

Since it is so tightly enclosed, the water is virtually tide-less. Currents, which cause its movement, are dependent upon the inflow of water, particularly that coming through the Strait of Gibraltar which is stronger than the current from the Black Sea. The current from the Atlantic continues along the North African coast, up the coast of the Levant, and west along the southern shore of Anatolia. Still moving westward, the current flows along the Greek coast and into the Adriatic. At Sicily, the current turns north along the Italian coast, then it flows along the coasts of southern France and Spain. Smaller, local currents exist in several areas such as the eastern and western coasts of Crete and off southern France. When sailors understand the force of the currents, maritime travel becomes easier.

Prevailing winds blow from both north and south into the Mediterranean. Strongest are the two paths of the Mistral which join over southern France; second in force is the Bora which reaches the Adriatic in the northeast. The Meltemi winds push down from the Dardanelles strait into the Aegean in the summer months and the Scirocco winds head northward into the Mediterranean along much of the African coast. The areas experiencing the strongest force of winds are the Aegean, the northern Adriatic, and the coastal area of southern France near Marseilles. Knowing and using the winds is essential to navigation in the Mediterranean. Thus, if the Mistral was blowing, it would provide power for eastward travel and if it was strong "then it and the eastbound north African current between them would carry the ship two-thirds of the way there, almost automatically, leaving the captain with no problem in seamanship more profound than managing to dodge Sardinia and Sicily."[2] In sailing westward, on the other hand, the task was to avoid the Mistral which, coming head-on, would impede rather than aid the journey. Recent evidence indicates that people had learned the nature of the currents and winds of the Mediterranean and appreciated the benefits and threats of sailing as early as 125,000 years ago.

The lands that surround the great sea and the large number of islands in that sea share many features. Low-lying coast is generally limestone or earth impregnated with lime and, thus, the soil is often thin. Certain river mouths, such as the Nile, Po, and Rhone, are especially fertile and, as a consequence, may be objects of desire to outsiders. The coastal land does not extend deeply into the hinterland which is regularly separated by mountains. Toward the interior, larger expanses of land take the opposite forms of arable plains and deserts depending on the prevailing climate of the region; the Saharan climate of Africa produces more of the latter while the more temperate climate of the European region results in more arable land. In the north, extensive mountain ranges and their spurs divide the plains from one another, producing serious challenges to unification between regions.

Broad regional differences exist between both the east and west basins of the Mediterranean and the north and south coasts. The two basins divide at the Sicilian channel between that island and the peninsula of Cap Bon in modern Tunisia. In addition to their different configurations, the western basin is smaller in size and more temperate in climate than the eastern. Mountains extend almost to the coastline, leaving a narrow strip of land by the sea in the west while they do not reach so near the shore in the east. Mountains are greater in extent and size in the northern Mediterranean lands than in the southern, a mixed blessing since in return for the valuable resources they provide they exact a regular toll in volcanoes and earthquakes. The southern Mediterranean lands, by contrast, are characterized by deserts: the Sahara desert seems endless with its 14,811,562 square kilometers relieved only by occasional oases. This contrast identifies another difference – namely in the rainfall, which is greater in the north and west than in the south and east. These differences influence a different pattern in the northern and southern regions of the Mediterranean basin.

For much of their long history, humans have been at the mercy of the environment as were the non-human inhabitants, especially when threatened with extinction during the great glaciations lasting thousands of years. In the final glaciation that continued until circa 16,000 before the present (BP), many of the large mammals and giant rodents disappeared. The human population plummeted. The authors of *Greece Before History* give a vivid image of the results: "A traveler sailing along the Greek coastline after the ice caps melted and the sea had risen to its present-day height would have seen wooded slopes and plains devoid of people, inhabited only by wild boar and deer, with sea birds, seals, and turtles massed on the shore."[3]

Climatic and environmental conditions of lands bordering or situated in the Mediterranean are capable of sustaining the life of plants, animals, and humans when a deep blanket of ice does not cover the earth. Much of the land is maquis and garigue – that is, rough land that can support a combination of shrubs such as laurel, myrtle, and wild olive; undershrubs including broom, daphne, and gorse; and herbaceous plants including clovers, grasses, and asphodel. True forests exist in northern and eastern regions, from the cedars of the Levant through the mountain forests of Macedonia and the Apennines to the significant forests of southern Spain. Most dominant are varieties of oak and pine. In addition to their fruit and timber, the forests were home to a number of wild animals: deer, bears, wolves, lynxes, panthers, leopards, lions, and boars as well as smaller animals. Regions without great forests also had a large complement of wild animals: lions, deer, and smaller animals in the north and the more exotic pygmy elephants and hippopotami, and monkeys of North Africa.

But the environment was becoming manageable. Melting of ice and warming temperatures extended the coastlines and some wild plants and animals had survived.

Human survivors also gained manageable resources. Widespread in the Mediterranean were sheep and goats. Transhumance of flocks of sheep and goats between summer and winter pastures became an increasingly common way of life for people living in the northern and eastern lands of the Mediterranean. Basic grain crops – wheat, barley, oats, and green millet – were also cultivated, as was a range of legumes, orchard fruits and nuts, grapes, and olives. For Lawrence Durrell, who lived most of his life in the Mediterranean, the olive tree describes superbly the basic requirements of a staple in the Mediterranean: "It seems to live without water although it responds readily to moisture and to fertilizer when available ... it will stand heat to an astonishing degree and keeps the beauty of its grey-silver leaf; ... the wood ... can be worked and has a beautiful grain when carved and oil."[4] These basic foods can also support a sedentary existence in upland area. Fernand Braudel, a French scholar who knew and understood the Mediterranean as well as any person can, painted a vivid picture with his description that "every mountain [in the Mediterranean region] has some arable land, in the valleys or on the terraces cut out of the hillside."[5]

The sea also contributed to the livelihood of humans even though its high salinity and exhaustion through its great longevity have made it difficult for some species of fish to survive in its waters. In the wide-ranging voyages of the ancient traveler Odysseus there were few occasions to dine on fish. Even so, a variety of marine life was present. The tunny is perhaps the most important fish; swordfish, octopus, and squid are present along with several varieties of shell fish.

The mineral wealth of the northern Mediterranean lands prompted travel. It was in the guise of a traveler for metals that Athena arrived on Ithaka to assist Odysseus' son, Telemachos, in his dealings with the suitors of his mother. It was a believable disguise. Copper was available in Cyprus, the Balkans, northern Italy, Sardinia, Anatolia, and southern Spain but, in the southern Mediterranean, only in the Sinai peninsula where there were also gold resources. The northern Aegean, Attica in Greece, and the Cyclades had silver resources; there are gold resources in the northern Aegean, the eastern Black Sea, Cyprus, and Spain; iron was plentiful in northern Italy and Spain; tin was rarer, although it was present in Spain, the northern Aegean, perhaps the Levant, and northern Italy. Base metals occur in much of the north as well as along the western African coast and flint and obsidian – the black volcanic stone – are found in Anatolia, and the island of Melos in the Aegean, the Lipari islands north of Sicily, and Sardinia.

Stretching between three continents where so many of the earliest developments in human history occurred, the Mediterranean experienced and supported a human presence even in the Paleolithic Age. As people learned to use its water for travel, ideas as well as people and objects moved between the northern and southern coast and from its eastern to western extremes. The ecological and geological diversity of the region produced a variety of cultures; however, groups of people were not greatly distanced from one another and there were geographical and resource connections between them. Life for Greeks was changed in every respect by the skill to course through Poseidon's realm. The legacy of that mode of travel is evident in the importance of shipping in contemporary Greece as well as in massive developments in Greek life brought about by Mediterranean neighbors from the time of the Romans, to the fall of the Byzantine Empire, to events of World War II.

The Physical Character of Greece

On AcroCorinth the sun faded
Setting the rock ablaze. And,
From the sea, seaweed's fragrant breath
Began to intoxicate my slender stallion.

With foam on the bit and the white of his eye
Glistening, he fought my grip,
Held close on the bridle,
Wrestling to leap into the horizon.

What was the hour? What were the many fragrances?
Was it the deep scent of the sea?
The distant breath of the forest?

Ah, would that the meltemi had lasted longer.
I would know how to clench the bridle
And the ribs of mythical Pegasus![6]

While the Mediterranean provides a unifying force to the lands that border it, there are distinct qualities in those lands. Greece shares more affinities with the eastern half of the Mediterranean and especially with the northern quadrant. The mountains, comprising roughly three-quarters of the land, are beautiful, as Angelos Sikelianos' poem describes, and they offer many resources but also serious challenges. The sea too provides great benefits but, at the same time, it presents major trials.

Awe and fear of the mountains have figured powerfully in Greek religious belief. Mount Olympus, reaching more than 10,000 feet, was easily accessible by the ancient gods but mortals did not attempt to reach its heights. Most of the mountain slopes are precipitous so that they appear to reach for the sky. Formed by two different tectonic movements, one system extends southward from Macedonia eventually into the northern and central Cyclades. In fact, the islands are peaks of now submerged mountains. The second system is to the west, formed as part of the formation of the Alps, and from the Pindos range separating Macedonia from ancient Epirus/modern Albania it extends through the Ionian islands, the Peloponnese, the southern Cyclades, and the islands of Crete, Karpathos, and Rhodes.

Many valuable resources are gifts of the mountains: stone; trees – especially the oak; minerals; natural springs closer to their bases; wild animals as well as grazing ground for domesticated animals that are brought from lower ground into higher summer pasture. However, human and animal use of the resources produces problems, particularly deforestation caused by overcutting of the trees or destruction of the trees by pasturing animals, especially goats.

The mountains themselves have unwelcome qualities; frequent volcanoes and earthquakes; thin soil; deep gorges that are traversed only with difficulty; the flow of silt down the river courses due to the winter rains. An intrepid traveler to Epirus in 1930, Nicholas Hammond (who would survive to become an eminent archaeologist and historian of ancient Macedonia) experienced all of these difficulties:

At one point where the river ran through a deep gorge between high peaks ... I found I was faced with a long scree, which extended from high up the mountainside to the lip of the cliff overhanging the gorge. I decided to run across it .... Off I went at full speed, but the whole scree began at once to move under me and my course was becoming a parabola leading to the cliff-edge, when I managed to reach the low branch of a tree, and pulled myself to safety. I lay flat, hearing the stones fall into the gorge ....[7]

Yet another contribution to human life in Greece is the regionalism that the mountains create. Travel between the lower pockets of land where settlements tend to be located is difficult in most cases, particularly in southern Greece and on the islands where few perennial rivers exist. And because conditions vary between these settlements, specific features of their cultures will differ; for example, a village high in the mountains will have a different set of resources than a lowland town and there are significant differences between northern and southern Greece: Macedonia and Thessaly do have perennial rivers which are absent in southern Greece and plains in the north are broader just as forests are more expansive. One answer to limited resources is to gain more from a neighboring area. Consequently, relations between the individual communities are more often unfriendly than cooperative. In antiquity, your nearest communal neighbor was often your worst enemy.

Sea-water defines the shape of Greece: to the east, the Aegean Sea separates the mainland of Greece from Anatolia and identifies the southern border of eastern Europe and, to the west, the Adriatic and Ionian seas separate the Greek mainland from the Italian peninsula. Islands in these seas, especially those closer to the mainland, will generally be part of the Greek world but they can serve as approaches to Greece for inhabitants of Italy. A second vital function of the sea is to provide access among the highly divided regions of the land. While the mountains make travel by land extremely arduous, inroads of the sea allow most settlements to exist within about 30 miles of its shore. From any point in the Aegean, and several points in the Adriatic, sailors are never out of sight of land. At the same time the sea serves to reinforce regionalism, dividing the land into smaller portions by its abundant bays, gulfs, and arms.

From the Aegean, travel into the Black Sea is possible and, since both seas connect with the Mediterranean, travel to the Strait of Gibraltar and beyond is relatively secure as noted above. Due to the poverty of their land, Greeks are likely to understand the rules of seafaring from their early history into the present. A general equation holds true: when Greece prospers, it will be active in seafaring; when conditions are poor, seafaring will be limited.

On the other hand, the sea provides its own challenges. Since the sea is tide-less, there are few estuaries to provide good harbors. And since heavy winter rains sweep silt from the mountains to the coast, deposits accumulate and often become swamp land that, without modern technology, tends to become a breeding ground for malaria-carrying mosquitoes. Even in the Bronze Age, as analysis of human bones demonstrates, malaria was present in several coastal regions of Greece.

In many respects, consequently, Greece and Poverty are step-sisters, as the historian Herodotus believed. On the other hand, the environment produced challenges that could be managed, given a high level of stamina in the inhabitants. A view that a culture's location determines its character is associated with the name of Hippocrates, the renowned physician of antiquity who lived in the fifth century BCE. Among the large number of writings associated with his name is a study entitled *Airs, Waters and Places* which associates human health with an individual's diet, environment, and the way of life. The author maintains that the differing character-istics of Asian and European peoples are linked to climate: the absence of major changeable climatic conditions in Asia produces a soft people while the more volatile extremes of Europe mold a tough people. Aristotle argued along similar lines in the fourth century BCE. Asian peoples are intelligent but lack spirit while Europeans are spirited although of less native intelligence.[8] Most fortunate were those situations between the two extremes. For Aristotle and Hippocrates the Greeks occupied the middle position and, hence, were both highly intelligent and spirited. Inasmuch as the physical environment of Greek life has remained much the same, these forces played an important part in its 9,000 year history.

Earliest Inhabitants

When humans chose to make their homes on the shores of the Mediterranean about 750,000 BP in the early Paleolithic Age, the physical nature of Greece was less inviting than that of other regions. Consequently human presence in Greece dates only from 300,000 or 400,000 years ago on evidence of a cranium discovered in a cave on the Chalkidike peninsula in the northern Aegean. Use of caves for occupa-tion describes the dependence of people on their environment, as does the use of readily available stone for their tools. The limited number of identified sites reflects a very small population until roughly 150,000 BP when the number of sites increased and included open-air as well as cave locations. An ability to survive in constructed sites reveals greater control over the natural environment. During the long duration of what is known as the middle Paleolithic Age to circa 30,000 BP, new tools such as harpoons, bone needles, and bows attest new practices – fishing, sewing, and new ways of hunting. Along with a growing tool-kit, humans became familiar with sea-sonality of certain food sources, knowledge that led groups of migrants to return seasonally to specific places that were remembered as providing sufficient food and water and protection at a fairly predictable time of year.

The interplay between nature and people produced more than a larger tool-kit, if the conclusions of neurobiologists and cognitive psychologists are correct. They argue that the impact between humans and their world has altered the nature of human cognition. Successful interaction with the environment stimulated biological change and, in turn, humans were able to transform their environment with the aid of new cognitive skills. These skills also aided developments in the tool-kit of humans. One of the major stages in this expansion gave rise to human speech as dif-ferentiated from the capacity of articulating sounds akin to those of animals.

In spite of these developments, population size remained small. In fact, it is esti-mated that by 20,000 BCE the total population of all of Europe was between 6,000 and 10,000 people. Major climatic changes were a significant factor in limiting the population as glacial conditions moved southward from the north and reached the northern Mediterranean.

Identity of the population in Greece is difficult to determine due to the lack of evidence. However, the nature of the practices and objects suggests a similarity with the Neanderthals who occupied much of Europe. Thus, it is believed that these peo-ple migrated into Greece from the north. However, our understanding of the most ancient of Greek history changes constantly. Very recent finds on Crete show that the earliest inhabitants of that island traveled by craft capable of open-sea navigation.

Whatever their identity and means of arrival, inhabitants in Greece found that life became easier with the end of the final major ice age in the Paleolithic Age about 20,000 BCE. The 10,000 years stretching from 20,000 to 10,000 BCE witnessed major innovations in many regions of the Mediterranean sphere including Greece; those innovations demonstrate a far greater control over the natural world. The Franchthi cave in the eastern Peloponnesus documents this pattern with evidence of human occupation from 20,000 to 3,000 BCE, the last phase of the Paleolithic Age. The earliest visitors to the site were small bands of seasonal visitors attracted by a perennial spring of water and the shelter of the cave itself. They hunted animals like the wild ass, gathered wild plants, and used flint tools. Successive occupants were similarly engaged but they took advantage of a wider variety of plants and animals (deer, bison, and wild goat), and gathered mollusks and caught fish – some as large as the modern tunny fish, which can weigh 200 lb or more.

Over time, people at the site learned enough about the ways of the sea to travel on it; obsidian from the island of Melos in the Cyclades south of mainland Greece identifies one destination. We have considered the presence of the sea in Greece where most communities are little more than a day or two from one of its bays. Currents and winds facilitate sailing. Thus the Aegean has been described as one of the "potential nurseries for the development of maritime technology and navigation."[9] Settlers at the Franchthi cave site are evidence of the potentiality of the Aegean.

By 6,000 BCE there are more varieties of animal bones at the site along with new plants. Not simply novel items, they reveal the revolutionary changes of domestication: a sizeable portion of the bones are those of sheep and goats, and among the plants are wheat and barley. At the same time, new tools such as sickles appear, pottery is introduced, and the area of occupation is extended. All signify the agricultural revolution. While this revolution is documented here with evidence of a cave site, its result was the emergence of settled farming villages as the dominant mode of life; the monumental discovery gave birth to a new age: the Neolithic, or New Stone Age.

Neolithic Period: Settled Life in Greece

One thesis proposes that the practice of agriculture spread from an original location probably in Anatolia across the whole of Europe beginning about 7,000 BCE. Settled life based on agriculture and animal husbandry can support and, in fact, requires a larger population than migratory existence. As additional land is needed first within Anatolia and eventually beyond Anatolia, the new form of community is dispersed, a dispersal that can be envisioned as a generational wave of advance. As the distance from the homeland of the earliest farmers increased, the more remote farmers would acquire new features from earlier populations and elements of the different physical environment.

The cave at Franchthi continued to be occupied but there was a second settlement outside the cave, an indication that the site could accommodate more people and that it could serve as a permanent, rather than seasonal, residence. Essentially, this development demonstrates the new way of life in much of Greece. Caves continued to have importance, but increasingly as religious sites; from circa 7,000 BCE people now lived in villages like Nea Nikomedia in Macedonia, where some 150 dwellers formed a community of twenty mud-brick houses, produced crops, and tended domesticated animals. Northern Greece was the favored location for the first settlements, not surprisingly, since the region has larger expanses of plains and low-lying hills than the steep, tightly packed mountains in southern Greece allow. The land is well watered, and there are more copious rivers.

Sesklo, one of the earliest sites in this area dating to circa 5,000 BCE, eventually covered approximately 30 acres and merits the title of "town" rather than village, with a population between 1,000 and 2,000 people. The main room of one of the houses measured 8.5 by 8.25 meters (about 28 by 27 feet), immense by comparison with previous structures and a sign of social, and possibly also political, differentiation. Neighboring Dimini had several concentric ring walls, perhaps to protect its inhabitants. This site had a main house situated on the crown of the hill. Crete was another location of Neolithic culture by the seventh millennium BCE. Settlers on that island, traveling through the island chain reaching from Anatolia or perhaps by sea from the mainland of Greece, are linked to Anatolia by similarity of objects, their agrarian knowledge, and animal husbandry.

These developments are enormous in their accomplishment and consequence. Humans are no longer at the mercy of their environment but have taken command of it not only in Greece but throughout much of the Mediterranean world. The nature of the culture and the time of its emergence will depend on the characteristics of the environment and the qualities of the human population. It is not surprising that the land of Greece was difficult to tame. By 10,000 BCE in the Ancient Near East, greater command was occurring in the domestication of plants and animals. The region of the Fertile Crescent, an arc extending through the highlands above the Tigris and Euphrates rivers, possessed a variety of wild plants and animals capable of domestication as well as good sources of water.

Domestication required larger groups of people to perform a variety of tasks and it also enabled larger numbers in a community. Previously 10 square kilometers was needed to sustain a single person; with domestication 1 square kilometer could support five to ten individuals. The new way of life became the preferred way of life. Anthropologist Colin Renfrew argues for the wave of advance effect as additional land was required for new generations of people. From its original location, agriculture and people spread eventually throughout much of Europe as well as in other directions. People and technology reached northern Greece and Crete early in the dispersal due to proximity by land and by sea.

Another aspect of this argument is to define the people: they are Indo-Europeans, as demonstrated by their language. The Indo-European family of languages has been dated to approximately 10,000 to 12,000 years ago and the earliest evidence points to Anatolia as its location. Greek belongs to this family of languages. The once-common language would gradually develop differences as individual groups encountered different environments and speakers of other languages, although retaining resemblances with related Indo-European languages. Thus those descendants of the original wave of advance who arrived in Greece brought domestication and their form of Indo-European, proto Greek.[10] If this view is correct, Greek speakers have been part of the story of Greece for some 9,000 years.

Kuria

Although we cannot name a person who defines the life of this period, it is possible to identify this way of life through an artifact, a contemporary depiction of a clay figure of a woman holding an infant. The figure comes from Sesklo, one of the larger Neolithic villages in Thessaly excavated by archaeologists. For want of a name, we have called the figurine "Kuria," which is the Greek word for "lady." We have chosen to imagine the woman with her child as representing a real person, instead of a goddess or religious figure, with the hopes that by presenting her in a specific context, we can provide a brief illustration of the way of life in Neolithic Greece.

The object itself represents the enormous changes in the lives of humans over the vast extent of the Stone Ages from a migratory existence to a settled village life defined by the domestication of animals and the cultivation of food. Initially, humans in Greece were at the mercy of the environment, using caves as homes, migrating in search of food, using stone to fashion tools. Gradually learning about the environment brought greater command of it: new tools created from the bones of slain animals, knowledge of areas where food was available at certain times of the year, and construction of temporary structures at these places. Such an economy required permanent structures.

It is not surprising that in humankind's earliest story, depictions on cave walls represented the most important living beings – animals, the source of life – with humans rarely if ever shown. And yet, with new skills in this changing way of life humans

Figure 1.2 Kuria. Source: Amy Absher

represent *themselves*. And the clay objects they created also serve as an excellent symbol of that transformation. Although baked, clay objects are breakable; thus clay wares indicate settled, rather than completely nomadic, patterns of sustenance. Beyond their utilitarian function as vessels, other clay objects represent houses and people.

One can imagine human emotion in this figurine – our Kuria – as her one arm wraps around the child, the other cradling, and the child's arm reaches to the woman's neck. And although we have no way to record the specific words she might have spoken to the child, we do know that Kuria's community would have spoken a form of Greek (proto-Greek) based on the common Indo-European language as previously discussed. It is easy to imagine – given the Greek oral traditions that follow – our Kuria singing the child a story.

It is significant that the figurine depicts a woman and a child. Within Kuria's settled community, perhaps of Sesklo, there were crucial tasks that women, children, and elders could and did perform: children could tend the animals, help with harvest; women wove animal fleece into fabric, stored and cared for the produce; the elderly possessed essential acquired skills such as the techniques of producing storage vessels for the surplus goods by potting and firing clay and knowledge of customs that were critical to the community's survival.

Pottery is the first material created by humans using a precise technology. Clay is abundant and can be molded into various shapes, then fired into durable forms relatively easily. Thus, objects can be – and have been – preserved, enabling us to trace developments over time. Improvements in quality and quantity of the clay objects strongly suggest growing specialization of skills and responsibility. Analysis of the composition of clay can identify the source of particular objects so that individual villages appear to have their own unique style of pottery, handmade and fired in pits and/or ovens also used for bread. Pottery evolved in style, skill, and purpose throughout the region. In the Early Neolithic period, the production of pottery was slight, perhaps about a dozen annually at the Franchthi cave; those pots were not used for cooking. Later, during the time when our Kuria might have lived, there was an increase in volume. Potters were now taking risks, firing their wares at temperatures high enough to produce unique glazes of metallic pigments fused to the clay's surface. By this time, the purpose of pottery was multifold, both utilitarian for cooking and storage, but also used in social exchanges or perhaps as gifts.

In Kuria's village, the decorative pattern of Sesklo ware was red and white, in repetitive squares or curved triangles or controlled flames. There is some scholarly debate over whether these first potters were predominately men or women. Kuria may have been a maker of pots herself, but if not, she could have used pottery for storage, decoration, and/or religious rituals.

Regardless of who did the shaping and firing of clay pots, all settlements had figurines in an astonishing variety of sizes, shapes, and types. And they were found everywhere in Neolithic villages from the Neolithic "kitchen sink" to the village dump or pit, just about anywhere. Scholars have noted that given the volume, figurines may have been as readily discarded as they were easy to make. Frequency of representations in the figurines provides us with a glimpse into the world they represent. Archaeology has revealed that this world is comprised of communal life in villages. It is interesting that female figures are more prominent than those of males. Animals are also represented; unsurprisingly, most are domesticated animals.

If Kuria had not lived in Sesklo, but in a nearby but smaller village, she would have had anywhere from a couple dozen to some 100 neighbors, all individuals living in closely spaced houses made of mud bricks on stone foundations. Their houses were rectangular, often with adjoining rooms the size of a modern closet. Some had two stories. Roofs would have been thatched and covered in layers of clay, with smoke holes. And although the technology to build these houses would be considered primitive by our standards, evidence suggests that the clay was sometimes painted in bright colors, windows and doors outlined in red and white decorations. Homes would have a central hearth or a hearth against one wall. Outside there would have been fire pits, ovens, and refuse pits as well. Sometimes houses were surrounded by enclosures. Given the climate, most villagers could have spent a great deal of time outside, cooking in ovens, tending to their crops and herds, or making tools and art.

Our lady would have likely tended to her infant as she went about the daily business of living, and she may have had other children. She might have helped to farm fields, and tools existed for the work; excavations of villages have yielded many artifacts. At home she would have used tools such as the clay spindle, whorls to spin yarn, and bone awls. She might have wielded the stone axe to chop wood, or left that activity for her spouse. She would have ground grains or cereals into flour on a quern (a base stone).

Food production was the greatest transition from the Mesolithic culture to the Neolithic; remains are preserved by carbonization of cooking fires or accidental destructive fires of the homes. Kuria may have provided meals for herself, her children, spouse, and other family based on communal or family stores. The villagers' diet involved grains (wheat and barley); legumes such as peas, fruit, and nuts; and sheep, goats, cattle, and pigs and the dairy products provided by domesticated animals. An outstanding archaeologist of Greece has described this world well:

> Inside the mud-plastered houses the main colors would come from woven textiles and painted vases. There would be beds of piled skin or brush, perhaps raised from the damp on benches of clay or stones. By day these bed or chipped stumps would serve as seats; by night the more valuable animals especially if they were pregnant, warmed by glowing charcoal or dung on the hearth. As in all Greek village life for the next seven thousand years, the outdoor court or street was a principal part of the home. The village itself was so small that it was essentially a family unit …. It controlled and apportioned neighboring fields and sources of fresh water. It maintained casual contact with other villages in the district but made no attempt to organize into larger groupings.[11]

The village, then, is the centerpiece of Greek life, and during Kuria's time, the village was likely an extended family. However, the artifacts tell a story of increasing sophistication in the economy: obsidian (a volcanic glass found in some quantity on the Cycladic island of Melos), exotic shell ornaments made of a spiny Mediterranean oyster have been found as far north as present-day Poland, honey-colored flint blades in Greece may have come from modern Bulgaria or Romania. Thus these Neolithic settlements must have had some kind of exchanges with other peoples, whether by bartered exchanges where the objects traveled farther than their makers or in the occasional long-distance trade. The presence of exotic goods in these Neolithic villages presents a different image than the common assumption about

"Stone Age" peoples. Kuria may have had some kind of jewelry made of shells or exotic stones, she likely would have had decorative pots in her home, a communal central room shared with relatives. Kuria, her family, extended family, and other Neolithic farmers were innovators because they had to be and, in so being, developed a particular material culture of long duration.

We cannot know what the clay figurine of the woman and child truly represented to the person or people who made her. There are many possibilities: perhaps the 'Kuria' figurine was an image of an idealized mother. The figurine may have served some kind of religious purpose. The mother holding her child could have been made to represent family members who died. A less dramatic interpretation is that the figurine was made of terra cotta because one villager had the time and inclination to do so. It could even have been a way to perfect the art of making a figurine, a more realistic and less abstract person than those mother goddesses found throughout Europe. Our Kuria could simply be a mother holding a baby made by a potter because he or she wanted to tell a story, or capture the moment. One must not forget that even in Kuria's time, there was likely the same human impulse to perfect a skill or craft. These farmers lived to eat well, store food, likely loved and argued with neighbors, buried their dead, decorated their homes, bartered for what they did not have. Above all, they created a material culture, and in so doing, continue to tell us their stories.

As the long story of Greece reveals, the importance of the family within its larger community has continued from the Neolithic Age to the present. What is more, the mountains and the sea have dictated that these smallish communities have been the center of Greek life for millennia.

Notes

1. Homer, *Iliad* 15.190 ff.
2. A. T. Hodge, *Ancient Greek France* (London: Duckworth, 1998), 27.
3. Curtis Runnels and Priscilla Murray, *Greece Before History: An Archaeological Companion and Guide* (Stanford: Stanford University Press, 2001), 30.
4. Lawrence Durrell, *Sicilian Carousel* (New York: Viking Press, 1976), 65–66.
5. Fernand Braudel, *The Mediterranean and the Mediterranean World in the Age of Philip II*, 2 vols., translated by S. Reynolds (London: Collins, 1972), 42.
6. Angelos Sikelianos, "On Acrocorinth," translated by Theodore Antikas and Carol Thomas.
7. Nicholas Hammond, "Travels in Epirus and South Albania before World War II," *Ancient World* VIII:1 & 2 (1983): 13–46; 39.
8. Aristotle, *Politics* VII, 7, 1327b20f.
9. C. Paul Rainbird, "Islands Out of Time: Towards a Critique of Island Archaeology," *Journal of Mediterranean Archaeology* 12:2 (1999), 216–234; 231.
10. Colin Renfrew, *Archaeology and Language: The Puzzle of Indo-European Origins* (London: Jonathan Cape, 1987). Significant support for the original home of the people is that DNA evidence from plant and animal suggests Anatolian roots.

    An early review of the wave of advance thesis in Colin Renfrew's *Archaeology and Language* in *Archaeology* (January/February 1987) by Curt Runnels reported that it was "received with a hail of protest." It was "revolutionary" and it "brushes away 100 years of arguments." Professor Runnels himself found it "a very good book" that "will make you think," and "your own view of European prehistory and archaeology will be challenged to the core" (88). Scholars are still thinking; there is no consensus a quarter of a century later. However, technological data including DNA analysis of human, plant, and animal remains has entered the picture. It has the support of increasing numbers of distinguished specialists. I have been increasingly persuaded of its merits in accounting for the Neolithic population of Macedonia and Greece and their way of life.

11. Emily Vermeule, *Greece in the Bronze Age* (Chicago and London: University of Chicago Press, 1964), 12 f.

Further Reading

Abulafia, David, ed. 2003. *The Mediterranean in History*. London: Thames and Hudson.

Beginning with the question "What is the Mediterranean?" chapters by specialists describe the history of that sea from prehistory to the end of the twentieth century CE. The abundant illustrations transport the reader into life in the lands circling the sea from deep antiquity to the present.

Barker, Graeme. 2006. *The Agricultural Revolution in Prehistory: Why did Foragers become Farmers?* Oxford: Oxford University Press.

This discussion of the agricultural revolution ranges widely from Asia through Africa and Europe to the Americas to answer the questions of why and how humans became farmers. Obviously Greece is not the main focus but the location of Greece has made the region an intersection in the process of the transition from hunting-gathering to settled agrarian cultures.

Braudel, Fernand. 2001. *Memory and the Mediterranean*, translated by S. Reynolds. New York: Alfred A. Knopf.

An extraordinary account by one of the greatest of European historians allows the reader to see the sea and its march to civilization from the Paleolithic Age to the Roman unification. The author's earlier two-volume history of *The Mediterranean and the Mediterranean World in the Age of Philip II* (Philip II of Spain in the sixteenth century CE) is a virtual encyclopedia of the Mediterranean world that provides a solid understanding of that sea.

Grove, A. T. and Oliver Rackham. 2001. *The Nature of Mediterranean Europe: An Ecological History*. New Haven, CT, and London: Yale University Press.

The scientist authors have produced a detailed, beautifully illustrated study that will appeal to everyone with a serious interest in the history of landscape. The illustrations, many in full color, are a reason in themselves to examine the characteristics and features of land "especially considered as a product of modifying or shaping processes and agents" (12).

Renfrew, Colin. 1988. *Archaeology and Language: The Puzzle of Indo-European Origins*. New York: Cambridge University Press.

In his preface, the author argues that "modern linguistics and current processual archaeology offer the opportunity for a new synthesis" (7). Early reviews were not largely positive of the success of his thesis. He continued to explore those categories of evidence together with traditional archaeological data. Just recently, DNA analysis has provided additional evidence that the success and spread of a settled agricultural way of life created a wave of advance settlement out of Anatolia in several directions, one of them across the Aegean toward Greece.

Renfrew, Colin. 2009. *Prehistory: The Making of the Human Mind*. New York: Random House.

The distinguished archaeologist/anthropologist/linguist examines the prehistory of humans before written records existed through such evidence as DNA analysis, radiocarbon dating, and artefacts. Without these tools, the depth of the human story was unknown until the mid-nineteenth century CE. And this evidence presents an understanding of intellectual as well as material developments from the time of the earliest hunter-gatherers.

Runnels, Curtis and Priscilla M. Murray. 2001. *Greece Before History*. Stanford, CA: Stanford University Press.

This readable, well-illustrated account of the earliest occupants of the Greek peninsula is based on the relationship between humans and their environment from the Old Stone Age through the Late Stone and Bronze Ages. It demonstrates that the "prehistoric societies were dynamic in a state of constant change, even if this change has to be measured in centuries and millennia" (154).

2

The Age of Heroes

Well into the nineteenth century, Greek history was still thought to date to precisely 776 BCE, the start of the record of Olympic victors. Only with the development of scientific archaeology was the antiquity of human life in Greece revealed. From the Paleolithic Age onward, the pattern of life echoed that of other areas of the Mediterranean, albeit with a somewhat later beginning. Although the size of the human population in Greece was small by comparison with other regions of the Mediterranean, human presence is attested between 400,000 and 300,000 years ago. As we have seen in the first chapter, a migratory existence slowly was replaced by village life based on agriculture and animal husbandry by 7,000 BCE.

By the end of this first phase of settled communal life in Greece – the Neolithic period – an increasingly wide spread of villages and towns existed on the mainland as well as on the Aegean islands. Agriculture was the backbone of their existence, but enlargement of the necessary tools fostered specialization, and the need for materials such as tin to create those tools stimulated seafaring. It is not surprising that the era around 3,000 BCE saw a second vast change in Greek history: the emergence of complexities akin to the way of life in the ancient Near East and Egypt.

Yet until the early twentieth century such a development was unthinkable: the earliest civilization of Greece known through the poetry of Homer was regarded as a product of wishful thinking. By accepting the historical reality of an Agamemnon or Oedipus, later Greeks had invented a world that never existed. In 1938, a classical scholar put the view clearly in stating that Homer "created a life that never was on land or sea. The men of his times were content to enter into and make their own a mythos of life." He did admit that Homeric poetry is powerful but it is no more historical than Keats' "Ode on a Grecian Urn."[1] Consider the "hero" Odysseus and his long-suffering wife, Penelope. He, a reluctant participant in the "Trojan War" for ten years, becomes, in the *Odyssey*, a beleaguered sailor attempting to return to his island home of Ithaca. In this endeavor he meets the Cyclops, Sirens, and Circe, who turns his fellows into pigs, and the Phaeacians who live in a never-never land, but he

Greece: A Short History of a Long Story, 7,000 BCE to the Present, First Edition.
Carol G. Thomas.
© 2014 John Wiley & Sons, Inc. Published 2014 by John Wiley & Sons, Inc.

finally returns to his home after another ten years – a home that no archaeologist has found. His wife has been faithful; in fighting off 108 suitors for her hand in marriage she is cleverly delaying a decision until she completes a woven shroud that she carefully works by day and unravels by night. A great story to be sure.

There were questions about the identity of Homer in antiquity but in early modern times that concern was joined to issues about the language of the *Iliad* and *Odyssey* to produce a hotly debated subject called the "Homeric Question," which has not been completely solved to this day. An answer centers on two issues: first, solid evidence, namely physical proof of a complex culture in the western Aegean as early as 3,000 BCE, contemporaneous with the earliest civilizations in the Near East and Egypt; and, second, an understanding of the "strange" language of the epic poems: the *Iliad* and the *Odyssey*.

The youthful discipline of archaeology began to address the first task in the second half of the nineteenth century, with surprising results. Heinrich Schliemann announced the discovery of the site of the Trojan War in 1873 at Hissarlik in the northwestern corner of Anatolia, and turned to the mainland in search of contemporary sites as homes of the attackers of Troy. His efforts uncovered Mycenae and Tiryns and he also sought Ithaca, unsuccessfully. At the start of the twentieth century CE, Sir Arthur Evans reported his success in unearthing the home of Minos and his Minotaur at Knossos on Crete. While it was clear that the excavations had uncovered something previously unknown, in the context of prevailing opinion and the inchoate state of archaeology such announcements were generally received with skepticism. Of "Troy" W. J. Stillman stated in the *London Times* of January 9, 1889, "I hope before long to put all the evidence … in such a shape that no one can doubt reasonable that 'Troy' is the Troy of Croesus" (i.e. from the sixth century BCE)

Yet there were believers and archaeologists who persisted in attempting to prove the reality of the "Age of Heroes." At Hissarlik/Troy refined techniques and inclusion of specialists from related disciplines were in place for a second major investigation from 1932 to 1938. Nine major levels dating from the early third millennium through two millennia demonstrated forty-nine catastrophes due both to natural and to human causes. Levels VI and VII were contemporaneous with previously excavated mainland sites and both revealed massive destruction. The head of this excavation added yet another site to the list of contemporary Greek sites associated with the war at Sandy Pylos, whose king was Nestor, at least according to the Homeric epics.

The most recent study of Hissalik/Troy, begun in 1988, employed highly technical tools including magnetometry, which uses a remote sensing device to read what lies below the surface. It produced evidence of a dense lower city of 5–10,000 people at the base of the previously excavated citadel that was ten times larger than the citadel site and protected by an ingenious ditch and palisade system. Just recently a missing element – people – was discovered in burials dating to the late second millennium. Finds of hydrologists using deep core boring to reconstruct the configuration of the ancient site have demonstrated that during the Late Bronze Age the bay between the two points where the Greek fleet was anchored according to the *Iliad* was considerably deeper and larger than it is at present. It has gradually been converted to a flat plain through silting.

Consequently, the Age of Heroes has a datable reality. It is now recognized as a time of growing complexity from circa 3,000 to 1,200 BCE, the period known as the Bronze Age on the Greek mainland, the isles of the Aegean, and the west coast of Anatolia. While impetus from civilizations of the eastern Mediterranean was essential, the Aegean peoples participated actively in affairs of the Mediterranean region and contributed elements of their own to the cosmopolitan way of life that emerged in the second millennium. Myth became history.

In more southerly areas of the eastern Mediterranean, this explosion was associated with the taming of rivers that could provide a regular source of water for crops, herds of animals, humans, and boats. In the Aegean, by contrast, there were few rivers to be tamed. Consequently, the complexity of life rested on other innovations that would produce a more diverse economy, larger towns, mechanisms of control, considerable social stratification, widespread trade, and other forms of contact with others. The key elements in the Aegean region were bronze technology; the addition of olive and grape cultivation to grain, legume, and pulse crops; and the discovery that certain natural resources – such as stone, which was plentiful – could be shaped into desirable objects for purposes of trade. Regular travel by sea provided access to necessary goods, particularly tin, which was alloyed to copper to produce bronze. That travel also produced customers for Aegean goods and thus stimulated construction of Aegean ships that could serve as carriers for their own products as well as for the goods of peoples who were not avid sailors.

The Role of Islands

The combination of elements seems to have occurred first in the Cyclades, islands of the south-central Aegean. The islands themselves are peaks of submerged mountains, many having no source of water other than rainfall. Even so, they became targets of opportunity as agrarian life expanded throughout Anatolia, then westward across the Aegean. The nature of agrarian life that was in place on some of the islands by roughly 4,300 BCE shows affinities with Anatolian culture. It was certainly carried by sea, since no land bridge remained.

The Cycladic islands were innovative in several respects: incipient bronze metallurgy dates to the late fourth millennium, poly-culture (including cultivation of the olive and grape) was in place by the third millennium, and crafting of products from marble was quickly perfected. One result was a population "explosion." A second consequence was a new complexity of life requiring specialists to create and carry products, to gain essential resources, and to organize communal life. These developments, together with a location that could serve as a laboratory for seafaring, drew the islanders into active contact with one another, then with more distant parts of the Aegean, and soon into the waters of the eastern Mediterranean.

Surviving representations of the boats indicate that they were longer versions of pre-Bronze Age dugouts: narrow, long, and low with a high stern, and propelled by oars. These long-ships are likely to have been a common sight throughout much of the Aegean Sea during the third millennium. Further removed, Cycladic ships appear to have reached the waters of the eastern Mediterranean: among incised pictures of

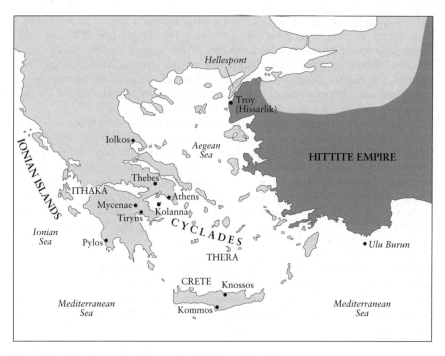

Figure 2.1 The Bronze Age Aegean. Source: Jason Shattuck

boats of various shapes and sizes discovered on the Carmel Mountain ridge in the Levant is an Aegean type of vessel.

Expansion in wealth of the inhabitants of the Cyclades is attested by physical remains. In a later Neolithic grave, the body was accompanied only by a painted footed cup and a pottery saucer. In a grave dating to the Early Bronze Age, by comparison, the body was accompanied by a footed vessel with stamped incised decoration, a marble bowl, an obsidian blade, an object shaped rather like a modern frying pan, a stone palette, and a grinder. By the body's feet were found another marble bowl with traces of red coloring, a seashell, copper tweezers, a carved bone tube containing traces of blue coloring, a straight bone tube with a copper spatula beside it, a bone pin with a bird head, two bone fragments perhaps from another pin, and two lumps of red coloring matter. Many of these objects could have had an on-going use among the living members of the community; thus their burial was a token of items that could be spared for another purpose. It is important to note that such wealth signals a monumental change in this unlikely habitat defined by mountains with limited resources. But the marble sculptures, products made from grapes and olives, and bronze objects attracted other peoples of the region, who would be drawn to a similar way of life.

First to build on the same skills were the inhabitants of a larger island, Crete, who raised the level of complexity to new heights. The earliest settlement had occurred by 6,000 BCE, accomplished by newcomers from Anatolia or northern Greece or perhaps both areas. A chain of islands extending from southwestern Anatolia to Crete would facilitate their travel but negotiating the stretches of water between the islands demanded ships. Thus knowledge of seafaring was an element of the intellectual tool-kit of the initial settlers and it would be a key factor in the growing complexity of life on Crete through the remainder of the Neolithic Age and would become far more evident in the Bronze Age culture from 3,000 BCE.

Other essential elements were the fairly extensive areas of land suitable for farming and herding that were capable of supporting a sizeable population. While Crete has its own mountains they do not divide the land into as many small regions as the mountains of the mainland and the islands do. There are only five main regions in its 150 by 20 mile extent. The island's location, opening north into the Aegean and south to the sophisticated civilizations of the eastern Mediterranean, makes Crete a likely intermediary in contacts within the eastern Mediterranean.

Over the three millennia of the Neolithic Age, population increase led to more settlements extending west across the island. As in the Cyclades, metallurgy and cultivation of the olive and grape enriched and transformed basic agricultural life. Increases in population, number of settlements, and contacts beyond the island continued in the Bronze Age.

During the third millennium, important towns located on the coast expanded and demonstrated greater specialization among their residents. In several locations, large "manorial" buildings suggest social and political specialization as well. Coordination of the activities of growing numbers of townspeople required delegation of authority and acceptance of that authority. Foreign objects in Crete as well as Cretan objects found elsewhere indicate that activity by sea was intensifying with the Aegean islands and with coastal sites in Anatolia, Egypt, and Libya. One Cretan site, Kommos on the Libyan Sea, appears to have been designed with needs of seafaring in mind: it had storage sheds for ships and a stoa-like building with an open colonnade and a roofed space at the rear wall to protect bins of stored goods.

Quite suddenly, about 2,000 BCE, the manorial homes of those who had benefited from and managed the changing world gave way to palaces at a number of places in the east and central regions of the island. At Knossos and other locations, palaces of dozens, later hundreds, of rooms sprang up to serve as economic, political, and cultural points of centralization located amid dense concentrations of people: 60–100,000 people lived in the area around Knossos – a true city. The appearance of records written in a script combining linear signs for sounds with an accounting system and pictograms of objects, known as Linear A, attests this revolution. Its stimulus was likely Egyptian writing that was well established in the third millennium. Cretan writing adapted its writing system to its own language and needs. The exact nature of that language is not known since, unfortunately, the script has not been deciphered.

On the other hand, its main use is revealed through the pictograms that accompany the script. The palace centers recorded one of their main functions as hubs for production and redistribution locally, with other centers on Crete, and in foreign dealings. Records include 100,000 sheep kept for wool production; numbers of vines and fig trees; allocations of grains; lists of bronze ingots; amounts of wool issues to women, presumably to weave; numbers of chariots and their wheels; numbers of swords.

Trading activity expanded during the four centuries circa 2,000–1,600 BCE into the central Mediterranean as well as in the eastern waters; the Egyptians knew the traders as the people of "Keftiu" (Crete) and the influence of Minoan crafts and skills is visible in the artistic traditions of both Egypt and the Levant. Closer to home, Minoan Cretans settled in towns on the Aegean islands and perhaps on the mainland of Greece itself, where their influence is also perceptible in the material culture. Since the tool of this influence was command of the sea, scholars have dubbed the accomplishment a "thalassocracy," meaning strength by sea. Although the view that Minoan culture was the creative force behind all cultures of the Aegean region is too extreme, the widespread penetration of the Minoan way of life cannot be dismissed.

The reality of such a rich civilization on Crete is recent, part of the "Homeric Question" mentioned at the beginning of this chapter. In the wake of Schliemann's discoveries at Hissarlik/Troy and on the mainland of Greece, Sir Arthur Evans determined to find a comparable contemporary reality for the "great city called Knossos where King Minos ruled and enjoyed the friendship of mighty Zeus," as Odysseus describes it to Penelope in one of his "lying" stories after his return to Ithaka.[2] In Evans' first year of excavation in 1900, he reported that "the earliest remains on Crete ascend 3,000 years into an obscurity that we cannot pierce."[3] In that year he uncovered the entire ground plan that closely resembled a labyrinth in which Minos was reported to have housed his Minotaur. A legacy of these discoveries is the name given to the civilization: Minoan Crete. As legend told, the naval power of Minos of Knossos commanded the sacrifice of young men and women from Athens to his Minotaur.

There is now solid evidence that such sea power drew Crete into international relationship in the first part of the twentieth millennium BCE. However, this thalassocracy would not continue into the second half of the second millennium. Destruction of most of the palaces by natural forces disrupted the fabric of Cretan life when shortly before 1,600 the Cycladic island of Thera was exploded into three chunks by a massive volcanic eruption that buried its main city and other parts of the island in an ash layer some 150 feet deep. Matter from the earth's interior spewed forth at temperatures of nearly 1,500 °F and the roof of an enormous chamber that had formed under the earth's crust collapsed, producing a caldera of 83 square miles (215 square kilometers). As the sea poured into the void, tidal waves of 70–100 meters high (about 230 to more than 300 feet) sped across the water. Crete would have felt the force of a wave traveling at more than 220 miles per hour (350 kilometers per hour) twenty to thirty minutes later. The force damaged, even destroyed, towns and ships anchored along the north coast of Crete, while volcanic debris would have polluted the land. Rebuilding did occur, but more interesting are indications of a new cultural presence at the main palace center of Knossos that point to people from the mainland of Greece. One clue is the change in the palace script; the newer script has been deciphered as an early form of Greek. In its weakened state, Crete may well have been a target for raids by others, which, if successful, might open an opportunity for occupation.

Not surprisingly, Minoan trading activity declines from this point in time while a mainland presence in the Aegean and other parts of the Mediterranean increases. Shortly after 1,400, Knossos, the last Minoan palace, was finally destroyed. If it had in fact been inhabited by mainlanders, as archaeologists and historians suspect, we may conclude that a center on Crete was no longer necessary; having been good students in learning the operation of a "thalassocracy," others could conduct the activity from other centers. The last centuries of the Bronze Age belonged to the Greeks of the mainland.

The Greek Age of Heroes

Inhabitants of the mainland were late contestants in the race toward complexity, which is somewhat surprising since the human story on the mainland has deeper roots than it does in the Cyclades and Crete, reaching back into the Paleolithic period. Signs of cultivation of plants and herding of domesticated animals occur earlier on the mainland than on Crete or the Cycladic islands, and elements encouraging greater complexity and increased density of population are visible about 2,800 BCE with the introduction of metallurgy and of domestication of olives and grapes. Village sites reveal greater wealth, more specialization, and tighter organization. The site of Dorion in the Peloponnesus, for example, was fortified and had space for 300 houses in addition to a small palace-like structure with attached artisans' shops and fifteen large storage chambers for vessels.

However, mainland settlements did not quickly achieve the complex society and economy of the Minoans. The five centuries from circa 2,100 to 1,600 were a time of transition from a proto-urban culture to the kingdoms that typify the last phase of the Greek Bronze Age. Regionalism fostered by natural features of the mountains and sea was a major factor in the process on the mainland that extends over 250 miles, north to south. Location and resources of each area promoted different ways of life. Thus the settlement at Kolonna on Aegina had monumental architecture and impressive wealth, while other settlements were tiny, poor, and isolated, and many were somewhere between these poles.

Overseas contacts were also instrumental in the transition, especially those with Minoan Crete, since the rise of impressive craftsmanship occurred earlier on Crete and those products influenced mainland culture. Contact with central Europe, where links with areas producing metal soon fueled the emergence of conditions akin to those of Crete, was also an important factor. Moreover, as noted above, certain of the mainlanders, assisted by the volcanic eruption of Thera, very likely took advantage of Minoan weakness in the late seventeenth century BCE. From the sixteenth century into the twelfth, people of the mainland became the predominant power of the Aegean. This late period of the Bronze Age in Greece is known as the Mycenaean Age after one of its most significant centers, Mycenae, which Heinrich Schliemann explored in order to find the other missing piece of evidence in the search for the Trojan War after he had discovered Troy in the buried ruins of Hissarlik. He excavated at other mainland sites, Tiryns for example, and later archaeologists added further impressive sites to the picture of Bronze Age Greece including Pylos, Athens, and Thebes. Currently, excavations in Thessaly at modern Volos are demonstrating the existence of a similar center known traditionally as Iolkos while a multi-disciplinary investigation on the western peninsula of the Ionian island of Cephalonia is seeking the home of Odysseus. The spread of these finds substantiates a complex way of life throughout much of the Greek mainland.

Results of these discoveries revealed that Mycenaean civilization revolved around several kingdoms ruled from citadel strongholds. Their territories were largely determined by circumstances of the environment. Careful examination of a topographical map will show that the realms of both Athens and Pylos were bounded by the sea surrounding their peninsulas and by mountains separating them from neighboring regions. Similar although not identical physical features define the other centers.

Another enabling feature was the craggy peaks on which the citadels were erected. Many of the citadels were also protected by massive walls which defined their relationship with the surrounding villages: the political center was deliberately separated from the populace over which it ruled. It may also identify a need for separation from a far more numerous population than that situated within the walls of the citadel. Archaeological study of the entire region of the kingdom of Pylos provides a population figure of about 40–50,000 living in villages and towns through the region. The population in the center has been estimated to have been about 3,000. Control was maintained by means of a hierarchical administrative structure headed by a *wanax* (lord). It is interesting to note that, in the *Iliad*, Agamemnon, king of Mycenae, is termed (w)Anax Andron, lord of men.[4]

Road systems allowed for the conveyance of goods to and from the center and for surveillance by investigators traveling in the chariots that the Mycenaeans loved to paint on their walls and pots as well as to drive through their kingdoms. A check on the flow of goods, land holdings, and personnel was kept in records written on clay tablets in the Linear script derived from Minoan Linear A: it is thus known as Linear B and was deciphered in the 1950s as an early form of Greek.

The contents of the tablets describe huge quantities – 3 tons of linen from one village, 100,000 sheep in the kingdom at one point in time. People who lived within the walls of the citadel had an enviable existence. The palace itself served as a residence as well as an official building and a place of production and storage. Houses near the palace were also grand. And the most important of the inhabitants were buried in graves filled with treasures or in the massive "beehive" tombs, each of which required roughly 60,000 man-hours to construct. Those who built such tombs, or who watched the sheep, or carded the wool were free peasants and slaves and specialists. The quantities of treasure buried in tombs were staggering: silver vases and vessels and pitchers; gold face masks and rings and bracelets; breastplates, diadems, goblets and vases; amber beads; alabaster; large quantities of copper, bronze, and obsidian; and boars' tusks. It is interesting to compare this wealth with that of the later Cycladic burials which also revealed the ability to remove precious objects from use by the living. The magnitude of the "removal" in Mycenaean Greece is overwhelming by comparison.

In addition to identifying the language of the tablets as Greek and revealing the wealth of the economy, the tablets provide another link with later Greek life: a number of deities are attested: Zeus, Hera, Poseidon, Hermes, Artemis, Athena, Dionysus, perhaps also Apollo and Hephaistos. Another name, but not in a religious context, is Da-ma-te, resembling the name of the goddess Demeter. Thus, of the great Olympians of Classical Greece, six certain and three possible deities figure in the Bronze Age records.

Respect paid to the more-than-human elements of their world is demonstrated in the archaeological remains of the palace centers. At Mycenae, for instance, an area covering three levels of the hillside had a processional corridor leading from a court-yard to a building which contained troves of unique clay figures. In the largest room of another building on the same level, a hearth was the dominant feature. Terms for priestess and priest occur on the tablets and they are associated with special land holdings. That these features come from the palace centers strongly indicates the importance of religion in the political authority of the Mycenaean rulers.

Other forms of control are also clearly evident in the records and the physical remains: walls surrounding and protecting the center; roads that reach out from the centers into the territory of the kingdom; inventories; orders for production. The strong presence of military activity in painted or sculptured representations as well as in actual weapons and armor describes the character of Mycenaean con-trol. Production of military equipment would serve purposes of trade and also make trade safer if the traders carried these weapons. Greeks of the late Bronze Age were renowned for both their products and their military activities: in fact the Hittite kings of the later second millennium knew these people, identified as "Ahhiyawa" (likely Achaeans, the Homeric name for the attackers of Troy), as troublesome intruders into their territory. It is important to remember that the Hittites at this time were one of the two major powers of the eastern Mediterranean, the other being the Egyptians.

Mycenaeans were known in part as participants in a close-knit network that connected the coastal regions of much of the Aegean with the eastern and central Mediterranean. Trade was a motive force of the dynamism and interaction of major powers in the Late Bronze Age and, as new evidence increases, its origins reach ear-lier and earlier in time. The find of a ship wrecked off the southern coast of Anatolia, at Ulu Burun, gives a graphic picture of the nature of this trade. Sailing port to port, the ship carried pottery from Cyprus, Syria, and Palestine; metal goods of Egyptian, Cypriot, Canaanite, and Mycenaean manufacture; glass from the Levant; a cylinder seal from Mesopotamia; an Egyptian hieroglyphic scarab bearing the name of Nefertiti; amber from the Baltic; and a length of elephant tusk probably from northern Africa. Other evidence reveals that sailing extended regularly into the central Mediterranean and had already penetrated the Black Sea. Finds in the Black Sea in fact indicate that the quest of Jason and his Argonauts for the Golden Fleece may be more than a fanciful tale. Ties of the Greek mainland with Italy and Europe, which had been established earlier, continued through the later Bronze Age.

Emporia where exchanges occurred were thriving centers. Ugarit in the northern Levant boasted a kingly palace, libraries, a navy estimated to have at one time num-bered some 150 ships, and a corps of chariots as well as an infantry force. When, beginning in 1870, Schliemann excavated at Hissarlik/Troy, he uncovered a settlement site on a high mound dating back to the early third millennium with subsequent forms extending into the first millennium. As we have seen, the most recent investigation at the site has revealed a city of between 5,000 and 10,000 res-idents and deep core drilling has found that the plain on which the site rests was a harbor stretching below the citadel in the Bronze Age. Thus Hissarlik/Troy may well have been a center of trade in the international exchange that characterizes the eastern Mediterranean region at this time. Such cities drew people from many lands whose mix produced a web of interactive influences visible in the arts, architecture, and ordinary products. It affected language, religion, writing, and social-political institutions. So significant were these links between cultures that the arts of diplomacy were honed. Surviving evidence contains correspondence between kings and pharaohs as well as between important kings and lesser lords. A group of Egyptian imports found at six Aegean cities dating to about 1,400 BCE has been read as the record of an Egyptian embassy sent to establish connections with a relatively new power. Marriage ties, too, were employed to further amicable relations. One example is the strong presence of Minoan culture at a settlement on the northeastern border of Egypt that may be a token of the presence of a Minoan princess married to the native ruler.

All relations were not amicable, however. At a battle in northern Syria early in the thirteenth century, the Hittite king led his force of 20,000 against the Egyptian pharaoh with his force of equal size. The result was essentially a dead heat leading to a division of authority with the Egyptian pharaoh claiming the area to the south of the site of battle and the Hittite king controlling the lands to the north, including Anatolia. During much of the rest of the thirteenth century BCE the Hittites would advance westward to the coast of the Aegean to enhance their sphere of control. A number of the records of the Hittite king concern a pest from a place called Ahhiyawa who is employing his chariots to do damage to the western fringe area of the Hittite realm. In one of these missives, the king writes of the struggle over Wilusa – which may well be Ilium – another name for Troy. The record also identifies a ruler at Wilusa by the name of Alaksandu; we remember that a key figure in the *Iliad* has the double name of Alexander/Paris!

The Hittite evidence combined with the archaeological evidence of sites such as Mycenae and Hissarlik/Troy as well as the militant character of Greek culture in the Bronze Age assists in a verdict that the *Iliad* and *Odyssey* do remember serious warfare in Anatolia in the later Bronze Age albeit in less than exact terms. The form of memory was oral tradition that surely was transformed in the five or more centuries before it was recorded in writing. Memory was also complicated by events throughout the eastern Mediterranean beginning shortly after 1250 when attackers known as peoples advancing by "land and sea" ended the international civilization of the Bronze Age. Damage to the interactive structure began in the late thirteenth century. By the mid-twelfth century, not only had internationalism disappeared, but the brilliant, complex culture that had profited from it had sunk into what is regarded as a Dark Age.

Penelope and Odysseus

Penelope and Odysseus belong to the culture of the Mycenaean Age and, perhaps, to its period of collapse. As Odysseus tells the Phaeacian king, Alcinous, on whose island he has been ship-wrecked, his kingdom was centered on Ithaka, "an island amidst many other islands that include Same, Doulichion and Zacynthos; Ithaka is low-lying in the sea and furthest to the west."[5] Odysseus' son, Telemachos, offers more detail about the island when he refuses the offer of three horses and a polished chariot proffered by King Menelaos of Sparta: he will not take the horses to Ithaca which "has no broad running courses nor grassy meadows; it is good for goats not horses."[6] Kingship had been in his family for three generations: his own father, Laertes, ruled before Odysseus, and his grandfather, Arkeisios, before Laertes.

Figure 2.2   Penelope and Odysseus. Source: Amy Absher

Penelope is the daughter of Icarius, who was the brother of Tyndareus, the king of Sparta, and father of Helen whose face launched not only a thousand ships but suitors for her hand of every young man of nobility. Odysseus was one of the suitors who gathered to win her hand. While in Sparta he saw the younger girl Penelope and asked for her hand in marriage. She was very young, barely out of childhood; thus the marriage was delayed for eight years. Less than a year after they were wed, the news of Helen's desertion of Menelaos for the Trojan prince, Paris, mounted a campaign of the kings of Greece with their men to punish the deed. Odysseus joined, reluctantly, since Penelope was expecting a child. Telemachos would be born after Odysseus had departed.

Odysseus, Penelope, their child, and his grandfather are a small nuclear family, more important than other families to be sure due to lineage, wealth, and good fortune. Others in their society have nuclear families of their own, similarly graded by the same factors. Close in status are the 108 suitors who live apart from the home of Odysseus and Penelope. Also present are people of lower status, some of whom are outsiders such as Eumaeus and Eurycleia, the faithful servants of Odysseus and his family, who were victimized by fate to be forced into servitude and taken from their original homes.

The privileged members of society live apart in more conspicuous circumstances. However, their occupations are common to others of lesser status in the realm of Odysseus. Laertes, once king, is now "retired" and farms his own plot; Penelope weaves expertly, so expertly that she deceives her suitors by her claim to be preparing a shroud for Laertes which she does diligently, only to unweave it at night. If we turn our thoughts back to the earliest settled villages in Greece, underlying features seem similar.

However, their world encompasses more than an individual region: Penelope is Spartan-born and such alliances are important in circumstances that produce international connections for purposes of trade, warfare, and alliance. Travel by sea is essential to those purposes. Odysseus speaks of war in Troy, sojourn in Crete, and his travels to places undefined, all describing wider travel in the Aegean, Ionian, and Mediterranean seas. Menelaos describes his own stay with Helen in Egypt after the Greek victory at Troy. One consequence of the interaction is the creation of guest friendship through the gift exchanges that figure prominently in the *Odyssey*.

To produce the wealth for gift exchange requires a variety of skills. The base of the economy in agriculture and animal husbandry demands a high level of competency in farming, care of animals, and weaving. Exercising leadership in the community demands the ability to command others by words and deeds. Odysseus is "wily," "cunning," clever at devising plans. The Trojan horse, for example, was his solution to capturing Troy. Respect paid to the more-than-human elements of their world is demonstrated in the archaeological remains of the palace centers. Unlike religion in the Mycenaean kingdoms, divine support to the Homeric heroes is personal. Athena figures most prominently in the *Odyssey*. She is Odysseus' almost constant guide on his return to Ithaka, telling him, "Here we are, the two shrewdest minds in the universe, you far and away the best man on earth in plotting strategies, and I famed among gods for my clever schemes."[7] In loving Odysseus, she has taken on the task of aiding his son, Telemachos, coming in disguise to push him into action against the suitors encamped in his home: "You are neither evil nor foolish nor has the craft of Odysseus passed you by so there is hope that you will succeed," she tells Telemachos.[8] In her own sphere, Penelope also has the attention of Athena; when she prayed to the goddess to protect her son from the suitors, "Athena heard her prayer."[9] Inasmuch as Telemachos was born after Odysseus left for Troy, Penelope has had to bear the burden of maintaining the family until her son can assume that role and she is subtly clever with delay tactics. And with Athena's help, her son is finally beginning to step into his father's role. Gratitude for divine assistance is joined to fear of divine power: Odysseus knows only too well the strength of Poseidon.

The world of Odysseus bears only a slight resemblance to that of the palace centers of the Mycenaean Age. Suitors of Penelope are encamped in his "home" which is not protected by a sturdy wall or by being located on top of a mountain. There are riches stored in his home but there is no sign of the collection and redistribution of goods that characterized Mycenae or Pylos or the other Late Bronze Age kingdoms. The staff of the royal family consists of some servants, many of whom are disloyal. In fact, the three loyal supporters are a goatherd, a swineherd, and an elderly "housekeeper" who was nurse to Odysseus and Telemachos. The scale of life pictured in *Odyssey* is much smaller: replacing the power of a centralized administration is the power of a man able to hold his own against contenders for his role. Odysseus is described as "like a god" (*isotheos*) because of his personal ability to rise above ordinary humans. He does not hold his position due to divine right.

The contrast between the Mycenaean Age and the world of Odysseus as revealed by archaeological evidence and the decipherment of the Linear B tablets has long been connected to the nature of our evidence for Odysseus' "kingdom." The epic is the result of oral tradition that would surely have changed over the long centuries between the twelfth century and the revival of literacy in the eighth century BCE.

We will examine the validity of this explanation in the next chapter, in which the "oral" account of the Late Bronze Age reveals the effects of the wrath of Poseidon, lord of the sea. The god was, metaphorically, furious with travelers in his realm in the later thirteenth and early twelfth centuries BCE as conflict raged throughout the eastern Mediterranean attributed to the "Land and Sea Peoples." The Hittite kingdom crumbled; Egypt became the "broken reed," the major emporion of Ugarit on the coast of the Levant was destroyed, and Hissalik/Troy may have been another victim; Mycenaean citadel centers were destroyed, some suddenly, others after several attacks. Some of the peoples facing attack moved to what they hoped were safer areas and some of the sea peoples eventually settled into now devastated locations. Odysseus' return recounted in the *Odyssey* that ended ten years after the fall of Troy may echo conditions that ended the Mycenaean way of life in Greece and returned conditions to the Neolithic village structure.

Notes

1. Samuel Bassett, *The Poetry of Homer* (Berkeley: University of California Press, 1938), 244.
2. Homer, *Odyssey* 19.202 ff.
3. Arthur Evans, "Minoan Culture Discovered in Crete," *Illustrated London News*, August 14, 1900.
4. The "w" found in the tablets of the Mycenaean Age disappears in later Greek. Thus *wanax* becomes *anax*.
5. Homer, *Odyssey* 9.23–26.
6. Homer, *Odyssey* 4.639–640.
7. Homer, *Odyssey* 13.306–310.
8. Homer, *Odyssey* 2.278–280.
9. Homer, *Odyssey* 4.767.

Further Reading

Barber, R. L. N. 1987. *The Cyclades in the Bronze Age*. Iowa City: University of Iowa Press.
  The Cycladic islands are enchanting and they are now known to have played a major role in the early history of Greece. This richly illustrated account that includes 200 photographs and maps begins with a comparison between the Ancient and Modern Cyclades. Then the author turns to the rediscovery of the earliest human settlement on the islands and their history in the Bronze Age.
Bittlestone, Robert, with James Diggle and John Underhill. 2005. *Odysseus Unbound: The Search for Homer's Ithaca*. Cambridge: Cambridge University Press.
  The "kingdom" of one of the major figures in the Odyssey has never been found although British businessman Robert Bittlestone has developed a team armed with top-of-the-line technology, such as satellite images, to search for that kingdom on the island of Cephalonia, particularly its western peninsula, which in antiquity may well have been detached from the main island. It is a fascinating adventure that some distinguished archaeologists are beginning to find probable.
Chadwick, John. 1958. *The Decipherment of Linear B*. Cambridge: Cambridge University Press.
  An exciting account of the decipherment of the Linear B script that was long and laboriously studied. Dr Chadwick was one of the major figures in the process. The decipherment

provided evidence of the identity of its users when deciphered as a form of Indo-European, specifically Greek.

Chadwick, John. 1976. *The Mycenaean World*. Cambridge: Cambridge University Press.

This "snapshot" of the Bronze Age culture on the mainland is a readable account drawing on archaeological evidence as well as the deciphered script of the palace centers by a distinguished British Classicist.

Fitton, J. Lesley. 2002. *Minoans*. London: British Museum Press.

The author is keeper of antiquities at the British Museum, a fine position for writing this study of Minoan Crete as well as its role in the contemporary context of the Bronze Age.

McDonald, William A. and Carol Thomas. 1990, 2nd ed. *Progress into the Past: The Rediscovery of Mycenaean Civilization*. Bloomington: Indiana University Press.

The study is an updated version of the first *Progress into the Past* authored by William McDonald. New information had altered previous views of the early history of Greece. Professors McDonald and Thomas cooperated in the revised publication.

Manning, Sturt W. 1999. *A Test of Time: The Volcano of Thera and the Chronology and History of the Aegean and East Mediterranean in the Mid-Second Millennium BC*. Oxford: Oxbow Books.

The role of the environment in history is dramatically demonstrated in the huge eruption of the volcano of Thera. It illustrates well the importance of interdisciplinary cooperation.

Strauss, Barry. 2006. *The Trojan War: A New History*. New York: Simon and Schuster.

The account is neatly situated into the nature of life in the Bronze Age; even the Trojan horse could be understood in the light of the nature of deceit in Hittite military strategy. Engaging and clear, the text is enhanced by maps and illustrations. It supports the historicity of the war recounted in the *Iliad*.

Thomas, Carol G. and Craig Conant. 2005 and 2007. *The Trojan War*. Westport, CT: Greenwood Press/Norman, OK: University of Oklahoma Press.

This approach to the question of the Trojan War locates it within the role of archaeology, the epic tradition, and the power of legend as well as the conditions of the Late Bronze Age. The authors also examine the role of Troy in the twenty-first century.

3

End of the Bronze Age
Slow Reshaping

The Dark Age

Evidence for the magnitude of the troubles during the late thirteenth century BCE and continuing into the twelfth is plain but identification of the cause of the disruption is difficult. Egyptian records describe the "conspiracy" of foreign countries which all at once were on the move, scattered in war. No country could stand before their arms. Although modern scholars call these attackers the "Land and Sea Peoples," they seem not to have been a unified body. Linear B tablets from the Mycenaean kingdom of Pylos describe the dispatch of rowers and watchers to the coast at the same time that the Egyptian pharaoh was expecting the arrival of foes and other written records describe enemies that were active in northern Syria, in the waters off Cyprus, and in Anatolia. By the early twelfth century, the two super-powers of the Late Bronze Age – the Hittite Empire and the Egyptian kingdom – had collapsed, the Hittite realm completely and Egypt falling into disunity. The Aegean kingdoms had been destroyed or survived only as refugee settlements.

Until recently, the favored explanation was destruction by invaders but evidence for such migrants is slim, if not altogether missing in the form of new objects or indications of new settlements. Rather, the earlier internationalism presents an important clue: something – or some things – affected the entire, interlocked region with different causes in the several areas. The trade network may have been damaged, or over-extended, or weakened by several years of poor agricultural productivity in some cases. Natural disasters may well have been agents: earthquakes, volcanic eruptions, and climatic change, which are frequent occurrences in Mediterranean lands, have serious repercussions. Internal problems in certain regions – assaults on citadel centers that possessed stores of food – may figure in the picture. Spread of disease through the interactive system may also have been a factor, as it has been in many other periods and places.

Greece: A Short History of a Long Story, 7,000 BCE to the Present, First Edition.
Carol G. Thomas.
© 2014 John Wiley & Sons, Inc. Published 2014 by John Wiley & Sons, Inc.

Whatever the cause(s), much of the last two centuries of the second millennium and of the period 1,150 to 800 BCE are justly titled the "Dark Age" throughout most of the eastern Mediterranean. Basic features of developments in the Aegean sphere included an almost total institutional change, although cultural continuity at a lower level of sophistication is evident. We tend to concentrate on the elite of the palace centers in discussing the Bronze Age. However, most of the inhabitants of the kingdoms controlled by those centers were farmers, herders, and practitioners of basic crafts living in villages and towns throughout the kingdom. Consequently, even if the centralized control disappeared, the daily life of the peasants could continue in the villages that had previously been united. This picture describes well the case of Greece: population declined drastically and deep poverty characterized the condition of survivors. On the other hand, the collapse of the kingdoms opened the path to the eventual rise of independent city-states by the Classical Age. Each was a community of small territorial size in which all full members participated in the communal well-being. The Greek term of that community is *polis* (often described as a city-state). The development would be slow but its roots took hold in the independent villages that managed to survive the time of troubles and the grim Age of Iron when, as the poet Hesiod declared, "men never rest from labor and sorrow by day and from perishing by night."[1] Living at this time, Hesiod describes the life he knew by wishing that he had been born before or after this Age or not at all. It is important to know that he lived at the end of the "Dark Age," when restoration of ordered community was under way rather than at its beginning that the world of Odysseus appears to represent.

The circumstances and the concerns of Hesiod and his village seem to bear certain resemblances to the circumstances of Penelope and Odysseus, especially in the importance of the nuclear family. But, there are many major differences. To understand the changes it is wise to appreciate the length and slowness of transformation that occurred between circa 1,200 and 700 BCE: 500 years. Examining the process of development century by century through individual sites discloses the interplay between retention and adaptation. Beginning with Bronze Age Mycenae, we will look next at Nichoria which reveals the tiny surviving settlement of a handful of people. Athens did survive complete destruction but became a small area of refuge that experienced influences from the larger Mediterranean sphere which would fuel recovery. On the island of Euboea, a small community that often shifted its location would venture well beyond the narrow strait of water on which it was located. Somewhat later, Corinth followed the same course of navigating the seas to become one of the major *poleis* of Greece. Then we return to Hesiod and his home on the cusp of the Classical Greek way of life.

Mycenae, perhaps the major kingdom of the Bronze Age, is an obvious point of departure. Signs of burning occur at three times. The first affected only certain areas of the citadel walls in the later part of the thirteenth century, likely propelling people to move within the walls. The second burning at the end of that century damaged most of the citadel; even though it was not deserted, the center may have lost control over the surrounding region. A final conflagration about fifty years later reduced Mycenae to a small community of little significance. In other parts of Greece as well, destructions took place – Pylos, Tiryns, Thebes, and some lesser damage at Athens – and survivors continued to live on most, but not all, of the citadel sites. However, control over the larger region was lost. Large numbers of former towns and villages were destroyed although some survived. Material culture reflects earlier forms, albeit in less sophisticated forms, not complete replacement by new introductions.

The citadel centers faded in the twelfth and eleventh centuries to be succeeded by tiny refugee settlements such as Nichoria, once part of the kingdom of Pylos. Nichoria's Dark Age inhabitants sought anonymity, living on their flat-topped ridge about a mile and a half inland from the Gulf of Messenia, well screened by a leading edge of low hills. The survivors may have followed a nomadic way of life for several decades, returning to a settled life around 1100 when some sixty-five people assembled one-room huts of mud-brick walls and thatched roofs, eking out an existence from crops and animals, and providing necessary goods through basic household crafts. The presence of one larger home suggests the existence of a village headsman who provided leadership for the community, perhaps in consultation with the elders of the group.

By the tenth century, darkness had lifted a bit in some places. Athens especially shows some vigor, not surprising since it did not experience the massive destruction of other sites and, consequently, served as a place of refuge for other Mycenaean Greeks. Tradition reports that the rulers of Pylos, descendants of Nestor, fled the burning Pylos by sea to take refuge in Athens and became members of its ruling line. Non-Greeks, too, appear to have been attracted to Athens for other reasons than settlement. Perhaps as one of few remaining ports of call it attracted traders from areas of the Mediterranean that had recovered earlier. It is likely, for example, that the new skill of iron working may have entered Greece through Athens.

Inhabitants of Athens also took to the sea in the eleventh and tenth centuries. Having a larger population than most contemporary sites led people from Attica, joined by participants from east-central Greece and the island of Euboea, to establish, or in some cases re-establish, settlements on the coast of Asia Minor. Other migrants from northeastern Greece found their way to the northern part of that coast in the late twelfth century. Over the next several centuries, the entire coastline as well as the off-shore islands would be inhabited by Greeks. Both the revival of seafaring and the identification of the Greek geographical sphere are essential to an understanding of Greek history from the so-called Dark Age to the present day.

Sustained recovery followed in the ninth century as members of some small villages took to the sea. Inhabitants of Lefkandi, on the island of Euboea, were especially precocious: initially the community was home to little more than twenty-five people but they were skilled in fashioning metal goods and bold in conveying these goods to locations reaching from the northern Aegean to the coast of the Levant to Ithaca and even southern Italy. In addition to trade, they began to form permanent enclaves in the northern Aegean and the central Mediterranean. In these distant places, they came to know peoples like the seafaring Phoenicians and the iron-working Etruscans from whom the voyagers from Euboea learned new skills – technological, geographical, and intellectual.

Archaic Age: Revival

Such vigor fueled a revival that has been named the "Renaissance of the Eighth Century." The key element of that Renaissance is the formation of the community known as the *polis*. A *polis* is a community of people within a defined territory. Since physical nature of Greece fosters division, territory is generally small. Each *polis* had a core for the coordination of life of its members but that core bore little, if any, similarity with a Mycenaean center. Rather it was the location for members of the community to manage the affairs of their state – it was a citizen-state. Originating from the early Dark Age villages, early *poleis* were small in size and population; thus participation of members who had roots in the territory was critical to the welfare of those who governed themselves.

That Corinth was one of the stars in this Renaissance is shown in its population growth, huge leaps in technology, a flood of new ideas from other cultures, and consolidation of a way of life within its limited territory. Corinth became a major trading power, creating products sought by others that used ingredients that had given rise to the complex economic culture of the Bronze Age: olives were especially valuable not only for their fruit, but for oil and perfume that required special vessels from the high-quality clay of the region. Corinth's location on the Gulf of Corinth allowed relatively easy seafaring both to the west and across the isthmus into the Saronic Gulf to the south made accessible by the construction of a track for moving ships from one body of water to the other. Eventually, the track would be another source of wealth from tolls paid by sailors from other regions. Corinth's inhabitants were willing to move to new lands temporarily as traders and permanently by establishing colonies along the coast and in coastal islands of the Adriatic and, eventually, across the Adriatic.

Contact with more distant cultures not only by Corinth but increasingly by other emerging *polis* communities is demonstrated by large temples and large-scale sculptures that show the influence of Egyptian craftsmen; a new style of warfare reveals knowledge of warfare in Anatolia; and alphabetic writing as well as artistic influence found its way from the Levant. Greece was once again connected with the larger world as it had been in the Bronze Age, though on a very different basis of political organization.

Greek culture had changed dramatically. By the mid-eighth century remnants of the Mycenaean way of life were difficult to see. Nor would the nature of that way of life be repeated in the second civilization of Greece during the Classical Age. Even though the small community remained the focus of life, villages were no longer controlled by a ruler housed in a central citadel; rather villages were the foundation of a community of people who depended upon one another for their good fortune. As a result, Greek society and culture differed markedly from Bronze Age culture in most aspects of life. Only after the conquests of Alexander of Macedon did Greece again experience the complex machinery of administrative control.

Yet the Greeks traced their roots back to the Age of Heroes by way of myths, legends, and epic poems as Hesiod's Five Ages reveals. It was through these remembrances that modern archaeologists discovered the actuality of the heroic past. Language, too, shows the persistence of practices and institutions reaching back into the second millennium. The Dark Age was not a wall of separation but a bridge of transition that reshaped an inheritance in accord with the difficult circumstances inherent in the Greek environment, made even more burdensome by the "Time of Troubles." There was continuity of people and their way of life in the wake of the disasters of the Late Bronze Age, albeit at a lower level of sophistication across the four centuries dubbed the Dark Age. A legacy of Mycenaean times remained although it was modified by the centuries of difficulties which brought a sudden reduction of the scale and quality of life.

Corinthian success was unusual. The end product of the reshaping by the late eighth century was smaller communities like Askra. It is useful to know that the Greek *poleis* would number 1,054 by the full Classical period. Most inhabitants were farmers; only the wealthier and braver farmers would be engaged in trade. Power, consequently, was not evenly divided among members of the community. New influences in the seventh and sixth centuries would produce changes in the specific structures of the community, even though traditional village life grounded in agriculture and herding persisted. Some stratification based on wealth and standing continued but the less wealthy and less eminent members of a *polis* gained important status. Askra is on the cusp of these changes: no longer Pre-Classical, it belongs to the first phase of the Classical Age of Greece, namely the Archaic phase defined so well by Antony Snodgrass:

> Before, they had been just another tribal society with fond memories of a better past; after, they were the expansive prophets of a new political system whose future must have seemed very bright. Before, they had orally-transmitted poetry of uncertain content and variable antiquity, which they were unable to record permanently. After, they had the songs of Homer and the means to write them down.[2]

Establishing Classical Greece

The two centuries from circa 700 to 500 BCE witnessed a rising tempo in the pace of life in Greece centered on the new conception of the Greek state. As evidence of the "Dark" centuries demonstrates, it was in the process of formation throughout them. In fact, its roots reached back to the independent villages of the Neolithic Age and to the villages subsumed in the extension of control from the Minoan and Mycenaean centers. Drastic population decline coupled with the inherent force of regionalism fostered life centered on small, largely isolated villages in the early Dark Age.

An important reason for the developments in the eighth and seventh centuries was a substantial rise in population caused perhaps by agricultural innovations, or improvements in climatic conditions, or a decline in the death rate of infants, or, perhaps, all of these factors. To extend land for farming and herding, communities pushed out into marginal land and toward neighboring villages. One result was that small villages found a common cause with neighboring communities that shared the same natural environment, expanding both their territories and populations as they merged into new, single communities. Athens is a good example of this process as the territory of the Attic peninsula was reunited following disunity during much of the Dark Age.

Often, however, affiliation did not provide a complete solution; consequently the young *poleis* were pushed to other recourses. One of the most notable responses was migration and colonization as members of many communities sought land and other opportunities far from the Greek mainland. Once again, topography and location directed this response. As early as the eleventh century, sailors from the island of Euboea were traveling into the northern Aegean and, by the eighth century, they and others were venturing into the eastern and central Mediterranean not only for purposes of trade but also to found settlements. Somewhat later, others navigated the tortuous Bosporus strait to penetrate the Black Sea while equally bold adventurers pushed even further westward toward the strait of Gibraltar.

It is likely that the first efforts were undertaken by individuals, probably the wealthier members of the communities who had both the resources to devote to constructing and equipping ships and also the produce and objects to carry as supplies and/or as trade goods. Soon, however, colonization became a deliberate *polis* enterprise with selection or conscription of colonizers, designation of a leader, and authorization from Apollo at Delphi. The designated leader of a colonial venture first consulted the oracle of Apollo at Delphi for advice and direction. Thus, over time, the Delphic oracle became a font of information. The new settlement would become an independent *polis*, not a subject of the founding community, although with ties of ancestry to be sure, but without officials from, or obligations to, the mother community.

Goals from the start were two. One was to gain access to necessary goods that were not available or not sufficiently plentiful at home. The early participation of Euboeans in the trade and commerce of Al Mina in northern Syria with the flourishing centers of the ancient Near East is proof of the importance of trade for the Greeks. Fertile land was also a goal as the choice of Syracuse in Sicily reveals. The two motives seem to have gone hand-in-hand and, surely for some, were joined by the opportunity for adventure. Hesiod spoke to his brother about seafaring with all of these impulses in mind: "If desire for stormy sailing excites you, I will advise you."[3]

Adventurers were among the seafarers. The Father of History, Herodotus, recounts the good fortune of the Egyptian Psammetikhos, who was one of several local leaders who wished to reunite Egypt under their own sway after Egypt's own Dark Age. To Psammetikhos came an oracle that "vengeance would come when bronze men appeared from the sea."[4] Those bronze men did appear when adventurers from the Aegean were driven off their course, landed in the delta, were hired to help Psammetikhos, and did so successfully.

The consequences of these successes were momentous. The Greek sphere expanded to include much of the Mediterranean littoral as well as the coast of the Black Sea, all dotted by independent *poleis* replicating those of the Greek Aegean. Access to new goods and products encountered in their different homes was a stimulus to specialized production with a goal of serving the needs of exchange. Contact with others also taught the Greeks new skills, techniques, and ideas. Greek pottery of the seventh century is named "Orientalizing" from the wealth of designs, styles, and shapes seen and adopted from the Ancient Orient of the eastern Mediterranean. Encountering monumental architecture and sculpture in Egypt was an impetus to learn the techniques of builders and artisans in order to undertake similar construction and fashioning in Greece. Contact with the Phoenicians, who had carved out much of the southern Mediterranean coast and the western region of Sicily for their own trading purposes, was the source of a return of literacy to Greece in the form of an alphabet adapted from the earlier Phoenician model.

From Lydia in Anatolia came knowledge of a new form of warfare – the phalanx with hoplites, equipped alike and marching in uniform rows and ranks, replaced individual combat and would remain the supreme tool of war until the Roman conquest of Greece in the second century BCE. Coinage, too, was learned from the Lydian kingdom. Stories, songs, views of divinity, and customs all flooded the Greek imagination.

Miletus flourished, not only on the coast of Asia Minor but in establishing new settlements of its own in the Black Sea. It is likely that its later significance also reflected its importance in the "Age of Heroes" as well as influences from non-Greek Anatolian cultures. One result of its widespread activity is intellectual: Thales of Miletus, the first known scientific-philosopher, wrote practical treatises and sought to explain the physical nature of the earth. In the next generation, philosophers Anaximander and Anaximenes were also Milesians. The question of the nature of the world animated the inquiries of the Milesians and philosophers throughout antiquity.

The outside influences were formative but the Greek mentality assessed and modified the inheritance in view of Greek needs. Greece did not become Egyptian, or Lydian, or Near Eastern. In fact, her own influence soon began to shape the other cultures especially in the central and western Mediterranean. More Greek vases of this period have come to light in Etruria than in most parts of mainland Greece. Alphabetic writing was passed on to Italy by the Greek colonizers there. Horace's words of the first century BCE that Greece captured by Rome captivated her captor have far deeper roots than the Roman poet suspected: Greece began to captivate her future captor many centuries before the *poleis* fell to Roman power.

Not all communities followed the course of colonization to accommodate a growing population. Although the Greek states bear a common name, each *polis* was independent not only in its political decisions but in its particular form of a way of life. The Greek language had dialectic differences; the Olympians were honored in a variety of ways; economic modes were diverse. Regionalism played a large role in the variety but self-conscious attitudes were equally important.

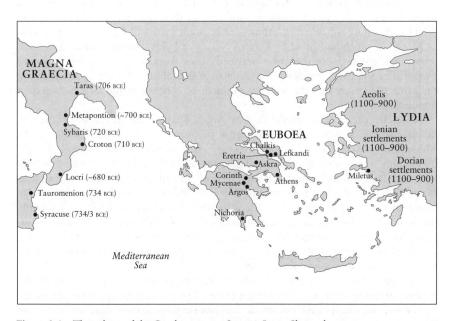

Figure 3.1 The sphere of the Greek recovery. Source: Jason Shattuck

It is not surprising that some of the first traders and colonizers were from coastal sites like the Euboean communities and Corinth, whose land was restricted by natural features or claims of neighboring communities. By the mid-eighth century, two Euboean communities had combined to establish an outpost on the island of Pithekoussai in the Bay of Naples. An attraction was access to the resources, especially metals, of the Etruscans in northern Italy. Further south, Corinth had targeted the site of Syracuse on Sicily by 733 BCE. Eventually movement from established Greek *poleis* would extend west to what is now France and Spain, to parts of northern Africa, and around the coastline of the Black Sea. The variety of cultures they encountered was immense, as Figure 3.1 reveals.

Efforts to found colonies and develop trade resulted in internal developments for those *poleis* that succeeded in their endeavors. As we have seen, Corinth, for example, began to specialize in production of marketable goods, such as perfumed olive oil, which required proper containers in the form of exquisite small vases. Physically, too, Corinth reflected the new activities in increasing urbanization: temples were constructed in the heart of the *polis* and on the isthmus, the latter temple fittingly dedicated to Poseidon; a potters' quarter took shape; ship building and bronze working were specialized crafts. The importance of these economic developments gave rise to changes in the social and political order. Rather than chiefs, such as those of tiny Nichoria in the early Dark Age, or powerful landowners, such as in Hesiod's Askra, oligarchies were created by a new form of wealth, gained from commerce and trade. The new order angered many, like Theognis of Megara who cried out in his verse that wealth not noble ancestry now was the basis of power. Theognis had the ancestry, not the wealth.

Landlocked Spartans did not take to the sea but rather solved the problem of population growth by expanding by land first in their own region of Laconia and then by marching westward to capture, after twenty years of fighting, the rich land of Messenia which had been the land of Nestor of Pylos. Original Messenian landowners became serfs for their new overlords, now working the land they had once owned. The solution provided both sustenance and laborers for the Spartans but at the same time it created the weighty problem of controlling the large subservient population.

Especially after a defeat in the field by Argos, Sparta hardened its institutions to define citizens as soldiers of equal status supported in their basic needs by the Messenian serfs and in other requirements such as manufactured goods by the inhabitants of neighboring villages. Unlike the serfs, the villagers exercised control over their local affairs but were directed by Sparta in all larger pursuits, such as warfare. For a time, the Spartans ended efforts at further territorial expansion. As an alternative, a series of bilateral alliances between Sparta and other states gradually produced the Peloponnesian League of states linked for offensive and defensive purposes. The need for military might was, consequently, a major factor in the economic nature of the Spartan state and also in the maintenance of an older political order headed by two lines of hereditary kings.

The territory of the *polis* centered on Athens combined the features of the regions of the Spartan and Corinthian states. The sea defined the territory to the east, west, and south of the peninsula. It is not surprising, then, that Athens would become a major naval power. But Attica was blessed with a fair amount of good agricultural land akin to Sparta's region; in the case of Attica it was distributed in four plains that were not separated by impassable mountains. Consequently the cohesion of separate small settlements was not as difficult as it was in some parts of Greece.

While Athens had not been destroyed by the problems of the Late Bronze Age, regionalism came to divide small groups of people from one another during the Dark Age. The chiefs of those groups were heads of families who were fortunate in their good, ample land holdings. Drawing together the once separate villages proceeded slowly but gradually produced a sizable number of local leaders who eventually agreed to cooperate in the affairs of a united community, acting collectively as members of a council that met on the Hill of Ares – the Areopagus – in Athens. Their enhanced powers gave them leverage in their local spheres. In fact, the early sixth century found many of the peasants of Athens reduced to a serf-like position with bondage to their lords.

These three examples of differing ways of *polis* organization and life come from three of the major *poleis* of the Greek world; they can be seen as part of the spectrum of different ways of life within the *polis* structure. It is important to recognize that the total number of *poleis* in the Mediterranean, Aegean, and Black Sea spheres was approximately 1,050. Specific physical conditions, locations, and prior history would create different forms of communal life through the entire Greek sphere. One similarity was the nature of relations with one's neighboring *poleis*. With space constricted by the physical environment, a community seeking additional agricultural land might be tempted to cross over the range of mountains to appropriate land on the other side. And this temptation defines much of Greek history from 700 to 336 BCE. The nearest *polis* was the worst enemy.

A fairly widespread similarity developed during the Archaic Age in the form of a growing resentment of the insignificant members of the emerging *polis*. During the seventh century the situation often led to the success of a single, powerful leader who championed the welfare of the "people" (*demos*) against the practices of the "lords." It is quite possible that such champions had the assistance of the peasants who now were engaged in the defense of their *polis*. One result of contact with other cultures was military: from the kingdom of Lydia in Anatolia, Greeks learned the value of equipping soldiers with the same armor, shields, and spears and organizing them in close formation of ranks and rows. Earlier practices reflected in the Homeric epics described heroes equipped with special armor and weapons and engaged in hand-to-hand combat with their opponents. Also significant is that the equipment was less costly; consequently, ordinary farmers could serve as troops in a formation where each member must cooperate with his peers.

The champions who aided the hoplite cause were known as tyrants by the Greeks after the non-Greek title *tyrannos*, used for powerful kings in Anatolia. Such individuals in a *polis* were not altogether altruistic; they were ambitious men but, in serving their own needs, they also limited the power of the aristocratic element. Advice from one successful tyrant to another was "Strike off the heads of the tallest heads of grain." By whatever means they removed opposition to their position – death, flight, the forced grudging accord of their peers – their actions weakened the hold of the aristocracy. With the limitation of aristocratic power, the middling levels gained a greater role in the affairs of the *polis*. As W. G. Forrest described the situation, the ordinary member of a community

> had not acquired a new political doctrine which insisted on a wider distribution of power ... [but] he could now see an alternative to [lordly] government, an alternative almost as noble as the [lords] themselves and just as rich, men already obviously favoured by the gods who could easily persuade him that they had been granted the ultimate favour, that Zeus had decided at last to punish 'the judges who grind men down' and had appointed human agents for the job (agents who with Zeus and 5,000 hoplite spears behind them could easily deal with 300 [lords] who had neither a better god nor better arms.[5]

The community first adopting the hoplite formation had a formidable advantage over its neighbors if and when it sought to expand its territory. Many identify that first hoplite force as Argos, a former Mycenaean center that had recovered early in the Dark Age. Its troops were known as the goads of war during the first decades of the Archaic Age. Their leader, Pheidon, described by Aristotle as beginning as a king but ending as a tyrant, actively attempted to expand in the Peloponnese, intervening in affairs in Corinth, defeating a Spartan army, and celebrating the Olympic games under his own presidency in the process. Such success in the field quickly taught other *poleis* that adoption of hoplite weapons, armor, formation, and tactics was essential to their survival, thus creating another largely common element of *polis* life.

Hesiod

We are fortunate that Hesiod's own description of the world in which he lived and his assessment of both its strengths and problems have survived. Living at the end of the Dark Age in the later eighth century and into the seventh, he stood on the verge of these developments. What is equally important is that his views of life are captured in written form. The two major works are *Theogony*, a "history" of the gods, and *Works and Days*, an account of life in the village environment that was becoming the geographical and organizational community we know as the *polis*. Hesiod's account does not reveal the full process of development from the end of the Mycenaean civilization into the earliest phase of Classical civilization, but it does allow us to sense the slow recovery. The poems have been dated on the basis of the elements of their language to 700–650, with *Theogony* being the older of the two poems.[6]

The Greek alphabet is also essential evidence for the continuity of the Greek story from deep antiquity to the present. Although the earliest form of writing in that story was not alphabetic, the Linear B tablets of the Bronze Age kingdoms have been deciphered as Greek. The destructions of the late thirteenth century BCE erased that form of writing. Renewed contact with the larger Mediterranean sphere led to knowledge of, and eventual adaptation of, the Greek alphabet. Hesiod's father may have played a role in that process, as a sailor in the Levant where he learned of the Phoenician alphabet, a critical element for the Greek alphabet. Although evidence of Hesiod's "education" is slight, the manuscript tradition of his works is valuable support of this history, as is the growing evidence of literacy in Greece from the seventh century.

The king of the gods set the generation of mortals. Kronos set the first two; Zeus set the following three. Hesiod's generation was the fifth. The gods first fashioned a golden race which was followed by a lesser silver race which, in turn, was succeeded by a yet more inferior race of bronze. Next, rather surprisingly, came a race of heroes – in fact demigods, some of whom fought at Troy for the sake of Helen. They, too, gave way to another age – the fifth age: Hesiod lived in this age of iron. Does the catalogue of metals describe decline, as the value placed on gold compared to the value of the other metals could suggest? One sign is that Hesiod reports Askra was "bad in winter, difficult in summer, never good"[7] and he certainly wished he had been before his own time.

It is interesting that archaeological evidence demonstrates that the use of bronze was replaced by iron technology in the transition between the second and first millennia. While Hittites had possessed the technology of producing iron in the second millennium, it was not dispersed until the widespread difficulties beginning in the late thirteenth century dissolved the Hittite kingdom, sending refugees – and their skills – to different locations. The worth of iron technology to the Hittites made it a well-kept secret. When knowledge of iron working was dispersed, it became one of the factors in the Greek revival at the end of the Dark Age.

A site has been identified in Boeotia that matches an ancient description of Askra. Earliest settlement dates to the late eleventh or early tenth century and continues through Hesiod's own lifetime into the third century BCE. Surviving evidence suggests a small farming village. The land is rocky but springs of water are abundant. A small hill may have served as a low acropolis although it is a miniature by comparison with the Mycenaean *acropoleis*. Not far distant, however, are much grander mountains that divide the plain from neighboring regions and serve as summer pastures for flocks: the Muses inspired Hesiod while he was pasturing sheep on the slopes of Mount Helikon. The sea, on the other hand, is a walk of a day or two depending on the pace of humans and animals.

Hesiod also relates how his father came to Askra from Kyme, a settlement on the coast of Asia Minor. Archaeological evidence confirms the correctness of traditional accounts of the migration, reporting the movement of mainland Greeks to the coastal area of Asia Minor after the turmoil beginning in the thirteenth century subsided.[8] Kyme was one of the settlements along the northern coast. A foundation date of 1,120 BCE was assigned by later historians with its founders identified as the grandsons of Agamemnon. The settlement gained importance through its location, which included a fine harbor, encouraging seafaring. It was also a neighbor to the landlocked small kingdom of Phrygia which was recovering rather more quickly than many areas from the Bronze Age disasters. Hesiod's father, perhaps named Dios, lived in Kyme but left when he was needful of a good life and sought it by traveling over the wide sea in a black ship. His sailing eventually brought him to Askra where he settled, married, and had two sons. Although life in Askra was primarily based on the land, Dios may have continued to sail, encouraging at least one of his sons to follow his example. Hesiod tells us that his brother, Perses, was seized by a desire for rough seafaring although he himself thought it foolish. Even so, *Works and Days* describes how and when to follow this dangerous course.

Figure 3.2　Hesiod. Source: Anne Lou Robkin

That poem also reveals the social and political developments of his *polis* community. Hesiod is worried about most matters and he airs his views powerfully. He gives advice on the proper way to work and provide a livelihood for one's family, a nuclear family akin to that of the Neolithic farming villages and of most people who lived in Bronze Age villages under the control of the citadel. Success, even mere survival, demands constant work which for most inhabitants of Askra involves farming the land and animal husbandry. As he reminds his brother: "Work, Perses, so that Demeter will favor you and will fill your barn with the necessities of life."[9] Lines 383 through 617 are essentially an almanac of what to do and when to carry out basic agricultural tasks. In this calendar, Hesiod is very concerned with the proper behavior of humans to avoid angering the gods and warns that men should "be mindful of the days that come from Zeus ... the wise counselor."[10]

However, there are differing shades of status in Askra, essentially between the ordinary peasants and the wealthier members of the community. Some of the more fortunate are able to engage in the trading of their surplus traveling by sea. His brother is keen to follow this path but Hesiod is wary and advises that Perses not load every bit of surplus aboard a ship that is likely to sink. Signs of a rising population are apparent even in tiny Askra. When the father of Hesiod and Perses died, the property was initially divided but Perses gained more than half with the aid of bribery to the gift-devouring "lords." Power rested with the few successful "lords"; it is interesting that Hesiod uses the word "*basileis*" (the Classical Greek term for "kings"). He can warn them that "the immortals observe those who with crooked judgments oppress others fearing the wrath of the gods not one bit."[11] All he himself can do is to advise them to "Beware ... straighten your decisions ... banish the twisting of justice."[12] There is no threat of a militant uprising by those who have been victimized.

Yet, Hesiod knew of the existence of a new development in the defense of a community when he traveled to the island of Euboea to participate in the funeral games held for Amphidamas of Chalkis, who was killed in a conflict with the neighboring *polis*, Eretria, circa 700. Both Chalkis and Eretria had followed in the pattern of Lefkandi as intrepid seafaring communities during much of the Dark Age. But they also depended on agriculture for subsistence and had the good fortune of sharing a fertile plain. Experiencing the growing rise in population noted in Askra fueled rivalry for control of more, perhaps all, of that plain by the two *poleis*. The nature and duration of the "Lelantine War" is uncertain; some believe that it attracted the participation of other *poleis* while others argue that it was seasonal and local. Archaeological evidence is clear on the development of massed infantry fighting in Greece in the eighth century, with the introduction of the hoplite shield by 675 BCE. Infantry tactics also allowed Pheidon of Argos to gain widespread conquest in the Peloponnese in the seventh century, as we have noted. While Hesiod does not describe infantry battles in Askra, he would have learned of their existence when he won his victory at Chalkis, probably by singing the history of the gods: the *Theogony*. This form of warfare persisted throughout the remainder of Greece's independent history both in the Aegean sphere and beyond in the colonized regions of the larger Mediterranean.

Hesiod knew of other commonalities. Greek was the common language throughout the wider sphere of Greek settlements although it had dialects that regionalism fostered. As the historian Herodotus put it, the Greeks must stand together against the Persians because they shared kinship and language as well as gods. The Olympians – many of whom are known from the Linear B tablets – were honored throughout the Greek world: Zeus was everywhere respected as the supreme god who commanded the thunderbolt and the weather, as the other eleven Olympians were honored for their own acknowledged spheres. However, since the deities assisted members of different *poleis* in various ways, the remembrance of the particular acts of assistance was shown in varying ceremonies and celebrations.

The division into hundreds of separate, independent polities akin to Askra defines the essential nature of the re-formed civilization of Greece across the more than four centuries following the collapse of the essential nature of the Mycenaean civilization. This division also conditioned the history of the following four centuries from the Archaic phase of the Classical Age, through the full Classical Age of the fifth century, to its self-destruction into the fourth century ending with absorption by another power in 338 BCE. Hesiod would surely have felt more at home had he been born later in the Classical Age rather than in a Mycenaean kingdom. Askra was a proto-*polis*.

Notes

1. Hesiod, *Works and Days*, lines 176–178.
2. Anthony Snodgrass, *Archaic Greece: The Age of Experiment* (London: J. M. Dent & Sons, 1980), 47.

3. Hesiod, *Works and Days*, line 618.
4. Herodotus II.152.
5. W. G. Forrest, *The Emergence of Greek Democracy* (London: Weidenfeld, 1966), 119, 121.
6. Richard Janko, *Homer, Hesiod, and the Hymns: Diachronic Development in Epic Diction* (Cambridge and New York: Cambridge University Press, 1982), 200.
7. Hesiod, *Works and Days*, line 640.
8. Thucydides 1.12.4.
9. Hesiod, *Works and Days*, lines 299–302.
10. Hesiod, *Works and Days*, lines 765, 768.
11. Hesiod, *Works and Days*, lines 248–251.
12. Hesiod, *Works and Days*, lines 263–264.

Further Reading

Dark Age

Sandars, N. K. 1978. *The Sea Peoples: Warriors of the Ancient Mediterranean, 1250–1150*. London: Thames and Hudson.

> The mysterious destroyers of the vibrant Mediterranean Bronze Age are identified through primary accounts of their activities, illustrations of their attacks, and descriptions of the results of their successes.

Tandy, David W. and Walter C. Neal. 1996. *Hesiod's Works and Days: A Translation and Commentary for the Social Sciences*. Berkeley and Los Angeles: University of California Press.

> Although Hesiod lived at the end of the Dark Age, he found life grim. However, he could not see that life in his small farming village was the basis of the emerging Classical Greek way of life. This translation of Hesiod's poem also provides a useful description of the man and his world with translation on the right-hand pages and commentary on the left-hand pages.

Thomas, Carol G. and Craig Conant. 1999. *Citadel to City-State: The Transformation of Greece, 1200–700 B.C.E.* Bloomington: Indiana University Press.

> The Dark Age deserves its name due in part to lack of evidence. It began with vast destruction of lives and settlements. Yet development over four centuries is demonstrated by the transformation of communal life. *Citadel to City-State* tracks the disappearance of citadel-based kingdoms through small, migratory groups eventually settling into diminutive villages. Some villages privileged by location began to improve while others sought better conditions by establishing wider contacts. Hesiod's Askra demonstrates the sum of these developments for the majority of Greeks in the late eighth century BCE.

Archaic

Boardman, John. 1999. *The Greeks Overseas: Their Early Colonies and Trade*, 4th ed. New York: Thames and Hudson.

> The long history of Greece is rooted in its role in the Mediterranean sphere. The author – a distinguished archaeologist and art historian – describes the return of Greeks to the sea after the destructions of the Late Bronze Age. The map of their return stretches from the Levant to the Atlantic and from southern Egypt to southern Europe.

Forrest, W. G. 1966. *The Emergence of Greek Democracy*. London: Weidenfeld.

> Recovery of stability brought new conditions to the lives of Greeks. One of the most significant was the new role of "ordinary" members of a community in managing collective

affairs. Such a role was absent in the Bronze Age kingdoms and Hesiod still complained about the power of a few men. The author explores its emergence over time through the forces involved and the societal changes it produced.

Hurwit, Jeffrey. 1985. *The Art and Culture of Early Greece, 1100–480 B.C.* Ithaca, NY: Cornell University Press.

As knowledge of developments in Greece following the Mycenaean collapse is predominately material, art historian Hurwit employs this evidence to describe the developments that link the Pre-Classical and Classical cultures of Greece.

Murray, Oswyn. 1993. *Early Greece*, 2d ed. Stanford, CA: Stanford University Press.

The author emphasizes three aspects: the history of ideas; the eastern Mediterranean unity; and the role of social customs. Primary sources are nicely embedded in a most readable account of Greek history from the end of the Dark Age through the Persian War.

Snodgrass, Anthony. 1980. *Archaic Greece: The Age of Experiment*. London: J. M. Dent & Sons.

Described as the "first major book on Archaic Greece to be written by an archaeologist," this account remains a classic. The period is seen as bounded by revolutions at both its beginning and end. Archaeological evidence is essential for understanding the structural revolutions. Documentation in the form of illustrations, charts, maps, and sites is excellent.

4

The Second Age of Heroes
Classical Greece

Developments that produced the *polis* way of life visible in embryonic form in Askra resulted in a second age of heroes. In fact, until there was proof that Greece was home to a sophisticated culture in the Bronze Age, it was the only heroic period in Pre-Classical Greek history. Several conditions were in place to project Greeks into an important role in much of the Mediterranean sphere. Not only had internal circumstances stabilized in the centuries following the collapse of the Mycenaean kingdoms but improved technology for basic subsistence was a factor in the increase in population. With limited land for increased production at home, Greeks had returned to the sea in search of fertile settings for new settlements as well as for trade. Although their culture was influenced by others, those influences had been folded into the indigenous Greek way of life. As the historian Herodotus reported, putting the words in the mouths of the Athenians, "We share the same kinship and language, devotion to the same gods, and a common way of life."[1]

On the other hand, the differences between the 1,000+ *poleis* and the rise in population in the eighth and seventh centuries BCE brought territories of the city-states closer together as more land was needed for basic agricultural and pastoral subsistence. In some regions like Attica, physical conditions fostered reunification of the entire peninsula, defined by the sea on two of its three sides and mountains on the third. What was emerging as the *polis* of Sparta unified an even larger region, initially by cooperation but increasingly by military force. The battle over the plain lying between Chalkis and Eretria on the island of Euboea as early as 700 BCE was noted in the previous chapter as demonstrating that one's nearest neighboring *polis* was often one's worst enemy. Greek contact with non-Greek states throughout the Mediterranean could be hostile as well as beneficial. Both types of conflict would result in a short-lived second heroic age. Yet, the culture produced by the *polis* would continue over the next 2,350+ years of Greek history, retaining its powerful influence into the present.

Greece: A Short History of a Long Story, 7,000 BCE to the Present, First Edition.
Carol G. Thomas.
© 2014 John Wiley & Sons, Inc. Published 2014 by John Wiley & Sons, Inc.

Mediterranean Impact

Greece was blessed in the developments of the later centuries of the Dark Age and during the Archaic Age that allowed more intrepid, or needful, inhabitants to begin to re-establish contacts with the larger Mediterranean sphere. Although the powerful kingdoms of the eastern Mediterranean had collapsed in the late thirteenth- and early twelfth-century disturbances, rejuvenation of great territorial states occurred in Egypt and Mesopotamia, while Greeks continued to struggle for survival in their tiny villages.

In the northern reaches of Mesopotamia, the Assyrians consolidated a strong state from which they swept to empire with their powerful military machine. Tiglath-Pileser III claimed during his reign from 745 to 727 BCE that he was "king of the world ... king of the four parts of the earth." Using tools of force, fear, and exaction of tribute, the Assyrians extended control from Egypt in the southwest across Mesopotamia toward the Caspian Sea in the northeast and into Anatolia in the northwest. These same tools, not surprisingly, produced determined opponents. The full empire, overextended in reach, survived for only a century in its fullest reach until the capital was taken by a coalition force from Egypt, Babylon, and Media in 612. Greeks knew the Assyrians but not intimately due to their distance from that empire. Yet there was some indirect contact: a Greek fleet was routed off the southern coast of Anatolia in 696 by the Phoenician allies of Assyria.

The three victors quickly began to reconstruct their individual territories. Egypt attempted to create a new kingdom until 525 when it was absorbed by a younger power in the Near East. Babylon expanded its control in Mesopotamia under somewhat shaky priestly control until that same younger power folded its territory into its own. The Indo-European Medes, who had settled in the west region of modern Iran, began to extend their territory on the defeat of the Assyrians until they too met "the younger power": the Persians.

Speedily, the Indo-European Persians dwelling southeast of Mesopotamia began to extend their holdings. The first independent king, Cyrus, took control of outer Iran, Mesopotamia, Media, and Anatolia during the twenty-nine years of his rule (559–530). Greeks also would know the Persians well as they extended their reach to the Aegean; Cyrus incorporated the coastal sphere which had for five centuries been populated by mainland Greeks who had established small communities along the coast. The son and successor of Cyrus, Cambyses, drew Egypt into the empire by 525. The most important task facing the third king, Darius, was internal unification of the vast territory and diverse cultures that had been conquered. His efforts were successful in building a solid structure which was aided by the view that leniency toward local customs would be more productive in fostering unity than Assyrian terror.

The vast territory was divided into regions, known as satrapies, each unified through a common code of laws, coinage, and system of weights and measures. Each satrapy was governed by a satrap with a hierarchy of other officials, all responsible to the central control of the Great King. A royal road stretching from Persepolis to Babylon to Sardis in Anatolia and an army of 250,000 were further forces of control and centralization.

With the task of unification accomplished, Darius turned to further expansion. Inasmuch as Persian control extended to the eastern coast of the Aegean, it was perhaps natural that he directed his attention across the Dardanelles toward the western fringe of the Black Sea inhabited by nomadic Scythians, surely no serious opposition to the strong Persian army.

Yet the guerilla tactics of the Scythians proved successful and the Persians withdrew, having accomplished nothing. Most important, however, was the reaction to this failure on the part of inhabitants of the western coast of Anatolia. Members of Greek *poleis* in coastal Anatolia determined that the time was right for gaining their independence. Planning their revolt in concert with one another, they realized the need for outside aid. Envoys sent to Sparta were unsuccessful – the Spartans refused to travel so far from home since removal of the Spartan hoplites from the southern Peloponnese would weaken the constant vigil over their subjected serfs. From Athens and Eretria on Euboea – both homes of the original migrants to Anatolia – they won the promise of ships and men: twenty ships from Athens, five from Eretria. Confidently, the Greeks took and burned Sardis, the Anatolian capital of the Persian Empire, in 498. Overconfidently, they withdrew and were, of course, easy prey for Persian retaliation. The revolt was quickly ended by 494.

More retaliation – a Persian counterstroke – was due for those ships from the mainland. The historian Herodotus, who described these events, believed that those ships were the cause of the major confrontation between the Greeks and the Persians. The first effort at reprisal two years later was thwarted by the treacherous winds off the Mount Athos promontory. Two years later, and by a different route, a fleet of approximately 200 ships carrying 25,000 men entered the narrow strait between Attica and Euboea. Eretria fell; then the Persians disembarked on the east coast of Attica at the plain of Marathon. In the hills, some 10,000 Athenians with a contingent of hoplites from the small *polis* of Plataea in Boeotia were anxiously awaiting aid from the Spartans, already famed as the outstanding land force of Greece. Phidippides (*the* Marathon runner) had run the 150 miles from Athens to Sparta to report the dire situation. No immediate assistance came from the Spartans inasmuch as they were in the midst of a festival to Artemis, certainly not a fabricated excuse but rather a commitment that could not be broken.

Strangely, the Persians aided the Greek cause by re-embarking a portion of their force to sail around the tip of the peninsula to pull into the harbor of Athens itself, now nearly defenseless. With forces more equalized and surely with concern for Athens and family members living in the *polis* center, the forces at Marathon attacked the Persians at a run killing 6,400, losing only 192 lives. Quickly they marched across the Attica peninsula to station themselves near the harbor as the Persian fleet was drawing in. Thus the second retaliation also failed.

Darius did not live to mount a third effort; it was left to his son and successor in 486, Xerxes, whose anger seems to have been intensified by the insult to his father's name and fame. Gathering a force estimated to have been about 250,000, and a fleet of 600 to 700 ships as well as a merchant fleet, he ordered that the Hellespont be bridged so that men and animals could walk across the water and that the treacherous Mount Athos peninsula be cut by a channel to avoid the winds that could be a threat to the fleet. He also managed to gain the neutrality of much of the Greek world so that as forces were stirring in the east, only Athens and Plataea and the league of Peloponnesian states had agreed to stand firm.

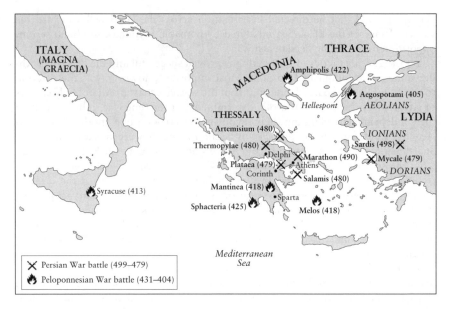

Figure 4.1 Classical Greece: Persian and Peloponnesian wars. Source: Jason Shattuck

By 480, the Persians had reached Macedon, reportedly draining the rivers of their water, so great was the thirst of the countless men and animals. From Macedon they moved southward by land and sea to meet the Greeks at the narrow pass of Thermopylae by land and off the northern coast of Euboea by sea. Greeks under the Spartan command at Thermopylae stood firm even after a traitor had informed Xerxes of a track leading to the back of the Greek force. That information trapped the Greeks between two Persian forces. The Spartan king/general, Leonidas, dismissed most of the other Greeks while he and the 300 Spartans remained to die in the struggle. With the defeat of the land force, the naval effort collapsed and southern Greece lay open to the Persian advance. Revenge for the ships that had aided the Ionian revolt was taken: Athens was burned although an oracle had prompted most Athenians to take refuge elsewhere. Consequently, both Athenian people and ships were spared.

Those ships were vital in the next confrontation in the autumn of 480: the Greek and Persian fleets assembled off the island of Salamis in the Saronic Gulf. Although the Greeks were outnumbered, the narrow waters seem to have worked to their advantage, causing confusion in the massed Persian fleet. So serious was the defeat of his force that Xerxes, who had been watching the action from a portable throne on the shore, fled back to Asia with the remnants of his fleet. The land force was left to winter in Greece and to negotiate with Athens.

Athenian determination was not shaken by the destruction of the core of the *polis*; to the contrary, that destruction surely fueled their determination. Greeks and Persians met again in 479 BCE at Plataea – the *polis* that had aided the Athenians at Marathon. Herodotus' account of the conflict makes it difficult to reconstruct the course of the battle but its outcome, with the death of the Persian commander, is clear. Traditionally, on the same day, the Greek fleet engaged the remnants of the Persian fleet off the coast of Anatolia and prevailed by sea. Victory was enabled by the timely desertion of the Ionian Greek portion of the Persian fleet to aid the mainland Greeks. The words of one Athenian participant in the battles are heady. Aeschylus, the composer of powerful tragedies, one of which was *The Persians* (performed in 472), reported that disaster awaited the Persians at Plataea "as recompense for their arrogance and godless thoughts. In coming to the land of Hellas they did not shrink from burning temples or pillaging images of the gods."[2]

In a short history of a long story why does the confrontation of the Greeks and Persians deserve so much attention? The outcome is remarkable but more importantly it reveals the basis for the Greek success in the fundamental nature of their reconstructed way of life. Greeks have regained sufficient control of their own environment to defeat a far greater force both by land and sea. Because of the wars, they interacted directly with the larger Mediterranean and Near Eastern spheres as they had during the later Bronze Age. However, the form of political life was no longer that of large kingdoms controlled by kings and their entourages ruling from walled *acropoleis*. The political form of independent communities created by the collapse of the Mycenaean world and maintained with difficulty over the worst of the Dark Age would continue. Within those communities, ordinary farmers were essential to provide the needs of the entire population – political, military, and cultural as well as economic subsistence. Thus the second age of heroes would not have kings as those heroes. Rather, the communal accomplishments of the citizens of the city-states of this second age merit the description of "heroic."

In addition, the intellectual sphere of Greek life by the fifth century BCE had attained a level that created admiration in other cultures. By contrast, the first Age of Heroes absorbed much from more advanced civilizations of the eastern Mediterranean sphere. The influence of Classical Greece has persisted to the present and is evident throughout much of the globe.

The victors at Marathon, Salamis, and Plataea may have been as surprised as the vanquished Persians. Mixed with that surprise was pride; they were a new race of heroes. Their accomplishment strengthened their view of the superiority of the Greek way of life centered on deep commitment to the *polis*. In the eyes of Aristotle, the *polis* originated in the need to sustain life but it thrived for the sake of a good life. Man (at least Greek man) was by nature an animal intended to live in a *polis*.[3] The bond between individual and *polis* in the fifth century provides evidence that most Greeks were of similar opinion in the aftermath of the Persian Wars. That bond produced a cultural outburst that ranks high on the list of the most prolific in the human story.

The Golden Age

According to the English poet Percy Bysshe Shelley (1792–1822), "We are all Greeks. Our laws, our literature, our religion, our arts have their roots in Greece. But for Greece, Rome the conqueror ... would have spread no illuminations with her arms and we might still have been savages and idolaters."[4] While many would judge this an overstatement, it is impossible to disregard the cultural influence of Greece on later cultures and periods of time. Classical Greece is one of a handful of ages conspicuous for the reach and quality of its cultural achievements. Most of the elements that constitute the influence reached an acme during the fifth century BCE in part due to the solid foundation created in the Archaic Age but also impelled by the unbelievable victory over the Persians. Greeks of the fifth century could claim the stature of their ancient heroes who, after all, had endured ten years of war to take the single citadel of Troy while they themselves had defeated, on land and at sea, the forces of a mammoth empire in a mere two years!

"Wonders are many but nothing is as wondrous as man" are the words of the Athenian tragedian Sophocles in his play *Antigone*.[5] These words express powerfully the mood of the Greek world following the unexpected outcomes at Plataea and Mycale. Expression of their elation is visible in every aspect of their culture which gave birth to the Golden Age of Greece. Four forces serve to define underlying features: a search to understand the nature and responsibilities of humankind; recognition of the essential role of the deities; preservation of accounts and records of human affairs; a demonstration of the greatness of *polis* life in the arts and architecture.

It is perhaps not surprising that the philosophical questioning that was already apparent in the poems of Hesiod and flourished in the early philosophic and scientific speculation of the sixth century expanded its scope. What we now call Classical Greek philosophy endeavors to understand the world and the human role in it. Thus it includes science, metaphysics, ethics, politics, and religion. Although roots of these subjects reached back to earlier periods, interest multiplied quickly in the late sixth and fifth centuries.

Many inquirers were curious individuals who sought to explain the nature of the universe: was there something permanent beneath the constant change that was apparent in the human experience? One answer was that one of the basic elements was water: it had three states and all that was alive was moist. A second basic element was air, which is invisible in its natural state and is the basis of life. The Pythagorean understanding that the basis of the universe is kinship of all life drew men together into a collective way of life that resembled religious orders of other times. Increasingly, inquirers became more scientific in examining the physical world. The atomic theory of the universe that everything is composed of tiny atoms that unite temporarily to produce living entities was advanced in the fifth century BCE. Specks in a ray of light, surely, are evidence! A more concrete form of questioning led to the attempt to define the nature of the world by exploring it in order to map it. Early efforts were bold in plotting maps of the world and, perhaps, even maps of the heavens.

A different goal is evident in the efforts of Hippocrates, from the Aegean island of Cos, who created a system for both analysis and treatment of medical problems. Writings associated with his name state his intention to discuss what man is and how he exists because it seemed indispensable to him that doctors must make such studies in order to be fully acquainted with nature. Understanding the natural conditions in which people live is essential to a proper diagnosis of their health. And, as we have noted, Hippocrates believed that the challenging nature of the Greek environment produced a hardy people.

Records of a different kind illustrate the pride Greeks took in their way of life and a need to preserve an accurate account of reasons for that pride. The father of history, Herodotus, was inspired to record his inquiry so that human achievements would not be forgotten, and that great and wondrous deeds by Greeks and barbarians would not be without their due glory. He especially wanted to show why the two peoples fought in what we know as the Persian Wars. And so the discipline of history was born. Homeric echoes in his account reveal roots in the earlier forms of oral history. However, its goal was new, as was its form: prose rather than poetry. On a smaller scale, inscriptional records now began to record the ordinary decisions of assembled citizens, to celebrate important affairs of the *polis*, and to pay honor to individuals who had been especially significant to the well-being of the community.

The role of citizens in the *polis* encouraged the emergence of "teachers." Young boys were trained in basic physical and intellectual skills. By the fifth century "wise men" known as Sophists traveled from *polis* to *polis* to offer instruction to others – usually for a fee – to enable them to attain virtue. Although Sophists had various approaches, a common feature was emphasis on proper, effective speaking, an essential quality in the increasingly participatory culture of the *poleis*, where an effective speech could sway an entire assembly or elevate a man to a position of leadership. Some identified Socrates of Athens as a Sophist although he denied that identity. We will look more closely at his role in his *polis* later since it neatly describes the multiplicity of citizen life in this "Golden Age."

In their pride, humans consistently paid tribute to the gods who had enabled the victory even to the point of participating in the fighting. At Salamis, Herodotus records, a phantom shape of a woman – Athena – appeared and called out to men in the fleet asking how long they would delay rowing out against the enemy: it was time to engage the enemy.[6] They obeyed and prevailed over the larger Persian force.

The deities honored had long been folded into every aspect of daily life; the names of many of the Classical pantheon of great gods are recorded in the Bronze Age tablets: Zeus, Hera, Poseidon, Athena, Hermes, Dionysus, and Artemis were present. In addition to the integral role of these and other deities in daily life, public celebration expanded in quantity and magnificence. In fifth-century Athens, for example, 130 dated festival days drew together members of the community in respect for the more-than-human members of the *polis*. Nor was Athens unique in demonstrating ongoing respect for the deities. The growing mastery of construction produced the marvelous temples, many of which still survive today. It is significant that they were often located on the most prominent natural feature within a *polis*: an acropolis was no longer the palace of a king but the structure for a deity. Religion could even bind the individual states together, at least temporarily, in the great games: at Olympia, Delphi, Nemea, and on the isthmus near Corinth. An estimated 45,000 spectators would gather at Olympia for those games in July and August. And, on the occasion of the games, warfare between *poleis* was prohibited, an impressive accomplishment given the proclivity of war between neighbors in Greece.

The emergence of dramatic festivals was another expression of the bond between mortals and gods. From roots in choral song and dance in various regions of Greece, the festival of Dionysus in Athens developed into a grand occasion that was a central event in the Athenian year and would soon spread to other *poleis*. At each dramatic festival, three tragedians chosen by one of the chief officials of the state presented a trilogy of dramas. Surviving plays of three tragedians – Aeschylus, Sophocles, and Euripides – explore elemental, eternal problems confronting humans, although the normal experiences of most people are not usually the kinds of challenges that face an Oedipus or a Medea. Eleven comic plays of Aristophanes survive; they too represent the issues that concern members of a *polis*, including Socrates, who was thought to be a "gadfly" in his *polis*, and how women of warring *poleis* determine to replace war with peace.

Fifth-century Athens has been described as the School of Hellas. In Athens the theatre was the school of the Athenians. Located in the core of the *polis*, the theatre was the site of an annual great dramatic and religious celebration involving hundreds of performers. The theatre's capacity was at least 17,000 people. The occasion celebrated Athens and the Athenians while reminding them in stark terms that the deities were aware of proper and improper behaviors of mere humans and would respond as needed. Actors and choral members interacted in words, songs, and dance on a platform raised before a circular, packed-earth orchestra surrounding an altar. Tragic performances tended to look to the past for their lessons – Oedipus, for example – while comedies drew from current issues – for example, finding an end to war by an ordinary citizen who decides to meet personally with Zeus.

The setting and nature of the dramatic form is fine evidence of the need for direct participation in affairs of the *polis* in the Classical Age. Not only were citizens essential to the political order of their state but management was done primarily through direct, oral communication. The power of the performance was diminished when the plays were read, which became possible probably in the fourth century. So powerful do they remain that their lessons are performed and read far beyond Greece today.

Other buildings of the fifth century mirror the same heroic vision as well as gratitude to the gods for their victory over kings Darius and Xerxes. Destruction by the Persians had created the need to construct new buildings in some places: Miletus had been destroyed after the conclusion of the Ionian revolt in 494 and Athens was demolished in 480. In the process of rebuilding ruins or constructing new foundations, more ordered *polis* centers began to appear. It is significant that notable refinement is evident in the public buildings: temples, theatres, stoas, and structures designated for *polis* management, such as facilities for members of the *polis* council or storage of archives, while domestic architecture was not so significantly refined. But the refinement was not completely innovation; rather it reflected an effort to hone the qualities of existing types, as the Parthenon in Athens reveals. Replacing an earlier temple on the acropolis that had a length of 100 Attic feet, the Parthenon extended over a length of 232 feet. The refinements of construction include a curved foundation, tapered columns, and tilted *metopes*, all intended to compensate for the view of spectators on the ground. This "perfect" building in which there is not a single straight line was constructed in eight or nine years with the technology of the fifth century BCE. Current restoration of that temple has been on-going for thirty-four years.

Figural arts also continued in the established mode but they too were visibly refined: sculptures became more naturalistic; red-figure vase painting replaced black-figure painting and enabled more detailed depiction. One notable feature of the paintings and sculptures is the closeness between mortals and gods shown by similarities in their forms as well as in their immediacy with one another. As in architecture, there was a search for perfect rendition.

Examples cited are often from Athens, a *polis* that gained a leading role in the cultural dynamism of the fifty years following the defeat of the Persians. One explanation for this role is that although Athens had been taken and virtually destroyed by the Persians, nearly the entire population had taken refuge, or was on board ship, or in the field against the Persians. Consequently, people could return to their territory to rebuild its physical core. Nor should euphoria be ignored: Athenians could return to the effort as victors. There were other victors, to be sure, but their homes had not been destroyed. Corinthians could return to their diverse lives in the northern Peloponnese and Spartans could return to their huge territory to keep their serfs under control. The Athenians had the unique opportunity to rebuild their *polis* and, in so doing, to influence life in all of Greece.

Athens' Rise to Dominance

Athens' rise was driven by the outcome of the conflict with Persia largely due to the fleet that the Athenians provided to the joint Greek effort; it was essential to the Greek victories, especially in the naval battle off Salamis and, the next year, in Asia Minor. Moreover, Athenians' special grievance over the destruction of their city by Persian forces was joined to their link with Greek states in the eastern Aegean and Black seas, where Persian control was still in effect. In 478 BCE, an assembly of all the Greeks was called, at which a proposed decree was accepted that representatives of the Greek states should assemble annually at Plataea, where the final land battle had occurred, and every fifth year celebrate the Games of Freedom. In addition, it was agreed that a levy should be made upon all of Greece for an on-going war against the barbarians, with only Plataea exempt and dedicated to the service of the gods because its territory had been the site of the final land battle.

Leadership went first to the Spartans, whose hoplite force was the best in all of Greece. However, their endeavors to direct overall affairs were ineffective due in large part to problems at home. Thus leadership passed to Athens. At a meeting of voluntary participants in the enterprise held on the sacred island of Delos, 143 *poleis* voted to contribute to the effort against Persia. An annual assembly on Delos would determine policy; Athens would command operations resolved by all, and would also provide a large part of the fleet; contributions from the member *poleis* and appointment of financial officers were arranged by the Athenians. Thus the Delian League came into existence, with delegates from member states vowing to keep the union until iron bars tossed into the water should float.

It is easy now to see potential dangers of the situation but at the time the goal of driving the Persians from the Aegean was accomplished in short order. In 469 (or possibly 467) the fleet of the Delian League defeated the Persian fleet in southern Anatolia at the mouth of the Eurymedon River. The Delian fleet gained mastery of the Aegean, which was the goal of the alliance. But the bars of iron would not float, especially as Pericles rose to prominence in Athens; he was yearly elected to the board of ten generals (one of the few elected positions in Athens at this time) from the middle 460s until his death in 429, with only two exceptions. Under his guidance the League was transformed from an alliance to an empire controlled by Athens. An important element in the transformation was knowledge of the machinery of empire gained through contact with Persia. A *polis* was becoming an empire and the transformation profoundly altered the history of Greece.

At first Greek ambitions for the Delian League were huge: the fleet was sent to Egypt to distract Persian attention from the Aegean sphere and to damage Persia by freeing the Egyptians from Persian control. At the same time, the Athenians undertook naval battles with their neighbor Megara and the island *polis* of Aegina, and voted to dispatch their land force into central Greece. In anticipation of hostility from neighboring *poleis*, construction was begun on long walls linking the center of the *polis* to its harbor in order to make the center unassailable, since siege machinery was still largely under-developed. Hostilities came soon: by 457, war had been declared by Corinth, Aegina, Thebes, and Sparta, the four other major states at the time. Three years later the force in Egypt was defeated with the loss of 30,000 men and much of the fleet.

Fear of reprisal from Persia played a part in the decision to remove the League's treasure from Delos to Athens, but the decision to have policy and assessments voted by the Athenian assembly – rather than by an assembly of League members – was a clear sign of the new status of the association. Certain legal cases were now tried in Athens and, to promote loyalty of members of the "alliance," the Athenians began to send citizens to live on the lands of their allies, a useful means of surveillance. By 439, only two free members remained in the League, which now deserved the title "empire." Members who wished to leave the alliance were likely to find the fleet in their harbor with fleet commanders asking if they wished to reconsider.

Athens benefited in many ways from the transformation: a tithe of one-sixtieth of the tribute collected was given over to Athens, which enabled the rebuilding of the *polis* center. Athens also became the hub of a large trading empire, allowing the collection of certain harbor dues and taxes. Athenian currency became *the* common currency; in a world in which coins betokened the individuality and independence of a *polis*, it was a signal that other participants in the trade system were less than independent. The comic poet Aristophanes stated boldly in the *Wasps*:

> And not with pebbles precisely ranged but roughly on your fingers count
> The tribute paid by the subject states and just consider its whole amount;
> And then in addition to this compute the many taxes and one percents,
> The fees and the fines and the silver mines, the markets and harbors and sales and rents,
> If you take the total result of the lot, 'twill reach 2000 talents or near. [In current monetary terms, several million dollars or even pounds or euros.[7]

Such tribute affected all aspects of *polis* culture: values, objects, practices, concepts, and institutions. Pericles, the greatest Athenian statesman of the period, described the result in almost chilling beauty:

> You must yourselves realize the power of Athens, and feed your eyes upon her from day to day, till love of her fills your hearts; and then when all her greatness shall break upon you, you must reflect that it is by courage, sense of duty, and a keen feeling of honor in action that men were enabled to win all this ...[8].

These developments made Athens a super-*polis* in every respect, including size. Its population became gigantic by ordinary *polis* standards. Altogether the population rose to a total of some 300,000 in the fifth century. Not all people living in Athens were equal: 168,000 were Athenians, 115,000 were slaves, and 35,000 were resident aliens. The task of managing life within the core of the *polis* and far beyond with other members of the Delian League was hugely demanding on its citizens.

The expanded role of the Athenian citizens made Athens one of the most democratic of Greek *poleis*. Participation was essential in military and political affairs for every citizen not occasionally but throughout the entire calendar year. Of the Athenians, only men over age eighteen were participants in citizen responsibilities. All major decisions were made by the Assembly, where all full citizens gathered at forty regular meetings each year and at additional meetings when events demanded decisions. A quorum of 6,000 was required; agendas were publicized in advance; anyone could speak and amend motions. Primary matters were defense, finance, food supply, qualifications of officials, and exile of citizens for wrongful actions. A smaller advisory body was the council of 500 members, selected regionally from ten artificial divisions of the citizen body and designed to ensure that all regions would be represented. Ten groups of fifty were selected by lot annually; a citizen could be a member only twice in his lifetime. Each group of fifty would preside over affairs of the *polis* for a tenth of the year and a portion of the current presiding committee was in place twenty-four hours a day to examine all business of the state in order to set it before the Assembly, where the final vote was taken. A third political obligation of citizens was to serve in the adjudication of law. Six thousand jurors were required every year; they were chosen from volunteers who were citizens and were at least thirty years of age. Those chosen were paid, minimally, for service. Inasmuch as the trials were held in Athens, many of the jurors would have lived in or near Athens.

Governance of Athens demanded active participation of its "ordinary" citizens, who could hold significant official positions that became increasingly numerous as Athens grew in power and size. The highest office was that of general: a board of ten was elected annually by the Assembly and an individual could hold office as often as elected. Qualifications were not demanding; one had to be at least thirty years of age and be able to attest to important matters such as whether the person treated his parents well, paid taxes, and performed required military service. Basic training existed for sons of citizens in physical training, literacy and mathematic reckoning, and music. Public training-grounds existed but much of the intellectual education was provided by private teachers, for a fee. It is not surprising that instruction in the arts of clear reasoning and persuasive communication with others drew many teachers – the Sophists mentioned earlier – to Athens. Physical "training" continued for every citizen from age eighteen with active military duty for forty years. Twenty-six thousand hoplites were needed for the infantry and, with Athens' new sea power created in the wake of the Persian invasions, thirty-four thousand were also needed for naval service. A small cavalry of approximately 1,000 was filled by those sufficiently wealthy to maintain a horse.

Citizen status required that both parents be Athenians. Citizenship also gave the right to own land in the *polis,* a right not extended to "foreigners" (e.g. resident aliens) even if they were citizens in another *polis*. By the fifth century, farming was not the sole occupation of all citizens; from the early sixth century, a father was to instruct his sons in both tending the land and another occupation. Roughly half of the population of the territory now resided in the core of Athens. The other half was distributed in the surrounding, larger territory and pursued a predominantly agricultural livelihood.

Socrates, Citizen of Athens: Wisest Man in the World?

One man thought of as a Sophist in his own time reveals the nature of life during this exhilarating time for a citizen of moderate standing. His name is Socrates; he was a citizen of Athens but also its "gadfly," due to the time and energy he spent in stinging its other citizens to lead virtuous lives. It is true that, akin to the Sophists, he endeavored to instruct anyone who would listen to him describe the path to virtue, but, unlike the "professional" teachers, he had no set curriculum, he did not charge a fee, and he did not travel away from Athens except when on campaign with the army. In fact, he symbolizes the iron-like bond between the individual and the welfare of his *polis*.

He was born in Athens in 469 BCE, the year that may have witnessed the Athenian success over the Persian fleet which ended the Persian threat to the Greek *poleis* in the Aegean and those along the coast of Anatolia. This was also the year that marked the beginning of Athens' rise to become the dominant *polis* in the Aegean sphere. As the son of Sophroniscus, a sculptor, and Phaenarete, a midwife, Socrates was qualified by birth to become a citizen at age eighteen.

Socrates learned sculpting and would practice it on the grand buildings of the acropolis constructed in his lifetime. He married, perhaps twice, and had three sons. With his family he continued to live in the core of the *polis*.

Socrates participated in the public responsibilities of all citizens, including military responsibilities. He proved to be an excellent hoplite, fighting in three major campaigns away from Athens. He was not a rower in the fleet nor was he in the small cavalry since he was not sufficiently wealthy to own a horse. As testimony to his

Figure 4.2   Socrates. Source: Robert Lejeune

capability as a hoplite-soldier, he saved the life of one of the generals during a battle in 431 who recounted that

> he stood the hardships of the campaign far better than I did, or anyone else, for that matter. ... [T]he way he got through that winter was most impressive. There was one time when the frost was harder than ever, and all the rest of us stayed inside, or if we did go out we wrapped ourselves up to the eyes and tied bits of felt and sheepskins over our shoes, but Socrates went out in the same old coat he'd always worn, and made less fuss about walking on the ice in his bare feet than we did in our shoes. They gave me a decoration after one engagement, and do you know Socrates had saved my life, absolutely single-handed.[9]

However, Socrates is best known as a philosopher, a lover of wisdom. A friend of Socrates asked the Delphic oracle to identify the name of the wisest man and received the response from the Oracle that, "Of all living men, Socrates is the wisest." When Socrates heard this reply he set out to disprove it and, in so doing, became notorious in his search for someone wiser than himself. The nature of his questioning is described in the dialogues of Plato, who was a pupil of Socrates; Socrates is the major figure of many dialogues as an interrogator. Socrates learned that some believed that they were wise, but that they could not describe their wisdom so perhaps the oracle was correct: at least he was on the path to wisdom. He believed knowledge was the key to virtue and happiness and that a person did wrong only out of ignorance. His daily activity in "instructing" others can be described as the quintessential product of classical Greek philosophy of the fifth century BCE.

We are able to picture Socrates' life in Athens through a variety of sources. His means of livelihood was sculpting, and a modern scholar believes she has identified his work on the Acropolis. Plato's *Dialogues* provides a vivid picture of his other activity, the search for knowledge. When he was not sculpting on the Acropolis, or at home with his family, or out of Athens serving as a hoplite in combat, he could be found in multiple locations, all of which give us not only an idea of his activities but also a picture of life in Athens itself. Plato has written of Socrates at a school (*palaestra*) for future citizens; participating in a symposium to engage in serious conversation, enlivened with wine; outside the area of the law courts and, for his own trial, inside one of those courts; in a private home such as that of Aspasia, "only a woman" but the mistress/wife of Pericles who guided Athens to its pinnacle; walking back from the harbor at Piraeus where he had paid devotions to the goddess; in other homes – for example, the home of an important Athenian or the home of a resident non-Athenian who lived in Athens because of its larger role in the Mediterranean world to which he contributed as a manufacturer of weapons; in the market place where speakers would draw great crowds; walking along the Ilissus River where – as his friend commented – it was convenient that Socrates was barefoot.

Socrates engaged everyone who was willing to listen to him: boys who were future citizens, citizens of Athens and even of other *poleis*, priests, Sophists, *metics*, and friends from all ranks of society. He drew great, diverse crowds of people, both admirers and those who argued against him. Cratylus says "You, Socrates, appear to me to be an oracle, and to give answers much to my mind."[10] Centuries later, Socrates has remained one of the best-known figures of the Classical Age of Greece. However, the developments in his *polis* of Athens offered extraordinary opportunities to all of its citizens.

The legacy of Athens is a birth of democracy where citizens determined Athenian policy at regular meetings of the Assembly. All citizens could serve on the Council, be elected to the board of ten generals, and serve as one of the 6,000 jurors selected each year. All could attend the tragic and comic presentations in the theatre, could learn from the Sophists and listen to the recitations of the father of history, Herodotus. Everyone – citizens, women, children, slaves, and resident aliens – could view the wonders of the physical core of Athens with the perfect temple to Athena gleaming on the Acropolis. Athens had become the core in another sense: as the force behind the coalition of *poleis* that were determined to keep themselves free from Persian control. The power and the wealth of Athens became immense.

Outcome: The Peloponnesian War

Socrates, unlike individuals highlighted in other chapters, demonstrates more than one major period of Greek history, namely the "Golden" Classical Age. His last years identify the dire outcome of Athenian greatness. Socrates himself was a victim. On the one hand, Athens attracted great numbers of people to its center, both intellectuals and *metics* who paid taxes in order to participate in the humming commercial life of the city. Yet, increasingly, Athens drew fear and hatred from other *poleis*, both from members of the now-involuntary alliance and from other *poleis* who were not allies of Athens, who were increasingly anxious over its dominance. What is often called the "First Peloponnesian War" erupted in 460 when Athens was constructing new long walls to surround the core of the *polis* and also building alliances with certain other mainland *poleis*. As a result, Sparta, Corinth, and Thebes formed a coalition against Athens. The year 457 BCE saw battles in Boeotia and, in 453, Pericles launched a naval expedition in the Corinthian Gulf. Major war was avoided when, in 451, Athens and Sparta agreed to a five-year truce. However, little was resolved and, in 446, a Spartan king led a force into Attica but, surprisingly, suddenly withdrew. In the following year Athens conceded loss of land power and a thirty-year truce was agreed between Sparta and Athens. Again, underlying tensions remained and *the* Peloponnesian War was under way fourteen years later.

Declaration of war on Athens by members of the long-standing Peloponnesian League directed by Sparta began a conflict that was waiting to happen. The Athenian citizen-historian Thucydides, who participated in and recounted the war, believed, "The real cause I consider to be the one which was formally most kept out of sight. The growth of the power of Athens, and the alarm which this inspired in Sparta, made war inevitable."[11] Deliberate provocations by the Athenians in the two preceding years raised anger to boiling point in 431 BCE.

The two combatants were Athens and members of its empire, on the one hand, and, on the other, Sparta with the members of the Peloponnesian League, which embraced much of the Peloponnese as well as large portions of central and northeastern Greece. The strengths of the parties differed considerably: Athens' strength was at sea, Sparta's on land. Consequently, strategies would differ. The Peloponnesians attempted to draw the Athenian hoplites into traditional combat for which they were better prepared in numbers and ability while the Athenians tried to damage the enemy by surprise coastal raids, refusing to do traditional battle with their hoplites. The persuasive powers of Pericles managed to restrain the Athenians, most of whom had been gathering inside the protective shell of the long walls. Those restraints were removed when Pericles, along with about a third of the Athenian population, died as a result of a plague that devastated the crowded city for three years. Athens sued for peace but the offer was refused by Sparta and for the remainder of the decade confrontations on the mainland as well as in the northern Aegean brought many deaths but no resolution. With the death of Pericles, his policy was replaced by direct confrontation with no decisive outcomes or victories. Consequently, in 421, a peace was negotiated.

Nothing had been fundamentally altered, however, so the peace that was meant to last for fifty years was almost immediately undermined. From 421 to 411, the theater of war expanded into the central Mediterranean, with a vast Athenian expedition to Sicily in 415. At the same time, hostilities grew more savage. Thucydides' account of a dialogue between Athenian generals and representatives of the small *polis* of Melos is unnerving. The Athenians admit that

> we shall not trouble you with specious pretenses—either of how we have a right to our empire because we overthrew the Mede, or that we are now attacking you because of wrong you have done us—and make a long speech which would not be believed. No; for your hostility cannot so much hurt us as your friendship will be an argument to our subjects of our weakness. ... [A]fter our withdrawal reflect once and again that it is for your country that you are consulting, that you have not more than one, and that upon this one deliberation depends its prosperity or ruin."[12]

When the Melians responded that they had confidence that aid would come from the Peloponnese, or the gods, or the fortunes of war, the Athenian reply was that in choosing between war and safety, surely, "You will not be so insensitively arrogant as to make the wrong choice." And after the Athenians took the city, they put to death all the men of military age and sold the women and children as slaves, although the Melians had surrendered unconditionally. The Athenians found themselves in a position similar to that of the Melians when their expedition to Sicily collapsed two years later. Most of the fleet was destroyed, with 4,500 Athenian hoplites lost along with 40,000 allied hoplites.

The magnitude of the defeat led to peace overtures to Sparta and a change in leadership in Athens in the form of an oligarchic revolution limiting citizenship severely, a form of government that accorded with that of Sparta. When the surviving fleet returned to Athens, however, democratic practice was reinstituted and, in its train, war continued. Thanks to Persian subsidies, both parties renewed their naval power – Sparta was now able to challenge Athens by sea while Persian monies allowed Athens to rebuild its fleet.

Meanwhile Persia, once the common enemy, profited from the continuing dissension in Greece. The last three years of conflict – 407 to 405 – witnessed naval battles in the sphere of Asia Minor. Victories see-sawed between the Peloponnesians and Athens: the first victory went to the Peloponnesians, the next to Athens, and the third and final to the Peloponnesians when they surprised the Athenians, captured their fleet, cut the vital grain route to Athens from the Black Sea, and starved the Athenians into surrender in 404. "As news of the disaster was told," the historian Xenophon remembered, "one man passed it on to another, and a sound of wailing arose and extended first from Piraeus, then along the Long Walls until it reached the city. That night no one slept. They mourned for the lost but more still for their own fate."[13]

Athens became a subject ally of Sparta and housed a garrison of 700 Spartans. Its long walls were demolished and its navy limited to twelve ships. An oligarchic government of thirty tyrants loyal to Sparta was established. The population of Athens was restricted to 3,000 citizens of oligarchic persuasion who now composed an "assembly" accountable to the Thirty Tyrants. Thousands of former citizens were driven out but many were taken in by other *poleis*. All judicial powers were also now in the hands of the Thirty Tyrants. The Council, also under the oversight of the Thirty Tyrants, was composed of 500 of the 3,000 citizens.

This transformation of one of the greatest of Greek *poleis* was sudden, severe, and devastating. However, it is important to remember that the new political order survived for only eight months. A modern leader led a small band of some thirty or forty opponents to the Thirty Tyrants. They were encamped in the foothills of Mount Parnes north of Athens and their number quickly increased to 700. In 403 the opponents took control of the Piraeus and the Spartan king intervened to arrange an amnesty along with the withdrawal of the Spartan troops. The Thirty Tyrants left Athens for Eleusis, a village in northwest Attica which they had earlier denuded of inhabitants, and democratic exiles began to return. Two years later, the survivors of the Thirty Tyrants made a final attempt to reclaim power with the aid of mercenaries. It failed.

Socrates lived through these events; he had remained in Athens even though he was not of oligarchic status in wealth or family or ideology. Perhaps he was not exiled because of his acquaintance with members of the Thirty Tyrants who had listened to Socrates' advice in former times. Because of this acquaintance, Socrates was asked to carry on certain tasks for the Thirty Tyrants. In 404 he was sent on the orders of the Thirty Tyrants, with four others, to arrest a wealthy *metic*, who was arrested, killed, and whose property was taken. Socrates, however, went home rather than accompany the others.

Five years later, when democracy was being rehabilitated, he was brought to trial on charges of corrupting the young and not believing in the state's gods. The true reasons for his trial are uncertain but surely they were connected with the time of the Thirty Tyrants. Returning citizens may well have associated him with the horrors of the Thirty Tyrants. A court of 501 juror-judges in the restored courts found him guilty but only by a small margin. And although his friends had arranged an escape from Athens, he refused the opportunity for a life in exile, choosing death in his *polis*. The Laws of Athens had spoken to him, he told his gathered friends. If he abandoned the state and its sacred laws that he had served for seventy years, the laws in the underworld would treat him as an enemy. He remained in prison to die by drinking hemlock in 399.

Debate continues over the issues that provoked the trial and its outcome but developments after 399 reveal that the Athens for which he died was also ending the *polis* life of the fifth century. Devastations of war led to a population decline of 25 percent; the base of the economy was nearly destroyed; widespread democracy was judged unworkable and the citizen population declined from 45,000 to 15,000; increasingly, official positions were held by specialists for long terms. Men like Socrates were no longer proper citizens. It is interesting to note that two of Socrates' students, Plato and Xenophon, left Athens for long periods following Socrates' death.

The reasons for their departures are more than personal responses to the trial and death of Socrates. The new political life of Athens drove thousands of Athenians from their *polis*. Xenophon became a mercenary soldier for a Persian prince contending for kingship of the empire. Plato traveled to Syracuse three times to assist in the education of a son of the current ruler in the proper role of a ruler. Plato's dialogue the *Republic* reports Socrates as believing that even sons of such rulers might be blessed with philosophic nature and, consequently, they could be educated to rule their states properly. A letter written late in his life reports that after the reign of the Thirty Tyrants in Athens, Plato wished to take part in political action. However, the *Republic*, dated to the period following Plato's first visit to Sicily, reveals his belief that the wisdom of a philosopher king would provide members of a *polis* with an orderly and secure life. The son of the tyrant did succeed his father but had not become a philosopher-king. Plato returned to Syracuse twice to continue the education; not only was he unsuccessful but he was in personal danger. After his return to Athens, his activities were centered on his school, the Academy, and his own writings.

Another guide to governing a state – the *Laws*, dating to the last period of his life – provides a vivid picture of Plato's changed view. The fundamental element is impersonal law. Thirty-seven guardians of the constitution between the ages of fifty and seventy guard the enforcement of the laws in all areas of communal life. Their dictates are very specific, from the permanent size of the community to ages when marriage must take place, religion, penal offences, and even how to deal with stray animals. Education into the rules of life is essential and is overseen by a Minister of Education who is one of the guardians. Since the community needs constant attention, a Nocturnal Council is permanently watchful. Although the community is known as a *polis* in both dialogues, a comparison of the two reflects the changing world on the heels of the Peloponnesian War.

Fourth-Century Greece

The larger outcome for Greece was a tragedy not only in the waste of life and resources but for the *polis* way of life. A world of more than a thousand individual states continued to foster alliances as well as wars. The eventual outcome came from a non-*polis* state, the kingdom of Macedon. The Greek *poleis* in 337 BCE were incorporated into the League of Corinth under terms set forth by King Philip II.

The first half of the fourth century saw attempts at empire by several main players who more or less repeated the scenario created by Athens in the preceding century. Athens itself, as a "subject ally" of Sparta, was loyal to Sparta in form, if not in spirit, until about 396 when a Spartan request for troops was denied. Even bolder was an Athenian alliance with Thebes in the following year. An important impulse to that alliance was Spartan conduct following the victory over Athens. Spartans tended to view themselves as the primary, if not sole, victors of the Peloponnesian War. Neglecting former allies such as Thebes and, in fact, garrisoning some of them, Sparta set about turning as many states as possible into Spartan subjects. Persian aid assisted those efforts but the price was the return of Asia Minor to Persia. In less than a decade after the collapse of Athens, a quadruple alliance of Thebes, Corinth, Argos, and Athens was concluded to challenge Spartan actions. Much of the fighting occurred in Corinthian territory, giving the name "The Corinthian War" to the indecisive and fitful battles that occurred from 395 into the next decade, when the new role of Persia in Greek affairs was dramatically shown in a manifesto delivered to delegates from various states. The manifesto is termed both the "King's Peace" after the Persian King Artaxerxes II and the "Peace of Antalcidas" after the Spartan who helped to negotiate the terms of the peace.

> King Artaxerxes considers it just that cities in Asia should belong to him, along with Clazomenae and Cyprus of the islands. The other Greek cities he thinks should be left autonomous, whether great or small apart from Lemnos, Imbros and Scyros, which should belong to the Athenians as they did of old. If either side refuses to accept this peace, I shall, joining the side wanting to accept it, make war on those people by land and sea, using my fleet and my resources."[14]

The Spartans were of the same mind, setting out to enforce this policy. An early example of Spartan policy was the successful siege of the Arcadian *polis* of Mantinea in the Peloponnese and the subsequent division of its inhabitants into five villages. The same spirit prompted the garrisoning of her former ally Thebes, and similar actions only strengthened the hostility of much of Greece. In the early 370s Thebes threw off the Spartan garrison, revolted from alliance with Sparta, reorganized its military machine, and quickly extended control in central Greece. At the same time, Athens was forming a second league, which eventually contained seventy members. Its purpose was to force the Spartans to allow the Greeks to be free and autonomous so that they might live in peace and friendship with one another. Thessaly, too, was unified under a strong leader who commanded the best cavalry in Greece as well as a standing force of approximately 20,000 hoplites.

Such rising internal pressure against Sparta exploded in 371 over the need to reaffirm conditions of the King's Peace. When Thebes alone was not allowed to make an agreement for her allies as well as herself, her delegates withdrew, an action regarded as cause for war by the Spartans. The two armies met at Leuctra in Boeotia where the 6,000 Thebans enjoyed a decisive victory over the 11,000 Lacedaemonians. Thebes then extended its scope, marching into the Peloponnese to sever Sparta's control of Messenia, then incorporating Thessaly, and building a fleet to challenge Athens.

As one might expect, these actions created a new coalition, now of Sparta, Athens, and Achaea against the common enemy, Thebes. The final battle of this round of attempts at empire was fought at Mantinea in the Peloponnese in 362. While nominally a Theban victory, the death of their brilliant and inspiring leader prevented the Thebans from taking advantage of their enemies. A peace was agreed based on the traditional condition of autonomy for every *polis*. As in the past, there was no machinery to guarantee adherence to the terms. Within three years, however, there would be a means of ending the incessant *polis* hostilities and the cycle of attempts at empire by the most powerful states.

The source of peace came from the north, in Macedonia, and was crafted by its king, Philip II. Philip's successes would effectively spell the beginning of the end of *polis* autonomy. This phase of Greek history merits a chapter of its own. Macedonian success would spur tendencies already apparent in the first half of the fourth century, namely the shift away from a *polis* perspective in political organization, a withdrawal of citizen participation from their common affairs, and the transfer of effective power from Greece to Persia and Macedonia; then, somewhat later, to Carthage and Rome. Still, in the events from 359 to 30 BCE, the *polis* way of life developed and embodied in the Classical period persisted and remained quintessentially "Greek," wars included. And this second age of heroes certainly persisted in its cultural legacy, which continues to the present.

Notes

1. Herodotus VIII.144.2.
2. Aeschylus, *The Persians*, lines 808–810.
3. Aristotle, *Politics* I, 3, 1252b and 1253a.
4. Percy Bysshe Shelley, Preface to "Hellas."
5. Sophocles, *Antigone*, line 322.
6. Herodotus VIII.84.
7. Aristophanes, *Wasps* 656–660.
8. Thucydides II.43. Revised edition of Crawley translation in Robert B. Strassler, ed., *The Landmark Thucydides* (New York: The Free Press, 1996).
9. The words of Alcibiades from Plato, *Symposium*, in *The Collected Dialogues of Plato*, ed. Edith Hamilton and Huntington Cairns, translated by Michael Joyce (New York: Pantheon Books, 1961), 219e–221b.
10. Plato, *Cratylus* 428c.
11. Thucydides I.23.5.
12. Thucydides, *History of the Peloponnesian War*, translated by Richard Crawley (1874), excerpts from V.89–111.
13. Xenophon, *Hellenica* II.2.3.
14. Xenophon, *Hellenica* 5.1.31, translated by J. C. Yardley.

Further Reading

General

Ehrenberg, Victor. 1968. *From Solon to Socrates: Greek History and Civilization during the 6th and 5th Centuries B.C.*, 1st ed. London: Methuen.

> A brilliant narrative of the main themes of the Classical Age of Greece. Its quality is demonstrated by its durability: a second edition was published in 1973 and a third appeared in 2011.

Forrest, W. G. 1966. *The Emergence of Greek Democracy*. New York and Toronto: McGraw Hill/ London: Weidenfeld.

> Included in Notes and Further Reading in Chapter 3, this study is an excellent resource for the on-going development of Greek democracy in the Classical Age.

Kagan, Donald. 2003. *The Peloponnesian War*. New York: Viking.

> One of a large number of studies by an outstanding scholar of Thucydides, the war he narrated and in which he fought, and the ascendancy of Athens.

Kitto, H. D. F. 1951. *The Greeks*. Harmondsworth: Penguin.

> The nineteen reprintings in many modern languages reveal the depth of the author's understanding of the ancient Greek view of the world. Why, he asks, did Greeks pay such attention to physical training and the Great Games?

Plato, *The Apology.*
> The account of Socrates' defense of himself to the jury of his fellow citizens is one of the best ways to understand the devotion of a citizen to his state. It also reveals how Greek life in the late fifth and early fourth century was moving in a difficult new direction.

Culture

Cornford, F. M. 1932. *Before and After Socrates.* Cambridge: Cambridge University Press.
> A short, insightful understanding of the long history of Greek philosophy.

Finley, M. I. 1981. *The Legacy of Greece: A New Appraisal.* Oxford: Oxford University Press, 1981.
> Fifteen essays by major scholars in their area of specialization describe aspects of ancient Greek culture and their legacy in subsequent ages.

Knox, Bernard. 1993. *The Norton Book of Classical Literature.* New York: W. W. Norton & Company.
> Three hundred selections of Greek and Roman authors of which two-thirds are Greek writers.

Pollitt, J. J. 1972. *Art and Experience in Classical Greece.* Cambridge: Cambridge University Press.
> A short introduction to the early history of the Greek arts provides the foundation for an account of the Classical period and its legacy to Hellenistic art. The discussion relates the arts to the larger social and cultural history of Greece.

Schoder, R. V. 1974. *Wings over Hellas.* Oxford: Oxford University Press.
> Photographs and commentary allow the reader to visit major ancient sites by flying, photographically, above them.

5

Incorporation into a Larger State

The Northern Neighbor: Macedon

Greeks had been well aware of the lands beyond their northern borders for centuries. The earliest farming villages were located in Macedonia and that settled way of life had spread south over the relatively passable link with northern Greece. Much later, during the Persian Wars, Macedonia had been a staging ground for the Persian invasion of Greece and, after the Greek defeat of the Persians in 479 BCE, contact continued inasmuch as the northern kingdom was a supplier to the southern *poleis* of important resources, especially metals and timber for ships. Even closer to Macedonia were Greek colonies that had dotted the coast line of the northern Aegean from the early centuries of the first millennium. Some had been planted along the coast of what would become Macedonian territory.

Its location on the northwestern coast of the Aegean made the small kingdom the node of connections not only for the Greek *poleis* but also more generally between north and south and east and west, drawing other peoples on its several borders into its expanding kingdom. Due to frequent incursions from all directions, creation of a strong state was difficult. One consequence was the view that Macedon and Macedonians were not major players in Aegean affairs until the fourth century BCE. That view needs revision.

There were various groups of Indo-European peoples in the region during the Bronze Age and interaction between other settlements and the Mycenaean kingdoms is shown in pottery finds as early as the sixteenth century BCE. The pottery is both imported ware and local imitations of that style. Not surprisingly, contact declined in the late thirteenth century as the Mycenaean world was engulfed in turmoil. Destruction also decreased the number of settlements within the territory that would eventually become the kingdom of Macedon. Of the sixty-eight sites in central Macedonia identified by 1990, forty-three were destroyed and twenty-five continued.

The initial impetus for a Macedonian kingdom can be dated to approximately 700 BCE when a clan known as the Argeads migrated eastward to inhabit a half-moon

Greece: A Short History of a Long Story, 7,000 BCE to the Present, First Edition.
Carol G. Thomas.
© 2014 John Wiley & Sons, Inc. Published 2014 by John Wiley & Sons, Inc.

shape of territory along the west coast of the Thermaic Gulf. Naming their center Aegae, after the Greek word for goats, showed their character as shepherds without a fixed abode. By this time in Greece, the *polis*, with its emerging hoplite phalanx, was solidly rooted. Consequently, for at least some of the Greeks, Macedonians were "barbarians." In fact, that view persisted into the fourth century: the Athenian politician and orator Demosthenes described Philip II, the Argead who created a kingdom extending from the Adriatic Sea to the Black Sea, as "not only no Greek, nor a relative of any Greeks; he's not even a barbarian from any decent place. He is a damn Macedonian from a country where you could never even buy a good slave."[1] As we will see, not everyone held that opinion.

The taunt that Philip was not a Greek raises the contested issue of Macedonian ethnicity, a question that has not been resolved due to the absence of written records in the Macedonian language. There is no ready answer.[2] However, our focus on the continuing nature of life in this eastern peninsula of Europe inclines to the view that Macedonians and Greeks shared cultures through their Indo-European origin and also because of their location in the same environment.

Shared ethnicity of Greeks and Macedonians certainly brought similarities of language: Macedonian has been identified as a dialect of Greek, specifically northwest Greek and the Greek alphabet was adopted for the written language of the kingdom, although only late in the formation of the kingdom. Earlier coins of the fifth century bear Greek alphabetic characters. Similar ethnicity would also be reflected in early institutions such as patriarchal kingship vested in one family among other noble lines, a council of elders, and an army assembly. The key point for our discussion of Greek culture and the question of continuity is that these institutions are reflected in evidence from Greece in the early first millennium but they were transformed by developments in the seventh and sixth centuries. On the other hand, Macedonian institutions retained the earlier forms. Religion, too, reflects important similarities such as the ancestry of the Argead line stemming from Zeus. Equally important was the ability of early Macedonian kings to appreciate, and incorporate into their culture, features of neighboring cultures that were akin to their own and valuable for the creation of a strong kingdom.

The earlier kings of the Argead line, from the late sixth century into the fourth, had some success in enlarging the kingdom and building a degree of centralization often by the recognition that adaptation of elements from neighbors was critical to their own success. Following the Persian defeat in 479 BCE, for example, Macedonian king Alexander I undertook confederation with adjacent kingdoms, aided by his innovation in infantry tactics. He had witnessed the success of the Greek tactics over the Persians in 480 and 479 when the Persians had first encamped in Macedon and, on their final defeat, had fled from Greece through Macedonian territory.

Macedonian kings also had an ability to recognize and draw on commonalities with many of their northern neighbors in language, ethnicity, economic conditions, political ideology, and common enemies. A confederacy of five regions was formed relatively early in the reign of Alexander I (circa 495–454), with the core of the original kingdom of Macedon becoming the hub. Later in his reign additional regions were added. From a narrow strip of land stretching some 60 miles along the coast, the kingdom was now roughly 6,600 square miles.

After his death, the interference of more powerful Greek states during the struggles of the Peloponnesian War largely demolished that unification until the late fifth century when King Archelaus (413–399) benefited from an absence of outside interference to strengthen the borders and to expand centralized administration from the new capital of Pella. However, in the first four decades of the fourth century the early efforts were nearly undone. Upon the death of Archelaus, kingship changed five times in less than six years. The fifth successor had a longer, though troubled, reign, to 370/69 and at his death his eldest son ruled for less than three years, and a second son had ruled for five when he died, along with 4,000 troops, in a massive incursion from the ferocious Illyrians driving over the mountains from their realm on the northwest coast of the Adriatic. The surviving brother, Philip II, was acclaimed Macedonian king by the army assembly and he faced the task of recreating a geographic and political kingdom.

Such an accomplishment was no small task. He was twenty-three and had virtually no army or wealth with which to create a state. And he had rivals, both in Macedonia and in neighboring territories. But akin to his predecessor Alexander I, he knew how to incorporate and build upon commonalities with his erstwhile neighbors. He dealt effectively with rivals for the throne and with Macedon's many foreign enemies during the twenty-three years of his reign and succeeded in consolidating a kingdom stretching from the Adriatic Sea to the Black Sea and from the Balkans to the north through Greece to the south, more than doubling the original consolidation of Alexander I. It now encompassed 16,680 square miles.

Near the top of his list of assets was his army, based on the original hoplite phalanx but reorganized according to the successful Theban infantry formation. Philip had been observant while he was a hostage in Thebes for three years during the time that Thebes was at the height of its success in the Greek sphere. Philip's soldiers were more mobile than the Greek hoplites, they drilled constantly, and were joined by special units of light infantry, cavalry, scouts, and crack troops. A career path in the military was a strong incentive for loyalty to the commander-in-chief, Philip. In addition to building the essential tool of military strength, Philip knew the value of greater centralization and achieved it through permanent defense of boundaries, tighter control of resources, and development of well-functioning administrative capabilities.

It was also essential to bolster his personal position as the Argead king. There were five other rivals for kingship of Macedonia at the time of his brother's death; although kings came from the line of the Argeads that line now had several branches. Thus, any Macedonian king had potential rivals in his brothers, uncles, and nephews. These claimants were often eliminated or, if allowed to live, brought under direct oversight of the king at his capital, Pella. Philip inherited a socio-economic structure in which aristocratic families enjoyed significant status and wealth and there were threats also in those once-independent kingdoms surrounding the core of Macedonian territory, a region that had only recently been re-consolidated. Heads of the powerful families could lay claim to a position similar to that of the Argead king. To assert his royal power against these kings, Philip created – or possibly enhanced – a cadre of subordinates in the form of young men of aristocratic families throughout the kingdom who were sent to the royal domain for training as future leaders. While creation of this corps was critical to effective military organization, in effect it held the aristocratic trainees as hostages for the good behavior of their fathers. Philip II demonstrated not a small amount of cunning in his kingship.

Other evidence shows him to have been a gifted diplomat both by his skill at dividing his enemies and through marriage alliance. Philip married seven- perhaps eight- times; most, if not all, of his choices were driven by political or military advantage. Philip stood ready to accept the invitations of the Greeks to help solve their internal problems, steadily advancing his sphere of influence southward, first into Thessaly and the Chalcidike peninsula, then into central Greece. As a result of his successes, he assumed positions within traditional Greek bodies. In Thessaly, for example, he was the *tagos*, an official who held command of the unified military force of the four regions of Thessaly and, as a member of the Delphic body of overseers, Philip joined one of the most significant organs uniting major Greek states. But, in spite of these positions, he had to continue his militancy especially when several *poleis*, the most important being Thebes and Athens, determined belatedly to take a stand against this very real threat to their independence. At Chaironeia in Boeotia, on August 2, 338 BCE, the Macedonian and Greek armies, numbering 30–35,000 on each side, met. The superiority of Philip's trained force and his own generalship, along with that of his son Alexander, gave the Macedonians a clear victory.

Thebes was garrisoned, Athens was spared. Of as much consequence were the actions of 337. Philip sought to arrange the boundaries among *poleis* in order to remove causes of conflict between them. He organized the League of Corinth, another sign of his familiarity with Greek methods of coalition: it was a defensive and offensive alliance between most *poleis* and Philip. A council of delegates would meet to determine joint action. All states were to be autonomous and no citizen was allowed to serve with a foreign power against Philip or the League. Finding a solution to the state of war between the Greek *poleis* won support from many individual Greeks. The Athenian Isocrates, unlike Demosthenes, recognized that the states "must cease their madness and spirit of enlarging themselves."[3] The Greeks could now be united for a proper goal: led by Philip they could battle against the real "barbarians" – that is, the Persians. If Philip were to succeed, Isocrates wrote, "nothing is left for you but to become a god."

When the delegates of allied states in the League gathered at Corinth in the winter of 337, they voted to undertake war against Persia with Philip as commander of a joint force. He was poised to begin because he was extending Macedon's reach eastward even while dealing with the Greeks states to the south. By the 340s, the Macedonians had marched eastward into Thrace and the Black Sea region where they viewed the Anatolian regions of the Persian Empire. With his diplomatic skills, Philip had gained Persian allies who were hostile to the Great King of Persia and through them he had knowledge that all was not well within that empire. In 336, he dispatched an advance force to Asia Minor under two of his most respected generals.

Philip's luck ran out before he could mount the full effort of war against Persia. In 336 at a grand celebration, he was assassinated in what was reported to be a petty, personal act by an insignificant man. Another tradition holds that a very significant person orchestrated the murder, namely his son Alexander who is reported to have complained that his father would leave no worlds for him to conquer. We may never know the true story but regardless of that uncertainty it is obvious that Philip's legacy allowed Alexander to find and triumph over those new worlds. We will return to the impact of Philip's legacy to Greek culture and its continuity after considering the nature of Macedonian and Greek relations following his death. Did Philip's efforts have a lasting effect?

Alexander III

Events that produced the new circumstances of Greek history began in the western Aegean but repercussions were soon felt from the Aegean Sea to the Indus River as Alexander, now king of Macedon, assumed the task that Philip had begun, but he vastly extended the scope. When Alexander died in 323 he was also Great King of Persia and held many other official titles. His own designs are largely unknown due to the absence of contemporary reports of people close to him or even accounts written by Alexander himself. A droll appraisal by Will Cuppy may not be far from the mark:

> Just what this distressing young man thought he was doing, and why, I really can't say. I doubt if he could have clarified the subject to any appreciable extent. He had a habit of knitting his brows. And no wonder.[4]

The monumentality of Alexander's accomplishment, on the other hand, inspired a number of accounts that allow the reconstruction of an outline of his dynamic, short life and its consequences for Greece.

Alexander's conquest would send Greece and most of the ancient Near East in new directions and that propulsion would win him the title Alexander "the Great." As in the Late Bronze Age, Greece and the East would be joined together even more closely than they had been a millennium earlier. The boundaries of the Greek political, military, and economic spheres would change dramatically: its culture would be re-molded by immersion in the cultures of the ancient Near East. Over time the commingled cultures of Greece and Macedon were further intertwined with the diverse cultures of the ancient Near East and Egypt.

With our attention on the interplay between the Greeks and their core environment, it is not surprising that exposure to the very different environment and people drawn together in the process of conquest produced major changes in the resulting "Greek" way of life. From the defeat of the Greeks at Chaironeia by Philip in 338 BCE to the fall of Rome in 476 CE, Greece was enfolded in sphere of others. Eight hundred-plus years is a long time to preserve earlier qualities of life under foreign control.

Born in 356 BCE, Alexander was the son of Philip II. His mother, Olympias of Epirus, was one of Philip's many wives. Trained in the rigorous physical requirements of a successful future king, Alexander was also provided with the tutoring of Aristotle to shape his intellect.

Aristotle's father, with his wife and their young son, had moved to Pella, where he became physician to Amyntas III, the Macedonian king. Aristotle offered his own service to Philip II as tutor to the youthful Alexander and his special colleagues. Even after the establishment of his school – the Lyceum – in Athens, Aristotle continued to aid Philip. The boundaries of the Greek *poleis* defining their physical identity within the federal League of Corinth, created by Philip, were drawn within the Lyceum. Aristotle is perhaps better known for his other contributions – to logic, metaphysics, ethics, politics, nature, the nature of life, the nature of the mind, and a great many other subjects. His breadth is a fine illustration of continuity in the longue durée of Greek history: while his work forms a coda to the intellectual world of Classical Greece it also provides a springboard to the Hellenistic Age. And that link is strengthened by his connection with Philip and Alexander of Macedon. Philip attempted to consolidate the tumultuous *poleis* disunity of the fourth century while Alexander triggered a new phase of Greek history.

Alexander was deemed sufficiently capable to direct Macedonian affairs at a young age; he was just sixteen when he acted as regent while Philip was on campaign and two years later he commanded the right wing of the Macedonian army at the battle of Chaironeia. On the murder of Philip in 336, Alexander was acclaimed king by the army assembly with the critical support of Philip's generals and aides.

He inherited a strong foundation: a unified kingdom, command of considerable resources, a strong infantry and redoubtable cavalry, control of Greece through the League of Corinth, and an ambition appropriate to one who claimed descent from Achilles on his mother's side and Heracles on his father's. This ambition seems to have been fueled by his mother, who is said to have told Alexander that his true father was not Philip but Zeus, who had visited her in the form of a serpent. Whatever the force of this assertion, Alexander's debt to Philip was essential to his own success.

However, the inherited foundation was not without weaknesses, particularly from kingdoms on the northern borders of Macedonia and arising from the still restive *poleis* to the south. In 335 Alexander was campaigning in the north when a report of his death sparked a revolt of the Greeks. A march of fourteen days brought the Macedonian army to Thebes, the center of the revolt, which was besieged, taken, and destroyed. Most of the rest of Greece submitted to the status quo. In the future, Alexander would make effective use of further revolts to obliterate other cities or peoples.

Within a year Alexander was ready to continue Philip's campaign against Persia. His military forces were a mix of Macedonian and Greek soldiers and marshaled some 30,000 infantry and 5,000 cavalry. He marched for the Dardanelles, leaving one of his father's most trusted officers, Antipater, as regent. On crossing the Dardanelles, his destination was Troy, where he could see the site of his ancestor Achilles' fame. Shortly thereafter he met the first Persian army at the River Granicus. Though almost killed in his bold tactical plan, his brashness was effective in awarding a clear victory to his forces. The army could then fulfill one of its goals: traveling along the coast, Alexander freed the Greeks – once again – from Persian control. The initial victory would be important in raising the confidence of Alexander and his force inasmuch as the resources of the Persian king were far vaster than those of the Macedonian king.

It was impossible, of course, to subdue the whole of Anatolia in short order. Thus, Alexander inaugurated what became a pattern throughout his campaign: after winning a decisive victory and at the point of entry into a new territory, he would designate a trusted subordinate to command a portion of the force while he himself moved on with the bulk of the army. Another of Philip's men, Antigonus the

One-eyed, was given the two-fold, demanding responsibility of pacifying Anatolia while maintaining an open link between the main army and Macedonia.

A detour into the Anatolian heartland provided knowledge of the interior. It also allowed Alexander to deal with the impossibly complex "Gordian knot" tied on the ox-cart of an earlier king – Gordius. An oracle promised that the person who could untie the knot would rule all Asia. He cut through it with his sword. The story gives us a good sense of Alexander's ambition. He then pushed on to Syria. At the head of that region, a second confrontation with the Persians was fought at Issus in 333. On this occasion, the Persian king, Darius III, personally commanded his army. He did not have either the leadership ability or the allegiance of subordinates that Alexander possessed so the result was a striking Macedonian victory with the capture of many members of Darius' own family, including his wife. The Macedonians continued along the coast, to Tyre, a major harbor for the Persian naval force. On the capture of Tyre after a seven-month siege, Alexander had virtually eliminated the fear of defeat by sea and he had detached Persia from the Mediterranean. It is not surprising, then, that Darius offered to cede to Alexander that part of his realm west of the Euphrates. Alexander obviously had a larger success in view, for he declined the offer.

Continuing on to Egypt, which was taken without a battle, Alexander initiated what would become another feature of his conquest (one might even say "policy") by the foundation of Alexandria. Eventually his foundations or cities would dot the course of his campaign and they, along with cities established by his successors, would provide the backbone of the new kingdoms that took shape after Alexander's death.

Another action in Egypt pointed to Alexander's own estimation of himself. Visiting the oracle of Ammon in the western desert, he learned the truth of his parentage although no record of the oracle's answer has been preserved. Perhaps he now believed his mother's report that he was the son of Zeus.

From Egypt his army marched to northern Mesopotamia where, at Gaugamela, they were met by a Persian force six times larger than the Macedonian army. The field had been arranged for the deployment of scythed Persian chariots which proved ineffectual when Alexander convinced his men that they must stand firmly in place, stepping aside only at the last moment to avoid the scythes. This third major Macedonian victory opened the door to Mesopotamia and to the Persian capitals of Susa and Persepolis. Acquisition of them provided treasure, an opportunity for Alexander to dismiss the Greek contingents since vengeance against the Persians had been exacted, and a reason for him to assume the Persian kingship. Darius was not dead but he was fleeing and would be put to death by his own men in the following year.

Alexander pressed on, however, since others now claimed the Persian throne. From 329 to 327, he tracked those contenders into Bactria and Sogdiana (now essentially Afghanistan) where he punished the claimants, married a Bactrian princess, and arranged that 30,000 native youths be trained in Macedonian fashion. With India just over the Himalayas, the troops continued into the Indus River valley where they were successful even against an unfamiliar military machine – elephants. Ready to move further eastward, Alexander was finally opposed by his men, who mutinied in 326. When his men could not be persuaded to change their collective mind, Alexander had to concede and from 326 to 324 his forces made their way back to

Mesopotamia by three routes: for some the route was the one that they had previously traveled; another path through which much of the force trekked was the cruel Gedrosian desert; and a portion sailed along the coast to explore the sea route between the Persian Gulf and India.

Babylon was their destination and it seems to have been the choice for a central point of the new realm. During the last year of his life, Alexander dealt with a tangle of problems that had arisen while he was out of contact with the original core of his kingdom and with those appointed to control it as he marched ever further away. The anger of the troops who were marching with him was rising to dangerous levels. It is reported that he began to make plans for the future but death prevented their fulfillment. Perhaps old wounds yet unhealed or fever from disease or even poison was the cause of his death on June 13, 323 BCE. He had conquered vast territories to form a geographic empire and he established some infrastructure by appointing commanders of regions. He had not formed a new functional empire because Alexander himself was the link in the variety of roles he played and he had not designated a successor. Tradition has it that, on his death bed, he gave his kingdom to "the strongest." As events would prove, more than strength was needed. Defining a long-term succession required half a century.

Alexander's Successors

Alexander was the main force both in creating the framework of a new form of state and in leaving no concrete plans for its development. During the early period following his death, there was a possibility that one person would succeed to continue Alexander's role. In 301 BCE that man was killed and with his death a second result emerged: Alexander's kingdom would be divided.

Antigonus the One-eyed was the potential single successor. Born circa 382 BCE, Antigonus was a contemporary of Philip II and, through marriage, he may have been connected to the royal Argead house. Defined as *Pellaios* (a youth of Pella), he was one of the young men raised in the capital to become officers and generals. Those who were successful would become the king's companions. Much of the training was physical, because not only as future officers would they serve and guard the Macedonian king, but they also performed this task as the king's boys. Antigonus was successful under Philip and when Alexander became king and organized for the campaign against Persia, Antigonus was given command of the 7,000 allied Greek hoplites. His life to this point in time indicates the importance of Macedonian institutions in his success. They would continue to shape his subsequent career.

Following the Macedonian victory at the Granicus River in 334, he was assigned the vital post of satrap of Phrygia in the north center of Anatolia, a position which entailed not only pacifying the extensive territory of the rest of Anatolia but maintaining lines of communication between Alexander, wherever he might be, and the kingdom of Macedon. Antigonus managed both tasks expertly. On the death of Alexander, he was confirmed as satrap in the territory that he had subdued. From 323 to 301 other Macedonian companions gained similar positions throughout the vast realm conquered by Alexander. The significance of Argead kingship remained powerful and Alexander's key subordinates endeavored to acclaim a successor for roughly twelve years.

Initially two ineffectual kings were selected: Alexander's mentally challenged half-brother (Philip III) and a newborn son of Alexander (Alexander IV). Real power obviously rested in the hands of Alexander's close companions. By 319, Antigonus was second only to Antipater, who had also been a companion of both Philip and Alexander and who had been left as regent in Macedon when the army crossed into Persian lands. With Antipater's natural death in 319, new contenders emerged, but Antigonus became leader of the Royal Army. However, in addition to Philip III and Alexander IV, a third Argead was also a potential king: Herakles was the son of Alexander the Great and Barsine, the daughter of a Persian satrap who had taken refuge with his family in Macedon. The family had returned to Persia but Alexander and Barsine met again when the Macedonian army was in Syria. Each Argead had strong advocates, not, however, sufficiently powerful to keep their candidates alive. Philip III was murdered in 317, Alexander IV in 311 or 310, Herakles perhaps in 310 or 309. With the removal of Argead successors, Antigonus was well-placed to become the single ruler of the conquests of Alexander.

In 306 he took the title of king, bestowing the same title on his son Demetrius, an act that pushed other contenders to claim that same title. Rising concerns about the power of Antigonus drove other successors to combine their forces. In 301 at Ipsus in Anatolia, Antigonus led a force of 70,000 infantry and 10,000 cavalry against a joint force of other contenders numbering 64,000 infantry and 10,500 cavalry. Antigonus was killed in battle; his son, who was his mature fellow general, escaped but the kingdom was divided among the victors.

In the following quarter-century, events produced three major new kingdoms – what remained of the eastern Persian Empire, Egypt, and Macedonia-Greece. The kingdoms were obviously not "new" as territorial entities but they were new in the direct commingling of Greeks and Macedonians with the diverse peoples of the conquered lands. The result has regularly been termed Hellenistic – that is, Greek-like – and Greek culture and people were extremely significant.. On the other hand, the term is unfortunate in that it ignores the on-going significance of Macedonians as well as the inherited cultures of the new kingdoms. A better term might be Megale (Greater) Macedonia, denoting the massive extension of Macedonian power that would persist over three centuries. Neither element – Greek nor Macedonian – would disappear as they were inserted into different environments.

Following the outcome at Ipsus, positions were reassigned. Alliances between these men continued as before, directed against others of their rank. By 280 most of the original successors were dead. Only one or two had died natural deaths but the more fortunate had been able to leave their kingdoms to heirs without a struggle for control. Such was the situation for Ptolemy in Egypt and Seleucus in Asia. Macedonia would require a struggle.

Those successors who survived the initial mêlée to claim kingdoms of their own had something of a plan of procedure which they inherited from Alexander. He had conquered a vast empire; hence as it had been won by the sword it must be maintained by military strength. Following the practice of earlier Argeads, Alexander recognized the value of non-Macedonian institutions in his short ten years of campaigning, perhaps most notably in his own claim to Achaemenid kingship, without,

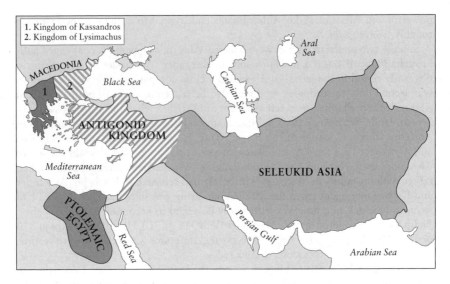

Figure 5.1   The Hellenistic kingdoms. Source: Jason Shattuck

of course, rejecting his Argead kingship. In addition, Alexander had retained existing administrative structures such as the division of territory into satrapies of Persia and the regional subdivisions of *nomes* in Egypt. His successors would find wisdom in following that precedent and they would also continue the foundation of cities that had been a prominent practice of both Philip and Alexander and earlier of Greek *poleis* by sending out colonies.

Just as important to the successors was the personal model that Alexander had set. Not one of them was certainly an Argead, although there is some suspicion about Ptolemy's parentage, and consequently, assumption of the Macedonian kingship was not likely. Once Philip III, Alexander IV, and Herakles had been put to death, succession in the Argead line ended. There were now many Macedonian kings rather than one of that noble lineage. Nor could any of the successors don the persona of the great Alexander although they followed his pattern of incorporating inherited institutions into their own rule. In fact, of the contenders for power in the years following his death, those most like Alexander were least successful. They also quickly learned that the force of earlier institutions and culture that they had inherited with their kingdoms could not be eliminated or even ignored.

Probably not the strongest, but perhaps one of the wisest, of Alexander's men was Ptolemy. He had been with Alexander in Egypt and, soon after the death of the king, decided that he wished to govern Egypt. Diverting the funeral cortege en route to Macedon, Ptolemy supported his claim through the symbolic link with the great conqueror and founder of Alexandria. Egypt under the Ptolemies enjoyed the longest life: 323/2 to 30 BCE when it was incorporated into the Roman Empire. Seleucus, another of Alexander's men, began to consolidate a kingdom a decade later when he established himself in Babylon, a key to the eastern part of the empire. Seleucid Asia endured, albeit in increasingly weakened form, to 63 BCE when it fell to Roman strength. Macedonia, the battle ground for many aspirants to power, would be restored only at the end of the struggle for succession: Antigonus Gonatas, grandson of two of Philip's and Alexander's most competent aides – Antipater and Antigonus the One-eyed – rebuilt the kingdom, which persevered from 275 to circa 168 BCE. It was named, after its creator, the Antigonid kingdom. There was a profusion of other states, but for two centuries the realms of the Ptolemies, Seleucids, and Antigonids determined much of the course of affairs in the eastern Mediterranean.

These three kingdoms shared many characteristics. All were large in territorial size and in population: Seleucid Asia comprised some 1.5 million square miles and Ptolemaic Egypt was home to 7–8 million people. In composition, the Greek and Macedonian element in the kingdoms of the Ptolemies and Seleucids was only about 10 percent of the total population. Consequently, while they were the elite of the Hellenistic states, Macedonians and Greeks were a small minority. To manage this situation of diversity the kings had to blend existing traditions and peoples with the newly introduced elements. Indeed, the blend is the reason for the name of this age: Hellenistic. Greek influence had earlier impacted Macedonia and it would now spread through the Middle East to become a dominant culture there, in its altered form, for ten centuries, until the Islamic explosion in the seventh century CE. By keeping the statistics in mind, we will understand reasons for the native resistance to "outside" control that grew in intensity in the second and first centuries BCE.

These heirs to Alexander all faced similar problems and employed tools of the same sort. Justifying their domination of non-Macedonian peoples required a strong administrative structure that incorporated long-established elements effective for the nature of the kingdom. The new rulers used existing local divisions within a central-ized administration in major cities. Foundation of new cities was a response to the need for a Greek element to serve as administrators and soldiers, as well as in trade and commerce. Alexandria, with its population of half a million reported by Diodorus writing in the first century BCE, is one of the most famous of these Hellenistic foundations but was joined by many similar cities especially in the Seleucid kingdom, where major cities such as Babylon had been key to administration in the Persian Empire and much earlier in the history of the ancient Near East. Earlier forms of political and social organization continued but they now were drawn from a far more diverse base than that employed by Greeks and Macedonians in earlier times.

Internal strength was essential to preserve Macedonian control but it was even more necessary in dealing with other kingdoms. The boundaries between kingdoms were regular battle zones just as the borders between *poleis* had been in Classical Greece. Therefore standing armies and navies of Greeks and Macedonians were essential tools. In Ptolemaic Egypt, military recruits largely from Greece and Macedon lived in colonies located in rural areas, while in Seleucid Asia they were settled in urban situations as well as in sensitive areas remote from the core of the kingdom. The policy of the Antigonids in Macedon also relied on several garrisons in strategic regions. Maintaining these tools was expensive, but a tightly controlled economy supplied a strong base of support through much of the Hellenistic Age.

Land, belonging to the king by right of conquest, was leased to others for a fee; rent in Egypt was usually one half of the yield of the produce. Much of industry and manufacture was a royal monopoly although actual production was leased to the highest bidder. Land was also granted to temples, both those dedicated to the practice of native religion and the temples constructed in Greek style for the Greco-Macedonian population. The religious architecture and religious practices demonstrate visibly the co-existence of native and imported cultures. Ptolemies and Seleucids alike appreciated the imperative to preserve and participate in the beliefs so essential to their mixed populations. The development of ruler cults underscores the role of religion in the Hellenistic monarchies. A cult of Alexander grounded, at least in part, in his own claim of divinity was a basis for the later cults, but native beliefs and practices were instrumental as well. The Pharaohs of Egypt were living gods, incarnations of Horus, and the Near Eastern traditions stretching back millennia deemed rulers as representatives of the gods. But their roles retained their Greco-Macedonian bases as well. The Ptolemies were pharaohs and assimilated Egyptian religious personas but they were also associated with Zeus and Apollo. The Seleucids also had dual religious affiliations. Just as the rulers had a two-fold religious status, the Greek deities themselves were joined by gods of the eastern Mediterranean, producing a synthesizing tendency that viewed gods with similar functions but different names as manifestations of one deity. Egyptian Isis, Greek Demeter, and Anatolian Kybele, for example, all were the Great Mother/Magna Mater.

Classical Greek philosophy also substantiated the power of kings. In his *Politics*, Aristotle maintained that "if there exists in a state an individual so preeminent … he should not be regarded as a member of the state at all. [He] should be rated as a god among men."[5] In arguing for kingships he also said that "people who are by nature capable of producing a race superior in virtue and political talent are fitted for kingly government."[6] Ptolemy II established a cult to his father and Seleucus' son, Antiochus, created one for his father.

The Greek subjects of Hellenistic kings also gained a different philosophy of their own lives that largely replaced the views of the fifth century. It was grounded in a search to find self-sufficiency and, perhaps, some happiness. Many were Skeptics who believed that nothing was known or could be known, so a wise person makes decisions on the basis of reasonableness. Cynics were somewhat more optimistic in believing that one should take what Fortune gives but should not become dependent on anything. Stoics, by contrast, emphasized the enduring quality of the soul as a fragment of the world soul. Happiness came through a life in harmony with the cosmos. Comfort for Epicureans was grounded in knowing that the universe was composed of countless, invisible atoms which sometimes combined to form bodies as they fell through infinite space. The bonds holding the atoms together were temporary so the compound bodies would fall apart. While the atoms of a person were intact, he or she should enjoy the simple pleasures of life.

Intellectual life generally was drawn under royal supervision and patronage. The Hellenistic Age saw the emergence of academies such as the museum and library at Alexandria where scholars were given generous salaries. Their task was to collect, edit, and classify the Classical Greek intellectual tradition. Eventually, some 700,000 papyrus rolls of that tradition were created and stored in Alexandria. Greeks of the Classical Age had no such capability for preservation of this literacy heritage. Now the heritage could be studied, corrected, and translated by scholars, to be preserved for posterity.

However, the character of Greek literature also changed with the new circumstances. The decline of the *polis* virtually eliminated certain genres such as tragedy, changed others – the comedy of manners replaced exploration of critical issues of the *polis* – and political history was superseded by efforts of systematic accounts of world-wide developments. The comic plays of Aristophanes, who openly criticized practices of the Classical *polis*, were replaced by affairs of ordinary people and their lives. The poet Menander was prolific; ninety-six known plays deal with conniving slaves, mistaken identity, grumpy old men, separated couples, and stolen babies in situations governed by Luck – often bad, sometimes good. Even when old genres were revived, they were peopled very differently than they had been earlier. Jason, hero of the Hellenistic epic poem about the voyage of the Argonauts in pursuit of the Golden Fleece, is often a victim of situations as were most people of the Hellenistic Age. Peter Green concludes that Jason is regularly "scared."[7] Finally, the pull of the royal court influenced poetry. A poem in honor of a lock of hair of a Ptolemaic queen turned into a heavenly star is but one illustration.

Confrontation with new methods and new materials produced a new golden age for Greek science. Major advances in physics, medicine, botany, astronomy, geography, mechanics, and math established the scientific base of knowledge that prevailed in Europe to 1600 CE. Rudimentary steam engines, water pumps, the heliocentric nature of the universe, nearly accurate calculation of the circumference of the earth, precise knowledge of the human body, and the beginning of infinitesimal calculus are a few of the stunning results. Discovery of a mechanism made of thin bronze resembling a primitive computer reveals the impressive level of technology. It was preserved after the ship on which it was carried was shipwrecked off the coast of the Ionian island of Antikythera in the early first century BCE. Modern experts have determine that its 30-some gears and the 2,000 characters inscribed on the object were employed to calculate movements of the stars and planets.

The growing insignificance of the *polis* as an independent state and the command of wealth by kings rather than by citizens of small, independent communities were both felt in architecture and the arts. Architecture continued to reflect the classical techniques but its purposes were changed by the rule of kings and their new, mixed cultures. Palaces and other buildings needed to manage their kingdoms became marks of royal power and coordination. New scientific knowledge also facilitated greater size that celebrated the royal power even if the product was not useful. Ptolemy IV ordered the construction of a ship 400 feet long and 50 feet wide, with its figureheads 70 feet above water. It demanded 4,000 rowers at its benches, managing oars 57 feet long. The vessel was never used.

The scope of that tradition is breathtaking: many of the Classical pantheon of gods were attested in the first Age of Heroes; the Greek literary tradition reaches back to the oral tradition of Homer; inquiry into the nature of the world can be linked with early Dark Age Greek settlements on the coast of Asia Minor; Classical art and architecture emerged from retention of certain features of the earlier tradition that were joined with skills acquired by contact with other cultures in the later Dark Age. Collectively they produced what has continued and continued: in his poem *Hellas*, Shelley declared, "We are all Greeks, our laws, our literature, our religion, our arts have their roots in Greece. ... But for Greece, we might still have been savages and idolaters."[8] The way of life fashioned in a particular place could survive, even prevail, in other places and times.

For most members of the native populations now under Macedonian rule, life continued much the same as it had done for centuries, even millennia: they lived in familiar locations, pursued the same occupations, and worshipped the same deities. Some natives, of course, entered the vast administrative structure and became participants in the new mélange of culture. On the other hand, for Greeks and Macedonians who were drawn to the Hellenistic cities and military colonies, life took a distinctly new turn. Many Greeks had left a *polis*, not as independent a community as it once had been but still possessing much of its original identity. Alexandria and Babylon bore little resemblance to Corinth or Athens. Occupations also changed: the immigrants were mercenary soldiers, administrators, engaged in commerce, or scholars. Their gods were joined by others.

For the Greeks in older traditional *poleis*, the changes were perhaps not as dramatic as they were for émigrés. Yet the vitality of the *polis* and the culture it sustained were ebbing even in Greece. During the time of Alexander, conditions of the League of Corinth were accepted through fear and inspired by the example of the Theban fate in 335. Yet, the larger *poleis* resented their dependence. The Spartans, for example, were influenced by Persian gold to attempt a revival of their power even while Alexander was in the heart of Persia. The attempt failed as did subsequent efforts to regain autonomy. On the death of Alexander, a number of states allied to assert their independence but the effort was quashed by 10,000 Macedonian veterans just returned from the East. The Greek states soon became pawns in the power struggles among the successors. Athens passed back and forth between the two contenders four times in a decade. As the third century wore on, the *polis* increasingly gave way to larger leagues forming through Greek initiative, to the will to power of great individuals, and to the active intervention of the major outside powers. Even so, the will to power of the *polis* did not die. The regionalism fostered by the physical nature of Greece had not been conquered. As late as the first century BCE, when King Mithridates VI of Pontus in northern Asia Minor sought allies to defeat common enemies, he gained Greek allies with his call for freedom for the Greeks. The Athenians were persuaded and restored democracy to their *polis*, albeit for a very brief time.

A poem by the Modern Greek poet Cavafy captures the enduring attachment to *polis* life by the no-longer-mighty Spartans during this period of decline when Cleomenes was king.

In Sparta

> King Cleomenes did not know, he did not dare—
> He did not know how he could speak so plain
> A sentence to his own mother: that Ptolemy required
> She should be sent to Egypt and that he should retain
> Her there in guarantee of their agreement;
> A very humiliating and unseemly proposal.
> And he kept on beginning to speak; and hesitating;
> And he came to his opening words; and kept on stopping there.

But this excellent lady understood him
(She had besides already heard some rumors about it),
And she began to encourage him to explain.
And she laughed; and she said of course she was going.
That in fact she was glad she could be
In her old age of use to Sparta still.

As for the humiliation—well she did not care.
A descendant of Lagos, yesterday's child, could never understand
The pride of Sparta; wherefore his demand
Could never in fact prepare
Humiliation for a Princess
Illustrious as she was, mother of a Spartan king.[9]

As the power struggles of the Hellenistic kings weakened the base of the kingdoms, a new threat to both what remained of the Greek way of life and that of the more recent kingdoms was strengthening in the west. Whether the Romans were drawn into the unending contention of the eastern Mediterranean or whether they viewed the region as ripe for conquest is hotly debated. A certain answer is unlikely. But it is clear that Romans had long known about the Greeks, not only those settled in the central and western Mediterranean and across the Adriatic on the mainland of Greece but also in the eastern Mediterranean. After the death of Alexander, Romans were increasingly drawn into the affairs of the eastern sphere. By 30 BCE, all the successor kingdoms had been incorporated into the Roman Empire, producing yet another commingling of Greek and other cultures.

The Greatest of Kings: Philip II

Alexander III of Macedon has been known as Alexander the Great since antiquity and the study of Macedonian history often focuses on the nature of this "greatness." Yet, Theopompus, a fourth-century BCE Greek historian, said in his account of the brilliant career of Philip II that Europe had never before brought forth such a man as Philip. Recent studies of his career have led to a reconsideration of the relative greatness of Philip and his son. We will award the title King of Kings to Philip II. Alexander is remarkable in the extent of his conquest and the short period in which it was done. He was an amazing, enigmatic person. The accomplishment of Philip is a more subtle and complicated achievement: from a point at which the Argead kingdom would disappear, he created a kingdom that included territory extending north to south from the Balkans to Greece (*sans* Sparta that no longer mattered) and west to east from the Adriatic to the Black Sea. He forged a plan for unification. Without the fruits of Philip's rule, Alexander would not have had the means to begin his campaign beyond the core of the kingdom and would not have inherited his many titles. Moreover, the product of Philip's effort would endure far longer than the brief consolidation of territory stretching from the Adriatic Sea to the Indus River. Such an admission need not diminish amazement at Alexander's brilliance and short-term success, and wonder at his inner being.

For additional support of the idea of Philip II as a King of Kings read the words reported to be Alexander's view of Philip's accomplishment.

In taking you on, Philip found you poor migrants, most of you clad in skins pasturing a few sheep in the mountains and fighting poorly over these sheep with Illyrians and Triballians and the nearest Thracians. He provided you with proper cloaks rather than skins, led you down from the mountains to the plains, turning you into true fighters against the neighboring barbarians so rather than relying on the natural strength of the land you trusted your own strength. He made you inhabitants of cities and provided you with laws and useful customs. Over those barbarians, by whom you and your possessions had been carried off and plundered, he established you as masters free from slavery and the role of subjects. He added most of Thrace to Macedonia and having captured the most convenient location on the seacoast he encouraged trade and commerce in the land, and allowed the peaceful working of metals. He made you rulers of the Thessalians, who had long filled you with fear, and by humbling the ethnos of the Phocians, he created for you a broad road into Greece that earlier had been narrow and difficult. He humbled the Athenians and Thebans, ever lying in wait for Macedonia .... Entering the Peloponnese, he settled matters there. And now named overlord of all Greece he took command of the army against Persia not for his own renown but for that of all Macedonians.[10]

Hyperbole is clear – not everyone wore skins and, in earlier periods, not everyone lived as recluses in the hills with their sheep. However, after the Illyrian invasion of 359 BCE, when Philip succeeded his slain older brother, a Macedonian kingdom did not exist. Philip was fortunate, clever, wily, and often brutal in gaining clear knowledge of the nature of Macedonia's enemies. Being a hostage in Thebes at the time of the Theban military reform he foresaw the advantages of the changes for the Macedonians. And, as king, rather than as elected official of a *polis* for a limited period, decisions were his alone to make. More than knowing his enemy and adapting elements for Macedon's benefit, he was well aware of the culture of Greece and its potential for Macedon.

After the critical rite of passage, namely survival and being acclaimed king, Philip dealt first with recovery from the massive defeat. Within his first year as Argead king, he reorganized the infantry in its formation, gear, training, and discipline. He structured better coordination between the cavalry and infantry, introduced new technology including siege machinery. His program of training youth from the entire kingdom in Pella produced a cadre of young officers. Land grants to soldiers and education for future soldiers whose homelands had been independent kingdoms fostered a sense of commonality that had existed earlier but had been jeopardized by the Illyrian invasion.

This accomplishment produces a picture of the region beyond the northern borders of Greece. How is it important for a history of Greece? Simply answered, Philip II as king of Macedon constructed the first national state in Europe in which Greeks would become prominent players with strange bedfellows from lands beyond its geographic nucleus including Epiriots, Illyrians, and Thracians. Alexander would add the peoples and territories of the Persian Empire using the tools and resources that Philip himself constructed.

Did this inclusion fundamentally alter the identity of the people and environment of the "system" of earlier ages in Greece? For two main reasons, the answer is no. First, the environment was essentially the same as that of the earliest settlements in the peninsula

Figure 5.2 Philip II. Source: Theo. G. Antikas

of Greece; consequently the regions were connected in nature and in proximity. Second, Greeks and Macedonians shared Indo-European ethnicity as well as the pattern of their earliest way of life in those regions that persisted from the Neolithic Age to the re-creation of the Macedonian kingdom by Philip – and beyond. Philip forged a new tool to unite the neighbors. Certainly military superiority was essential. In addition, his keen knowledge of the Greek way of life brought appreciation of similarities. His answer was the creation of a federal state incorporating Greeks and Macedonians.

After defeating the Greeks in 338, Philip created a new league – the League of Corinth – with himself as its leader. It demonstrated clearly the Macedonian power over Greece but it also created a new order within Greece in which Macedon and its king would be its core. Arranging settlements with individual Greek states was an essential first step. The boundaries of states were defined, perhaps through the assistance of Aristotle, whose connection with Macedon began when Aristotle's Greek father came to Pella as a doctor and it had many facets over a long period of time. With the territories of all *poleis* defined, a common peace was declared. Philip made it known that if any *polis* attacked another he would aid the injured state and make war against the offender.

After reaching the individual accords, a governing council was created of delegates from the allied states with the exception of Sparta, which refused to participate since it would constitute servitude. Decisions were taken regarding joint action in the council, which also served as a court to arbitrate disputes and to proceed against those who violated the decrees of the League. Its leader – Philip – was both the chief political official and military commander-in-chief. In addition, the League gained another role against the true enemy of its members: a campaign against Persia. An advance force was dispatched to Asia Minor in 336.

The League of Corinth resembled earlier coalitions such as the Peloponnesian League and the Delian League. But it differed in an essential respect: it was a federal state under a new conception that all members would retain their independent identity while gaining a participatory role in a far more extensive entity. The organization required a two-tier political structure, both essential to its success. This use and transformation of an existing Greek political structure showed Philip's genius in overcoming the *polis* dilemma.

In the short term and in the longer history of Greece, the league structure would be critical. In 338 it settled conflicts among Greek *poleis* and between them and Macedon. Consequently, it was possible for Philip to initiate a joint military effort against Persia and, subsequently, for Alexander to execute. As Alexander moved further from the Aegean, the League's role became less important but without it Alexander would not have been able to achieve as much as he did. In fact, he fostered other leagues in the conquest of the East. Under the successors, not only did the League of Corinth survive but new leagues emerged. Antigonus the One-eyed and his son Demetrius revived the League of Corinth with themselves as its leaders/commanders-in chief. Antigonus also founded the League of the Islanders centered on the Cyclades in circa 315–314. After the death of his father in 301, Demetrius struggled to carve out a realm of his own, dying before he could succeed. The task fell to Demetrius' son, Antigonus Gonatas, who reunited the territory that was essentially Philip's realm. He used the tools of Philip II.

Definition and centralization of the realm echoed Philip's pattern. Force was essential to define its extent and, thus, the military structure that Philip had honed was critical but understanding of the earlier political organization of his kingdom was equally necessary. The territorial organization had to be reconstituted. Pella was the capital of Macedonia, which was divided into districts, each under a governor. Land outside of Macedonia belonged to the king by right of conquest: Antigonus governed Thessaly as Philip had (as the *tagos* of the four regions); other regions were governed through generals; and at the *polis* level local political structure preserved its own form. A structure of democracy or oligarchy or aristocracy could be tolerated as long as citizens were not openly hostile to Macedon as they had been until the last years of Philip's reign. Greeks were not yet quiescent.

Antigonus enjoyed a long rule – until 239 – and it paved the way for a restored League of Corinth under his successor, Antigonus III/Doson. In the confusion of much of the third century, small communities in isolated, economically poor regions of Greece were driven to make common alliances with one another in order to survive challenges of the larger *poleis*, a situation reminiscent of the successful Athenian drive to power in the fifth century. The response of the endangered communities was to unite as a league. Leagues emerged in Arcadia in the mountainous center of the Peloponnese, Achaea in the northern hump of the Peloponnese, and Aetolia in the mountainous west of central Greece. All of these regions are conspicuous by their absence from the earlier story of Greek history.

Individual communities retained their own local identities to manage life within the community but created a collective structure composed of an assembly open to every citizen that met at fixed times during the year to decide policy, make laws and constitute a federal court, and to elect a head and other officials. In addition, members of a federal council were elected by league units in proportion to their military strengths. Smaller than the assembly, the council could meet often and whenever necessary. Some leagues produced a federal coinage and many built a religious center.

Polis spirit had not disappeared, especially in Sparta under kings who were determined to recreate the extensive realm of Classical times, an effort that included Arcadia and Aetolia, whose fear of the newly energized Sparta led to an alliance with Macedon. Antigonus Doson agreed to aid Arcadia and Aetolia, but only by invitation. He was invited into the effort in 224, and subsequently he defeated Sparta in 223. Afterwards he reconstituted a new League, this time a league of leagues which preserved the autonomy of its members. All league decrees had to be ratified by individual members, a council dealt with peace and war, and the king of Macedon presided as president and commander-in-chief.

The consolidation from the third to the first century is important in several respects. Earlier *poleis* cores endured but increasingly as cities. The force of regionalism had been moderated by a new political and economic concept: the consolidation had its beginnings in the "state" which, one could say, Philip II established. And as the Romans became interested in the eastern Mediterranean, they dealt largely with leagues. Later, under Roman control, technology would further help to manage the physical difficulties of the environment that needed to be overcome by creating yet greater centralization. However, the environment and geographic region of Greece had not been fundamentally altered; only in the late nineteenth and early twentieth centuries did modern skills begin to join valleys between mountains and bays separated by promontories. Anticipating a much later chapter in the Greek story, the effort continues to the present day and the identity of the people dealing with that environment is also continuous. The city-states of the Golden Age of Greece may have been conquered by the Macedon kings but Macedonians themselves were akin to Greeks in their ethnicity. Greece had been incorporated into a new and larger state and its way of life, although modified, was preserved and incorporated in all of the successor kingdoms. Our search for continuity proceeds into Roman times in Chapter 6 when Greece became part of Rome's empire.

Notes

1. Demosthenes, *Philippic* III.31.
2. Hughey, J.R., et. al., "A European population in Minoan Bronze Age Crete." *Nature Communications* May 14, 2013.
3. Isocrates, *Third Letter to Philip*.

4. Will Cuppy, *The Decline and Fall of Practically Everybody* (New York: Holt, 1950), 45.
5. Aristotle, *Politics*, 1284a.
6. Aristotle, *Politics*, 1288a.
7. Peter Green, *From Alexander the Actium: The Historical Evolution of the Hellenistic Age* (Berkeley: University of California Press, 1990), 210.
8. Percy Bysshe Shelley, *Hellas* (1821), preface.
9. *Poems by C. P. Cavafy*, translated by John Mavrogordato (London: Chatto & Windus, 1951), 174.
10. Arrian, *Anabasis (Campaigns) of Alexander* VII.9.2–5.

Further Reading

Macedonia and Macedonians

Arrian 1971. *The Campaigns of Alexander*, revised ed., translated by Aubrey de Sélincourt. London: Penguin.
    The most reliable primary source.
Borza, Eugene N. 1990. *In the Shadow of Olympus: The Emergence of Macedon*. Princeton, NJ: Princeton University Press.
    The author provides a picture of the change of the kingdom's status as a backwater to a major power in the eastern Mediterranean. His understanding of that change is based on first-hand knowledge of the region as well as a long and distinguished career of teaching and scholarship. It is accessible to non-specialists as well as specialists.
Briant, Pierre. 1996. *Alexander the Great: Man of Action, Man of Spirit*, translated by Jeremy Leggatt. New York: Harry N. Abrams.
    A brief, beautifully illustrated study by an outstanding scholar of the Persian Empire in which Alexander figured prominently. Professor Briant has also become fascinated with the nature of Alexander's fuller life and career.
Gabriel, Richard A. 2010. *Philip II of Macedonia: Greater than Alexander*. Washington, DC: Potomac Books.
    Philip II has become a popular subject for books. This study presents a view of the king as unifier of Greece not only through military success but through his means to create a federal constitution incorporating Macedon and Greece, thereby establishing the first territorial state in Europe.
Green, Peter. 1991. *Alexander of Macedon, 356–323 B.C: A Historical Biography*, revised ed. Berkeley: University of California Press.
    Beginning, as it must, with the importance of Philip II, this engaging account succeeds in fulfilling the author's purpose "To strip away the accretions of myth, to discover—insofar as the evidence will permit it—the historical Alexander of flesh and blood" (p. 487).
Thomas, Carol G. 2007. *Alexander the Great in His World*. Oxford: Blackwell.
    The intent of this study is to turn to the world in which Alexander lived to seek forces that shaped his life and to ask what qualities a Macedonian king must possess in order to confront those forces successfully.

Hellenistic Age

Erskine, Andrew, ed. 2003. *A Companion to the Hellenistic World*. Oxford: Blackwell.
    The interesting variety of subjects and authors provides an understanding of the historical developments from the death of Alexander to the death of Augustus as well as specific

aspects of the culture including religion; social and economic conditions and changes; and art and literature.

Green, Peter. 1990. *From Alexander the Actium: The Historical Evolution of the Hellenistic Age*. Berkeley: University of California Press.

This justly praised, extensive account of the new world resulting from the success of Alexander, totalling 739 pages of text and illustrations, 167 pages of notes, and 19 pages of select bibliography, may be daunting. A shorter alternative by Green is *The Hellenistic Age: A Short History* (New York: Modern Library, 2007).

6

Graecia Capta
Roman Control

The legacy of Classical Greece to the following three centuries was strong enough to determine the usual name by which those centuries are known – the Hellenistic Age. However, the majority of peoples and environments differed significantly from earlier periods. The official end of the age is dated to the death of the last ruler of the longest surviving of the kingdoms, Ptolemaic Egypt, which was incorporated into the Roman Empire in 30 BCE. The word "Hellenic" did not figure in its designation under Roman rule: Greece became "Roman Greece," or *Graecia Capta* as the Roman poet Horace described it. By the first century BCE Greece was one of many provinces of the empire and its provincial name was Achaea.

In our search for continuity, it is essential to ask if Greeks and their environment had been so changed from the time of Alexander to 30 BCE that the system or way of life had been completely altered. We argued in the previous chapter that Greek peoples remained prominent within the individual kingdoms and that their culture had exercised a dominant role within the new territories. Now we must ask how a provincial status within a non-Greek empire affected continuity of Hellenic people and their way of life. To anticipate an answer to the question of continuity, life within the compass of Rome would preserve and even invigorate the established Hellenic culture in the comparable environments of Greece and Italy. The Adriatic Sea allowed easy access to one another and their common Indo-European identity brought language similarity as well as other cultural features.

The peninsula of Italy is akin to that of Greece in geographic features. Seventy-five percent of the land is mountainous, and those mountains divide the land into regions. Bordered by seas on three sides, the Italian coastline stretches 4,700 miles. Longer and thinner than the Greek peninsula, its total land mass is more than double that of Greece. Italy does not have a great number of rivers but more of them are perennial than those of its eastern neighbor. These geographic likenesses fostered similar means of subsistence, forms of communities, and interaction with the larger Mediterranean sphere via the sea.

Greece: A Short History of a Long Story, 7,000 BCE to the Present, First Edition.
Carol G. Thomas.
© 2014 John Wiley & Sons, Inc. Published 2014 by John Wiley & Sons, Inc.

Connections between the peoples of Greece and Italy reached deep into the past. Evidence now indicates that the Neolithic settlement in Greece in the seventh millennium BCE was part of a continued westward transmission into Italy later in that millennium. The carriers of settled agrarian life were related as Indo-Europeans with earlier roots in Anatolia. Even the legendary history of Rome's founding is linked to Greek tradition. Its founders – Romulus and Remus – were said to be descendants of Trojan Aeneas who had survived the fall of Troy to the Greeks to endure his own "Odyssey" in search of his destination, Italy. We do not intend or need to look for the truth of Aeneas' story, or even for proof of his existence; rather, what is of interest is that this tradition reveals a sense of early links between the Romans and Greeks on the part of the Romans.

Other better-documented connections occurred around the time of the settlement of Rome, dated by the Romans to 753 BCE. During this period Greek adventurers were beginning to sail again to western waters in search of resources absent at home and, shortly thereafter, to locate lands for new settlements. As we have seen in Chapter 3, the heel and toe of Italy, as well as much of the eastern coastal area of Sicily, were settled by Greeks as *poleis*, so thickly, in fact, that the area came to be known as *Magna Graecia*.

To the north of the Tiber were Etruscans, whose origin and identity is debated. One possibility is that they were driven from the eastern Mediterranean in the "time of troubles" at the end of the second millennium BCE and resettled in northern Italy. Becoming the most powerful people of Italy in the early Iron Age, the Etruscans held Etruria – that is, modern Tuscany from the Arno River to the Tiber River and from the Apennines to the Tyrrhenian Sea. Internal development in the ninth century BCE is testified by archaeological evidence. The population grew, villages coalesced and increased in size, and the Etruscan sphere expanded south to the Campania for agricultural as well as commercial purposes. The northern city-states possessed mineral resources and the technology to work them skillfully. Traders from the eastern Mediterranean were drawn to Etruria and imported goods reveal the growth of Greek trading activity from the later eighth century onward.

Etruscan domination resulted in the growing importance of Rome as a link between Etruscan activities to the north and to the south of the Tiber River. Rome came under Etruscan control until 509 when the Etruscan overlords were expelled. A more powerful, enlarged Roman state began its slow, seemingly methodical expansion throughout the Italian peninsula. By the later fourth century, Rome's borders abutted the territory of the Greek *poleis* in southern Italy.

Greeks of the post-Classical period also had a strong interest in Italy. Alexander's death produced a number of would-be kings seeking new kingdoms. In the early decades of the third century, one of Alexander's younger successors was Pyrrhus, of the kingdom of Epirus on the eastern coast of the Adriatic, who was persuaded to bring his forces to *Magna Graecia* in southern Italy and Sicily with the hopes of ending disputes among the more powerful of the Greek states there; the *polis* spirit of warfare was endemic in the colonial settlements as well as on the mainland of Greece. He won a few victories in Italy and Sicily but the major consequence of his intervention was to draw Rome into the conflict. After being defeated by the Romans, Pyrrhus returned to Greece in 275 BCE with his depleted troops, causing more confusion there until he was killed in a raid on Argos in 272. By that same year, Rome had annexed the Greek states of southern Italy and incorporated the territory into the Roman sphere through alliances.

Roman control was now within sight of the Greek sphere in Sicily, separated only by the narrow Strait of Messana. The usual clash between Greek *poleis* in Sicily soon required intervention, drawing Rome into that contest. This engagement, however, also drew in powerful imperial Carthage whose reach extended from North Africa throughout much of the western Mediterranean. Not only would the war involving Rome and Carthage decide the future of Greek Sicily but it would have a far more sweeping aftermath. This First Punic War (the Latin word for the Carthaginians is "Poeni") gave the Romans a victory over Carthage in 241 but a Second Punic War was inevitable after the Carthaginians had rebuilt their empire. Roman victory in the second confrontation thrust the Romans into even wider participation throughout the Mediterranean.

This second confrontation—Hannibal's war, as it is designated after the famous Carthaginian general – began in 218 with a Carthaginian invasion of Italy from the north that quickly produced a dire situation for Rome both in military defeats and in dissolution of Rome's system of alliances. Eventually the field of battle returned to Carthage where the Romans scored a decisive victory in 202. The treaty concluded in 201 brought Sicily, Sardinia, and Corsica into the Roman domain not as allies but as provinces, defined as the geographical regions managed by Rome. Moreover, as the dominant power in the western and central Mediterranean, Rome made alliances with eastern kingdoms that would inaugurate two centuries of Roman interventions in dealings of the Hellenistic kingdoms.

Initially, the intervention was welcomed – for example, when the Romans defeated piratical peoples nesting along the northeast coast of the Adriatic. The region became a Roman protectorate and the Greeks' means of thanking Rome was admission to the Olympic Games. Macedonian kings were reviving the consolidation of Macedonia with Greece while some former *poleis* were striving to return to their independent status of the Classical Age. The very different goals led to four so-called Macedonian Wars in which Rome was a major player.

Antigonus Gonatas had been relatively successful in re-establishing the association between Macedon and Greece that Philip II had achieved. In effect, he attempted to return to the earlier form of kingship, to build a shield against northern enemies, and to return Greece to Macedonian control. By his death in 239, Macedon was a powerful player in affairs of the eastern Mediterranean. Unfortunately for Greece, Rome was becoming a participant in eastern affairs in the period shortly after Antigonus' death.

Four wars quashed the accomplishment of Antigonus Gonatas. The first war resulted from the declaration of war against Rome by a descendant to the Macedonian kingship. Betting on the success of Carthage and Hannibal in the Second Punic War (218–201), Macedonian King Philip V planned to aid the Carthaginians by invading Italy from the east. While Macedonians did not carry out the invasion, Rome remembered the intent. The second war between Macedon and Rome began with Rome's ultimatum to the Macedonian king in 200 BCE to end the warfare in Greece, clearly not a simple task. It brought the Roman army to Greece to win a victory over the Macedonian army in 197. Macedon became a restricted independent Roman ally, while Greece was a free protectorate.

The Macedonian king was not submissive and attempted to rebuild the strength of his kingdom, leading to the third war and another Roman success. Macedon was divided into four republics and hostages were taken from Greece for the good behavior of their countrymen. The final war was the result of a rebellion by a pretender to Macedonian kingship. After the Roman victory at Pydna in 148 BCE Macedon was made a province with a Roman governor and tribute.

In that same year, a Greek revolt from its status as a Roman protectorate raised swift Roman reaction: Corinth was burned to the ground and all of Greece came under the control of the Roman governor of Macedonia. By arms and administrative structure, the Romans had accomplished the feat that had eluded the Macedonians through their efforts in creating the League of Corinth by Philip II and the League of Antigonus Doson. The future of the eastern Mediterranean might be predicted: the ruler of the kingdom of Pergamum in Anatolia willed his kingdom to Rome in 133 BCE as a token of Rome's momentum and the Hellenistic rulers' fear of it.

Thus, the first century BCE witnessed the completion of Roman control of the lands around the Mediterranean Sea. At the start of that century, of the major Hellenistic states, only Seleucid Asia and Ptolemaic Egypt remained independent. Seleucid Asia, now a shadow of its former greatness, fell to Rome in 63 BCE. In the Roman reorganization of Aegean and Levantine states, Crete and Syria became provinces while the Greek cities were, in theory, free but most paid tribute. They

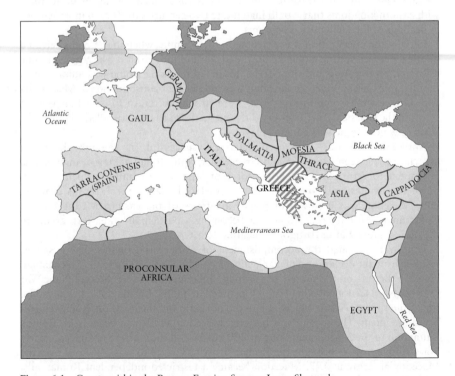

Figure 6.1   Greece within the Roman Empire. Source: Jason Shattuck

were now, of course, no longer city-states – that is, *poleis*. The Ptolemies aided their own demise through incessant rivalry for the throne, infighting that served to lure ambitious Roman generals to the banks of the Nile. The kingdom and its last ruler, Cleopatra VII, attracted first Pompey, who had been granted command of the entire Mediterranean in 67 BCE; then Julius Caesar, who acquired major power after Pompey's death; and, on Caesar's murder in 44 BCE, Mark Antony, who intended to secure his own power in the East. The first and the third met their deaths in Egypt. Even Caesar's assassination in Rome may have owed something to his connections with non-Roman Egyptian ways, perhaps envisioning himself as a monarch in the tradition of Alexander and his successors. Romans had expelled their last king in 509 BCE and had no wish to return to a monarchy. Cleopatra herself was not welcomed in Rome when she came with Caesar. Her ancestry was likely one reason for her treatment: it blended Macedonian, Greek, and a touch of Indo-European Persian. Her language of rule was Greek but her other eight languages included Egyptian. On the other hand, she is an interesting example of the continuity of Hellenic culture.

One Roman man who could not be lured by Cleopatra was the adopted son of Caesar, Octavian, who fought for Roman values over the "decadent" values of the East. At Actium, in northwest Greece, his fleet was victorious in 31 BCE over that of Antony and Cleopatra. And although they escaped back to Egypt, Antony and Cleopatra took their own lives and, in 30 BCE, Egypt became a special type of protectorate. Octavian lived to settle conditions in Italy and throughout the empire, accepting the title *princeps* (first citizen), as well as the honorific name Augustus (the August One).

Even though the Greek East had been defeated by Roman legions, Hellenization of Rome had been constant throughout the period of Roman expansion. Roman soldiers, governors and their entourages, and other Roman officials were affected by the Hellenic culture they found in the East. Greek objects and people – hostages, envoys, professionals, traders, and slaves – found their way to Italy in such numbers that the poet Juvenal (60–130 CE) viewed the result as frightening and stated his opinion in the following three selections from his *Third Satire*.

> Now let me speak of the race that our rich men
> dote on fondly.
> These I avoid like the plague, let's have no coyness about
> it.
> Citizens, I can't stand a Greekized Rome. Yet
> what portion
> Of the dregs of our town comes from Achaia only?
> ...
>
> Furthermore, nothing is safe from his lust, neither
> matron nor virgin,
> ...
> Since I'm discussing the Greeks, let's turn to their
> schools and professors,
> The crimes of the hood and gown.[1]

Important Romans understood the nature of current Greek rule in the eastern Mediterranean and used that knowledge to their advantage as the careers of Julius

Caesar and Pompey the Great demonstrate. Even more discernible was the Hellenic influence on Roman literature, philosophy, and art. The lines of Virgil, who composed the Roman epic about Aeneas, are plain in identifying differing spheres of excellence of Greeks and Romans:

> Let others fashion from bronze more lifelike, breathing images –
> For so they shall – and evoke living faces from marble;
> Others excel as orators, others track with their instruments
> The planets circling in heaven and predict when stars will appear.
> But, Romans, never forget that government is your medium!
> Be this your art: to practice men in the habit of peace.
> Generosity to the conquered and firmness against aggressors.[2]

One of the earliest works of Roman literature was the Latin translation of the *Odyssey* by Livius Andronicus, half-Greek, who lived in Tarentum in southern Italy, the only Spartan colony.

Roman Administration

Rome's expansion necessitated major changes in its institutions as well as its intellectual life. With the earliest extension of Roman territory in Italy itself, new peoples could be joined to Rome as friends. These personal relationships that sometimes were associated with formal alliance were entitled *amicitia* (friendship). Allies were theoretically independent but they were obliged to contribute troops to aid Rome. Another form of inclusion into the Roman sphere was that of creating client states, a relationship between Rome and non-Roman states based on mutual advantage but where Rome was the superior partner.

Successful expansion beyond the Italian peninsula required different solutions. Victory in the first war with Carthage led to the annexation of Sicily, Sardinia, and Corsica with the status of provinces. The Latin word *provincia* defines both a region, which these islands clearly were, and a sphere of influence. Most new territories were won by the sword and thus a provincial charter was drawn up by a commission consisting of members of the Roman senate and the military commander who had led the victorious Roman legions. The charter defined rights and obligations of the various cities and towns within the province. What did not yet exist in the Roman political structure was an official who could exercise authority in the province. An answer was found in extending the period of office of the two highest Roman official positions: the two *consuls* and the *praetors*, which were initially also two but increased in number over time. Both offices granted their holders full power – *imperium* – which would be needed to manage all affairs of people within their control. By prolonging their term from one year to two, and eventually longer, *consuls* and *praetors* would serve their original year in the traditional positions while in the second they would act as governors – *proconsuls* or *propraetors* – in one of the provinces. Sent with a small staff composed of both lesser officials, such as financial agents, and personal family and friends, their responsibilities were to keep order internally within the province, to protect its frontiers, and to collect taxes from its peoples.

Greece was drawn into this scheme gradually at the conclusion of the Second Macedonian War when Rome replaced Macedonia as the principal power in the Balkans. Macedonia was not made a province but rather became a "friend and ally" of the Roman people. Greece was free, paid no tribute, and had no Roman troops stationed in its territory. At the Isthmian games in 196 BCE, when a Roman herald announced the return of Greek freedom the applause was so thunderous that birds flying overhead were said to have fallen dead from the sound. It would be interesting to know if this status reveals Roman appreciation of the kinship between the two peoples. If so, that appreciation did not prevent the change in status after the two further Macedonian wars. After the defeat of Macedon in 168 BCE, the kingdom of Macedonia was replaced by four "republics," while defeat of Greece in 146 brought Greece under the control of the provincial governor.

Connections between Macedonia and Greece with the Hellenistic kingdoms in the eastern Mediterranean had drawn support for the cause of Greece and Macedonia from the Hellenistic kings. Another motive for this support was the fear on the part of rulers in the East of the rapidly rising Roman power throughout the Mediterranean. Not surprisingly, their actions did not deter the Roman advance and Roman troops continued to push eastward into Anatolia and the Levant.

Kingdoms had proliferated since the original division into three major realms. Especially noticeable was the fragmentation of the vast Seleucid kingdom, originally extending from the Mediterranean to Bactria and into Anatolia. Thus, Rome was confronted with too many kingdoms to deal with simultaneously. With some, the Romans could form a degree of friendship and cooperation, although again Rome generally had the upper hand due to its military might and the changing structure of government as newly acquired regions were incorporated. These kingdoms became "clients" of Rome; that is, they were under Rome's patronage. The degree of Roman management depended largely on both the power of the "client" king and kingdom and on acquiescence to the status of Roman overlordship.

The first century BCE witnessed almost constant warfare, with many contests fought in Greek territory by strong-minded generals or kings from both Rome and the Hellenistic East. The will to power on the part of ambitious individuals was as keen now as it had been in the wake of Alexander's death, as Romans like Pompey and Julius Caesar fought one another for power, enhancing Rome's territory into the bargain. Not only were Roman troops in northern Africa and the eastern Mediterranean, they were also marching west into Gaul and north into German territory. Adding territory to the Roman domain brought wealth and fame to powerful individuals as well as to the Roman state. The wealth of the Hellenistic East was an especially strong magnet. Recognizing the value of their kingdoms, rulers of independent realms – as well as nominal rulers of "client" kingdoms – were equally ready to fight to maintain their independence.

Victory did come to Rome but only after huge damage had been done to the Roman state. The century from 133 to 30 BCE is correctly defined as Rome's "civil war." It stemmed from the creation of an empire by a republic, success that stretched the efficiency of republican institutions and demanded numerous armies and commanders. Responses to the situation varied enormously between the three classes within the Roman state: the senatorial class of patricians whose members held the highest political positions; the proletariat of small farmer-soldiers, who could vote in an assembly if they resided near Rome; and a new moneyed class, the equestrians, who were becoming wealthy on the business of Roman expansion. In effect, the three groups fought for control, often one Roman army against another Roman army. Leaders were successful generals – Marius, Sulla, Pompey "the Great," Julius Caesar, and Octavius Caesar – who fought for their own power as well as against foreign enemies. When several attempts to restore order had failed, Octavius, the nephew and adopted son of Julius Caesar, rose to a position of nearly uncontested power after his victory over the last independent Hellenistic kingdom, Egypt, in 31 BCE. His victory was followed by the suicides of Mark Antony and Cleopatra as Roman troops entered Alexandria the following year. Surprising many of his contemporaries, who once thought of him as a man with a name but no authority, Octavius endured to reshape the Roman state from republic to empire.

Some Republican institutions were preserved, such as official positions and the senate, but now overarching authority was vested in this leading citizen or *princeps*. The early imperial Roman state bears the title Principate. New developments strengthened the central power of the *princeps* as a cabinet of officials took shape alongside a *concilium* of special advisors to the *princeps*. Introduced as well were a secretariat and a civil service drawn from middle-class professionals – the equestrians – rather than from old aristocratic families. A regular career path emerged for aspiring civil servants: following ten years of military service, one could gain the status of a *procurator* governing a small sensitive area, such as Judaea or Damascus, or management of the mint or of the gladiatorial games. If successful at this level, one of the more important *prefectures* might be won: governance of Egypt, direction of affairs of the city of Rome, command of the fleet, superintendence of the grain supply, or command of the praetorian guard, the only troops now in Italy.

All of these innovations were a boon to the provincial system which had become a means to power and wealth for ambitious and/or greedy figures during the second and first centuries BCE. Now provinces were either senatorial or imperial, a distinction that depended on the need for a military force within a province. Only imperial provinces had an army. The *princeps* was loath to place command of a portion of the army in the hands of a would-be rival and, consequently, retained ultimate authority in situations where significant military strength was necessary. Governors were still *proconsuls* or *propraetors* who took small staffs with them. Also present in the provincial staff was a special legate whose loyalty was to the *princeps*.

Greece became the province of Achaea under the eye of a proconsular governor and usually it was without a military contingent, a status that suggests a strong degree of tranquility throughout the region. The governor's staff was small, estimated at one official for approximately 400,000 provincials. As a result, local Greek civic leaders provided most of the governmental administration. Roman policy continued that of the Hellenistic kings by relying on urban units to form a network of local control that now was linked with central administration in Rome. Since numerous town and city centers had existed for centuries in Greece (many were the cores of former *poleis*), it was not necessary to create large numbers of new cities in

Greece, although some were founded to orient Greece westward toward Italy. Thus, long-established centers endured or were re-established and their individual state structure looked very much like that of the Classical Age: there were assemblies, councils, and officials.

The great difference was that these bodies were no longer independent. Greeks were warned by Dio Chrysostom, an orator and philosopher living in the first century CE, not to be riotous in assembly when a Roman official was near. More graphically, the Greek philosopher and biographer Plutarch reminded the Greeks that "above your heads are Roman boots."[3] The nature of participation also changed since Romans relied on members of the upper classes to manage local government. There was a marked decline in participation of ordinary citizens that had existed in the classical *polis*. Although there were few major revolts, reliance on the wealthy for local political management worked to the disadvantage of the lower classes with respect to their political involvement and economic well-being.

Responsibilities of local leaders were limited to matters of maintaining public services and buildings, keeping order among the population, collecting taxes, and paying to Caesar that which was Caesar's due. Taxation amounted to some 3.5 to 4 percent of a person's annual income, a high sum for a peasant family. As a modern scholar has observed, "men in the ancient world shared modern opinions about taxation."[4] On the other hand, Rome provided services: military protection, useful constructions like aqueducts, and aid in hard economic times. For some two centuries, the Mediterranean coast enjoyed a welcome peace following on the heels of the previous centuries of turbulence. Much of its population, especially in the eastern part of the empire, was willing to extend cult honors to the *princeps* and to Rome, just as Greeks had previously granted to the reigning Ptolemy or Seleucid. Mainland Greeks had felt the power of centralized might at Chaironeia in 338 BCE. Three hundred years later their remembrance of autonomy and true independence was very dim.

Life in the Province of Achaea

In spite of the many features of Greek culture enduring from earlier times, the *Pax Romana* (Roman peace) brought considerable change to the lives of Greeks. Perhaps most important was the on-going disappearance of the *polis* way of life. The *polis* had been deprived of its autonomy under the Macedonians and now the important former *polis* centers were urban entities subservient to the ultimate power of Rome. In addition, its internal structure was now equally altered. The essential link between the core of the *polis* and its larger territory, already weakened, was severed as political, economic, and religious affairs cut across the old *polis* borders. Some surviving *polis* centers might long for past days of independent statehood but that situation was beyond retrieving under the Roman administrative structure. The new city foundations that were decreed and made possible by Rome did not have a tradition of freedom to remember and to regret the loss thereof.

The cities themselves were the basis of local administration under the immediate supervision of the Roman governor. As was Rome's custom throughout the empire, urban life was encouraged and, consequently, populations grew in size and density.

Corinth had a population of 80,000. Economic needs were one "magnet" drawing people to the cities from rural areas; benefits gained through imperial benefactions – aqueducts, baths, temples – were a second. Similar features had been of major importance in the old *poleis*, of course, but now much of the planning was undertaken by central Roman administrators.

Local affairs continued to be conducted by Greeks holding official positions and serving on city councils; their business was keeping order, raising funds for necessary local expenses, and meeting tax obligations to Rome. If a member of one of the Greek cities wished to pursue a more significant political career, the solution for most was to become a soldier in the Roman auxiliary forces for a term of twenty-five years or to enter the Roman civil service. Some Greeks managed to attain more significant positions in the central Roman structure. Although it was not impossible for Greeks to gain Roman citizenship while retaining citizenship in a Greek city, it was not a frequent occurrence.

The importance of cities – and an increase in the density of their populations – brought a decline in rural activity. The rural population of Corinth was a mere 20,000, for example, a fourth of the size of the urban population. In the Classical Age, by comparison, the distribution of population in highly urbanized Athens was 50 percent rural. Marginal and inconvenient land was neglected, pastoralism increased, and small farms were swallowed up in large estates. For example, when a Roman traveling in Greek waters was shipwrecked, he was taken in by a family of squatters living on a deserted estate. Agriculture became the source of wealth for a small landowning class of powerful families and it was not impossible for prosperous citizens of one city to hold land in several regions. Imperial largesse assisted this development as the emperors could make grand gifts to helpful friends: Augustus made a gift of the whole island of Kythera to one Spartan. The labor of many was necessary on such grand domains; with the employment of such laborers we can sense the roots of later serfdom. Not unexpectedly, a growing divide between the wealthy and the poor marched in step with these trends.

The general economic well-being of Greece declined as world trade now by-passed mainland Greece for more favored ports of the eastern Mediterranean such as Rhodes. One story describes the time that a large ship sailed into the Piraeus harbor of Athens having been blown off its course. So unusual was the presence of a great ship that the whole city of Athens walked to the harbor to see it. However, this picture is overly bleak. Greek products continued to be desirable: olive oil, flax, marble, and limestone for cement had a market. And parts of Greece drew visitors because of their past greatness as well as their current attractions: Athens was one of *the* places to receive an excellent education. Cicero – Roman statesman, orator, philosopher – gained much of his knowledge through Greek models and, upon determining that his son would be educated in Athens, he arranged that his son be "provided with a bill of exchange for as much as is necessary."[5] Roman citizens who came to Athens to study knew their Greek.

Certainly, Greece was changed by contact with Rome. Incorporation into the Roman Empire inserted Greece into a new kind of cultural unity that is detected in art and architecture, religion and philosophy, and language. Strong elements of the new unity are Hellenic. Stoicism, one of the four major Hellenistic philosophies, was widely embraced by Romans as it was perhaps the philosophy most akin to the

Roman mentality. Grounded in a belief in the universality of a world soul and each individual's possession of a parcel of that soul, Roman Stoicism maintained that individuals must fulfill their responsibilities in a virtuous, dedicated fashion.

Another feature was the imperial cult to Rome and its emperor which stretched through the empire. Julius Caesar recognized the power of the Ptolemies that bestowed divinity on the ruler of Egypt. Latin was the language of administration and business throughout the empire but inhabitants of the provinces preserved their own languages. Roman roads, aqueducts, planned cities, temples, baths, forums, and basilicas were physical evidence of similar form and construction from the Black Sea to Gibraltar and they embodied earlier traditions of architecture of their location.

Yet, the Greek contribution to Roman life was potent, especially as the flow of movement brought Greeks westward as well as Romans eastward. The significance of the contribution is as impressive as the length of the list of Greek influences. Greek was the second language of the empire and, in Greece, it was used for all but official Roman inscriptions and correspondence. Corinth offers an interesting snapshot of the comparative force of the interplay between Greek and Roman elements and the role language has on changing a culture. Destroyed for its role against Rome in 146 BCE, Corinth was re-founded in 44 BCE as a Roman colony populated largely by Roman freedmen whose language was naturally Latin. Over time its Roman character was increasingly Hellenized. By the early second century CE its language was officially Greek.

Romans may have been drawn to Stoicism and Epicureanism due to the qualities of those philosophies that were appropriate to their culture. But it is important to note that earlier philosophic traditions also found their admirers in Rome. Greek gods as well have a major role in Roman life and many found their way into the Roman pantheon: Zeus and Jupiter are akin in their roles and Apollo appears in both pantheons without a change of name. Major cult centers of earlier times continued their appeal especially to Roman visitors.

Classical and Hellenistic art and architecture were fundamental to Roman works. When Rome was founded, traditionally in 753 BCE, it was a small, insignificant settlement. Already, inhabitants of Greek colonies being founded in southern Italy and Sicily were creators of increasingly fine pottery and structures. The Etruscans, who ruled Rome until 509 BCE, admired Greek pottery so highly that much of the archaeological record of Greek pottery derives from Etruscan Italy. *Magna Graecia* continued to influence the Romans in both material and literary products from the earlier stages of Roman history to the period of Roman imperial rule.

An especially interesting goal of Greeks who came to know Rome and the Romans well was to explain the Greeks to the Romans and the Romans to the Greeks. We have mentioned one of the first links through writing in the translation of the *Odyssey* into Latin by Livius Andronicus. Somewhat later, Quintus Ennius came to Rome from a town in the heel of Italy in 204 BCE, received Roman citizenship, and taught Greek and Latin to children of important families in Rome while pursuing a prodigious career of writing works in both Roman and Greek traditions. More widely known are the works of Plutarch (circa 50 to 120 CE), who was a priest at Delphi for thirty years, gained Roman citizenship, and composed the parallel lives of Greek and Roman statesmen and soldiers, pairing a Greek example with a Roman example to demonstrate the characters of both to his dual readership. Later,

Ammianus Marcellinus (325–391 CE), born into a respectable Greek family, rose to high command in the Roman army and, as an ex-soldier, composed a history extending from the end of the first century to the mid-fourth century CE. Of thirty-one original books, only the final eighteen survive. Although his native language was Greek, he wrote the history in Latin and is regularly identified as the last great Latin historian of the Roman Empire.

By the lifetime of Ammianus, internal and external threats produced fifty years of anarchy during the third century CE, which nearly caused the collapse of the empire. The period saw twenty-five recognized rulers and fifty pretenders to imperial power; of these, only one died a natural death. Since the tool necessary for success in the struggle for the throne was the army, portions of the Roman army were turned against one another, a situation that threatened the entire administrative structure of Rome.

At the same time, the build-up of pressures from beyond the borders of the empire demanded constant armed vigilance. Increasing numbers of tribal groups abutted the northern boundaries of the empire while major new kingdoms – especially Parthia, now established as a new Persian Empire – threatened from the east. Even in times of a strong economy, the costs would be burdensome but in the third century agricultural productivity was declining, pirates were again a threat to trade by sea, and existing wealth was used unproductively. With the population falling precipitously, tax burdens were back-breaking. Ammianus Marcellinus wrote that "Some, becoming weary of life and light, sought a release from their miseries by hanging themselves. The treasury is empty, the cities are exhausted, the finances are stripped bare."[6]

Unexpectedly – in view of the situation of the empire and the failure of so many previous contestants – the son of a freedman clerk, who had risen through an army career to great esteem, was nominated by the army of the East for the imperial purple. After defeating the army of the West, Diocletian became the next in the kaleidoscope of emperors. Unlike his predecessors, however, he managed to survive twenty years of power to retire in 305 CE and was one of the very few Roman emperors to retire voluntarily. In those years, the empire took on a new appearance that was essentially an attempt to eliminate problems experienced during the preceding fifty years.

First there was the necessity of creating an orderly succession. Diocletian's solution endowed two emperors with full power – *imperium* – as *Augusti*, with two junior rulers, the *Caesari*, sharing the burden of preserving the empire. The *Augusti* were to govern for twenty years, and then retire to allow the *Caesari* to assume the role of *Augusti* and to nominate their juniors. This division of power among four rulers would be beneficial by allowing imperial oversight in various parts of the many provinces, all of which were threatened from beyond the borders. It might, however, reveal a growing division between sections of the huge empire. In fact, although Diocletian preserved this scheme during his rule it quickly collapsed when he retired.

More administrative changes were essential to strengthen Rome's provinces. The size of the provinces was reduced, producing several hundred rather than the twenty-eight under Augustus or approximately forty at the end of the second century CE. Individual provinces were grouped together into twelve dioceses. The *praetorian prefect*, once commander of the only legions in Italy, gained general control over the provinces.

For greater predictability of requisite skilled groups, people were fixed to the professions of their fathers: if one's father was a peasant farmer, that occupation would be inherited by his sons, the sons of soldiers became soldiers, and the sons of workmen followed their fathers' crafts. Another attempt at fixing produced the Edict of Maximum Prices in 301 CE. A similar effort to secure the traditional Roman values focused on proper respect for the Roman gods as well as the imperial cult to Rome and Caesar, which was needed to confront a new religious belief that was eroding the traditional Roman values; to eradicate that force, Diocletian persecuted those Christian believers.

Perhaps to safeguard his own position, as well as to prolong his life, Diocletian's reign saw a growing divide between the ruler and the ruled. He was no longer "leading citizen" but now *dominus* or lord; thus, this late period of Rome's history is often termed the *Dominate*: its ruler was *dominus* (lord) rather than *princeps* (leading citizen of the early empire). The emperor's very appearance embodied the division between himself and his subjects.

> On state occasions he was attired in silken robes of blue and gold, to symbolize the sky and the sun; his hair was dressed to imitate the sun and sprinkled with gold; upon his head rested a jeweled tiara; a collar of pearls was around his neck; over his breast flowed necklaces of rubies and emeralds; his fingers wore rings flashing with precious stones; his finger-nails were gilded; his shoes were of red Persian leather with golden soles. He carried a scepter terminating in a gold ball typifying the globe and tipped with a golden eagle, in whose talons was a splendid sapphire, symbolic of the blue of heaven.... Immediately upon the entrance of THE Presence every person in the throne room sank to the floor in oriental obeisance and remained prostrate until The Sacred Presence was seated, when he was permitted to kiss the hem of the imperial robe.[7]

Through the rigid ordering of Roman society that could be compared to a stiff corselet Diocletian tried to save the empire but the corselet needed adjusting to function a while longer.

The adjustment came from the single successor to Diocletian, Constantine, who put an end to the scheme of *Augusti* and *Caesari* to become sole emperor by eliminating his rivals. Like Diocletian, he recognized the inadequacies of a single capital at Rome and created a new capital at the entrance to the Black Sea at the location of an ancient Greek colony, Byzantium. Re-founded as the *polis* of Emperor Constantine, Constantinople would serve in the East as Rome served in the West. Need for several spheres of command resulted in the division of the empire into five prefectures, three in the West and two in the East, each controlled by a praetorian prefect, essentially a military commander. Each prefecture, in turn, was divided into dioceses controlled by vicars, while each diocese was divided into provinces under governors.

Glue of another kind was found in the adoption of a new state religion, Christianity. It is claimed that Constantine prevailed over his final rival for power in 312 CE with the support of a heavenly sign of the cross. While his true motivation is debated, his foundation of Constantinople as a Christian capital is clear. Though successors might attempt to return Rome to its earlier cults and practices, Christianity not only spread through the Roman world but was inserted into the workings of the state. Constantine's government was drawn from bishops as well as generals and counts.

Greece suffered through the years of reorganization and anarchy although the mainland was a battleground less often than it had been in the second and first centuries BCE. In the long run, it would profit from the importance of Constantinople especially after 395 CE when the empire was officially split into halves: the Western Empire centered on Rome and the Eastern Empire anchored in Constantinople. This division had lasting consequences but not in favor of Rome. "The Greek East attained a remarkable political achievement when in the late 3rd and 4th centuries it donned the ponderous armor of the Roman Imperium, an armor which the Latin West could no longer support, and wore it successfully for so long."[8] By donning that armor, another incarnation of Greek culture emerged: the millennium-long story of the Byzantine Empire. On the one hand, the empire restored an independent Greek state and, for much of its history, was a powerful player in Mediterranean and European affairs. On the other hand, it transformed much of Greek culture in its organization and in its religion.

Polybius: A Greek Captive Praises Rome

We are fortunate to be able to see Roman success in Greece through the eyes and words of one of the Greek hostages for the good behavior of his countrymen, Polybius (circa 200–circa 118 BCE). He was the son of a major political leader in the early second century as Rome's interest in Greece was becoming keener. Polybius participated in events in both Greece and in Italy. He also is an historian who wrote forty books on the developments of his time; only five of those books survive. But the content is sufficient to describe the author as an historian as well as a participant who provides an eyewitness account of his subject that allows us to understand the Greek perspective of the fortunes of *Graeca Capta*. Not only did he experience the success of the Roman incorporation of Greece into its expanding sphere, he understood how it had occurred and why it might be a positive solution to the existing situation in the larger Mediterranean world.

He wrote that the task of the historian is "to record with fidelity what actually happened and was said, however common place this may be."[9] Polybius also acknowledged that authors would be partial towards their own country but should not make false statements about it.[10]

He was born in the time when individual *polis* communities were unequal to the pressure of kingdoms. In order to survive, the solution to Greek factionalism was resurrected by the establishment of federal leagues which incorporated the individual *poleis* – originally orchestrated by Philip II and revived under the Antigonid Macedonian kings. Among the first to move in this direction were the small *poleis* in the northern Peloponnese, known as Achaea. The Achaean League had blossomed in the third century, eventually uniting sixty *poleis* and covering an area of 8,000 square miles. As we have seen, Macedonian King Antigonus Doson saw the possibility of ending the continuous warfare between states by means of consolidation. The Achaean League was a good example, but was not the only successful league. In 224 BCE Antigonus Doson created a league of leagues that would act, together with Macedon, at the highest level of common concerns.

Polybius' father, Lycortas, was *strategos* (president and/or general) of the Achaean League for two terms at a critical time in the league's status. He cooperated with the equally powerful leader in the league, Philopoemen, to defend the league successfully against the Spartans in 223 who refused to relinquish the power of their *polis*. In 207 Lycortas was instrumental in the death of the Spartan king in battle and, when yet another Spartan king was murdered in 193/2, he was a key player in adding Sparta to the Achaean League. The young Polybius was groomed to follow his father's path and, along with his father, Polybius was a member of an embassy to the court of the Ptolemies to broach the possibility of alliance. At the youngest age of qualification, Polybius held the league office of "cavalry commander" for 170/69. Advancement to the league office of *strategos* seemed assured.

Dealings of the Achaean League with Rome made Polybius' advancement impossible. Although Roman troops had been withdrawn from Greece in 194 following their victory over Macedonian King Philip V in 196, Roman concern over Greece and Macedonia remained. Greeks were equally concerned about Roman intentions. In fact, the Achaean League embassy in which Polybius participated sought support from the Ptolemies in case Roman legions returned. Rome had allowed Philip V to remain king of a much smaller Macedon but all of Greece south of Mount Olympus was freed from Macedonian control. Greek leagues and cities were not taken under formal Roman control. Rome would be watching events in Macedon and Greece but from Italy.

The incorporation of Sparta into the Achaean League was not welcomed by the Romans. Nor did Romans look kindly on the expanding activity of Macedon under Perseus, the son and successor of Philip V. These activities brought Roman legions to northern Greece for a third Macedonian War from 172 to 168 that ended with the total defeat of the Macedonians; the kingdom was divided into four republics. The status of Greece remained ambivalent. The Roman senate intervened in local conflicts and attempted to weaken the Achaean League by separating members from it and, more importantly especially in Polybius' case, by removing league leaders. A list of a thousand unreliable Greeks who were to be exiled contained the name of Polybius. He was shipped to Rome. Although the Achaean League would suffer by his fate, Polybius was extremely fortunate; and, because of his settlement in Rome, so too are people who are interested in the history of this period.

Without his *Histories*, we would understand far less about the period from the perspective of leading Romans who were directing the monumental rise of Rome's power in the second century BCE. Polybius' good fortune was that he became a member of the entourage of a leading Roman family, the Scipios, whose members were major officials of the state with stunning achievements both in diplomacy and military command. Cornelius Scipio Africanus is especially famous for the defeat of Hannibal. The Scipios' larger circle included other noteworthy officials and intellectuals such as the Greek Stoic philosopher Panaetius and the Roman poet Terence, individuals who suggest the breadth of interest and identity of its members. Much of the remainder of Polybius' life would be entwined with the Scipios. We owe his account of the events between 220 and 124 to the seventeen years that he was officially in exile. When finally free to return to Greece, he delayed, traveling with Scipio to Spain and Africa in 151 and to Carthage in 146, when the party also ventured to test the waters and winds of the Atlantic Ocean. Then he assisted the Romans with the settlement of Greece following the conclusion of the Fourth Macedonian War in 148. His wider travels continued, stretching throughout the Mediterranean Sea from Sardis in the Aegean, to Alexandria in Egypt, and to Spain.

Polybius had earlier training for historical research. He produced an account of Philopoemen, a driving force of the Achaean League and a close friend as well as a colleague of Polybius' father. Unfortunately, the biography does not survive. He also had personal understanding of the Achaean League, both through his father and his own important role. His education in the structure of the Roman state came from some of its most significant and successful individuals and included Roman generals, consuls, and jurists. He was sufficiently proficient in Roman negotiations to be involved in the Roman settlement in Greece. Polybius' education in Roman culture was equally powerful. He gained vital understanding by travel to sites like Carthage and by engagement in embassies. The surviving books are sufficient to assign Polybius' account to the category "eyewitness history," a branch of the larger field of contemporary history. The span of his account falls largely in his own lifetime and so he was discussing people he personally knew. Thus, the historian had first-hand knowledge, access to witnesses of events, and other written sources to describe the flow of events over time and the causes of that flow.

Figure 6.2   Polybius. Source: Jozef Sedmak/Dreamstime.com

In short, he witnessed the transformation of history in the Mediterranean world. His account is not "one thing after another" but an analysis of the process. In his own words:

> There can surely be nobody so petty or so pathetic in his outlook that he has no desire to discover by what means and under what system of government the Romans succeeded in less than fifty-three years in bringing under their rule almost the whole of the inhabited world, an achievement which is without parallel in human history.[11]

In his account of Polybius and his history, F. W. Walbank makes the case that Polybius' purpose was to explain Rome to the Greeks both by offering practical advice to Greeks in their earlier dealings with Rome and later, after Roman power was complete, by offering advice about how to embrace that power as well as how to access its nature.

The result is central to the picture we are building of the long story of Greece. Polybius understood the nature of international relationships in the Hellenistic Age only too well: it was dominated by violence between major kingdoms and between smaller units within them. During the years between 323 and 160 BCE, there were only six years without major wars among the large kingdoms. And now there were new major kingdoms growing in power and scope – Carthage and Rome in the West, Parthia in the East. *Poleis* still had to contend with leagues and leagues fought one another in attempts to expand. Polybius experienced the outcome in the contests between Greece and Macedonia as well as between Rome and Carthage. Not surprisingly, one of his beliefs was in the naturalness of war and that expansion of territory was desirable;[12] in fact, he considered successful expansion of territory to be a sign of good government. On the other hand, the desire to expand would cause anarchy on the international level since international laws did not exist.[13] Consequently, Fortune (*Tyche*) would step in to decide an outcome of the on-going cycle of violence.

Rather more positive for the future was Polybius' view of the Roman constitution because, by the second century BCE, it had merged the positive qualities of each form of governance: monarchy, aristocracy, and democracy. And by this time Rome had brought under its control almost all of what Polybius defined as the inhabited world. One wonders, however, how free Polybius felt to describe his Roman patronage to Greeks, especially after the sack of Corinth in 146 although he openly condemned Philip V's destruction of Thermon, the center of the Aetolian league.[14]

Beyond Polybius' interpretation of the course of history, he is useful as a figure in our examination of the continuity or discontinuity of the fundamental elements of Greek culture in the period in which he lived and which he described. Due to his long exile in Rome as a member of the Achaean League who was fortunate in being included in the sphere of powerful Romans, did he sense that inclusion of Greece into the vast realm of the Roman Empire would completely transform the deeply rooted Hellenic "system?" In other words, did Polybius' exile make him more "Roman" than Greek and, more generally, did Roman influence change the Greek way of life beyond recognition?

A strong case can be made for the answer "no." As a province, Greece had been returned to its smaller environment as the eastern peninsula of Europe. During the

Roman Empire, economic life had been adjusted to close reliance on the resources of that sphere. Political structure now focused on individual centers; to be sure they were no longer *poleis* but they were urban cores of earlier city-states. The old Greek gods lived on, although challenged by Christian beliefs that were expanding through much of the Mediterranean. Hellenic art, architecture, philosophy, and scientific thought had earlier been spread widely, in the Greek language as well as translated into other languages. Greek remained the language of the majority of people in the original core of the Greek territory. The intellectual history of Greece still had a lasting influence on Rome. For example, the Roman emperor Hadrian, who ruled from 117 to 138 CE, has been titled "Graecula" for his fondness of Greek culture. He completed the temple of Zeus Olympius at Athens, which had been initiated in the sixth century BCE, and then founded an organization of member-cities from the Roman provinces of Achaea, Thrace, Asia (Asia Minor), Crete, and Cyrene. Each member sent representatives titled Pan-Hellenes to meet in Athens as a council of the Panhellenion presided over by an archon. Could the events be echoes of the Delian League or the Athenian Empire? The Panhellenion had a longer history than either that league or empire, persisting until the mid-third century CE. The echoes of the Greek way of life continued in spite of, or perhaps even because of, Roman influence.

Notes

1. *The Satires of Juvenal*, translated by Rolfe Humphries (Bloomington: Indiana University Press, 1958), lines 60–62, 111, 115–116.
2. Virgil, *Aeneid* VI.847–853, translated by C. Day Lewis.
3. Plutarch, *Moralia* 813 F.
4. Chester Starr, *The Roman Empire, 27 BC–AD 476: A Study in Survival* (New York and Oxford: Oxford University Press, 1987), 77.
5. Cicero, *Epistulae ad Atticum*: XXII, 24.
6. Ammianus Marcellinus XXIV.3.5.
7. James W. Thompson and Edgar N. Johnson, *An Introduction to Mediterranean Europe, 300–1500* (New York: W. W. Norton & Company, 1937), 11 f.
8. Lynn T. White, ed., *The Transformation of the Roman World: Gibbon's Problem after Two Centuries* (Berkeley and Los Angeles: University of California Press, 1966), 106.
9. Polybius II.63.
10. Polybius XVI.14.6.
11. Polybius I.1.5.
12. Polybius VI.50.3.
13. Polybius V.67.11–18.2.
14. Polybius V.11.5.

Further Reading

Alcock, Susan E. 1993. *Graecia Capta: The Landscapes of Roman Greece*. Cambridge and New York: Cambridge University Press.
    The study provides an historical and graphic picture of Greece under Roman rule from circa 200 BCE to the declaration of universal citizenship through Roman territory in 212 CE. As an archaeologist, the author paints a vivid picture of the rural landscape and also of life for Greeks who continued to live in the cities.

Bowersock, G. W. 1965. *Augustus and the Greek World*. Oxford: Clarendon Press.

This brief account of the consolidation of the Greek and Roman spheres until the first *Princeps* of the empire offers a clear picture of the outcome of the Roman victory over the last of the Hellenistic kingdoms.

Eckstein, Arthur M. 2006. *Mediterranean Anarchy, Interstate War, and the Rise of Rome*. Berkeley and Los Angeles: University of California Press.

The study is addressed to both historians of the ancient Mediterranean and political scientists. Chapter 4 describes the crisis that began in the Greek Mediterranean, the fifth chapter turns to the western Mediterranean, and Chapter 7 examines the Roman decision to intervene in the eastern sphere with the consequences of that intervention.

Green, Peter. 1990. *From Alexander the Actium: The Historical Evolution of the Hellenistic Age*. Berkeley: University of California Press.

The author describes the interaction from the eastern perspective.

Gruen, E. S. 1984. *The Hellenistic World and the Coming of Rome*, 2 vols. Berkeley: University of California Press.

A magisterial study of the interaction between the eastern Mediterranean world that emerged after Alexander's death and the period when Rome expanded throughout the peninsula and began to look to or be drawn into the affairs of the larger Mediterranean.

Starr, C. 1987. *The Roman Empire, 27 BC–AD 476: A Study in Survival*. New York and Oxford: Oxford University Press.

A readable survey of the whole of imperial Roman history from the features established by Augustus and changes over time to the collapse of the structure in the western Mediterranean.

Walbank, F. W. 1972. *Polybius*. Berkeley: University of California Press.

Greek Polybius who became a Roman captive and eventually a man of importance in Roman affairs is the "person" who illustrates life in the early stages of *Graecia Capta*. The author demonstrates the value of Polybius for understanding the change in the status of Greeks.

White, Lynn. (Ed.). 1966. *The Transformation of the Roman World*. Berkeley: University of California Press.

Essays by Mortimer Chamber, "The Crisis of the Third Century," and Speros Vryonis, "Hellas Resurgent," are especially relevant to this period.

7

Power Returns to Greece
The Byzantine Empire

The foundation of Constantinople as a new, Christian Rome did not save the Roman Empire but it did establish the roots of a different empire in the eastern half of the Roman sphere. Greece, Macedonia, and the northern Aegean became its core and, in time, it extended into Anatolia and beyond. Thus it resembled the empire configured by Philip II, expanded by Alexander III, and re-configured by the successors of Alexander.

Its name derives from its capital, the ancient *polis* of Byzantium, founded as a colony in the seventh century BCE. The strategic location on the narrow strait into the Black Sea gave the settlement lasting importance. The role of Constantine in the fourth century CE in saving the Roman Empire is often identified as the birth of a new empire. In assuming sole command of the Roman Empire he re-founded Byzantium as Constantinople, namely the *polis* of Constantine. Later, when the existing territory of the Roman Empire was officially divided into two separate realms in 395, each with its own emperor, the roots of a new kingdom grew deeper. With the last emperor in Rome deposed in 476, the reigning emperor in Constantinople became the sole survivor of the Roman imperial system. It is not surprising, then, that the inhabitants of the territory under control from Constantinople knew themselves as *Romaioi* and their state as the Roman Empire, although their language was primarily Greek and a majority of them were Hellenes. Today the achievement of the Eastern Romans is generally known as the Byzantine Empire.

If we date the empire's origin to the re-foundation of the *polis* of Constantine, the empire had a life of more than 1,100 years until the capture of Constantinople by the Ottoman Turks in 1453. In fact, it has been described as the Eternal Empire. But its history was not uniform either in territorial size or internal structures of governance. One persistent feature is the constancy of threats from every direction. Consequently, five phases allow a more realistic understanding of the Byzantine Empire.

First was its emergence within the Roman Empire, beginning with the rule of Constantine I (306–330) through the death of Justinian I (518–565), who failed to reassert control over the territory of the old Roman Empire. In the second phase,

Greece: A Short History of a Long Story, 7,000 BCE to the Present, First Edition.
Carol G. Thomas.
© 2014 John Wiley & Sons, Inc. Published 2014 by John Wiley & Sons, Inc.

successors to Justinian struggled to maintain territorial control against formidable enemies, to create a functional structure of governance, and to foster naval strength for trade as well as military purposes. The Byzantine Empire was among the most powerful, wealthy, and highly civilized states in Europe and the Near East from 820 to 1056, the third phase of its life. A shorter fourth period was marked by internal dissent coupled with the growing threats of enemies from Sicily and southern Italy, other European states, Anatolia, and the Balkans. It ended with the capture of Constantinople by the Crusaders and the division of territorial fiefs to the western lords. The period 1204 to 1453 witnessed restored control to the Byzantine emperors, who enjoyed a precarious success in the thirteenth century. An especially ominous development was the fourteenth-century expansion of the Ottoman Turks into Europe that eventually surrounded the core of the empire; Constantinople was taken in 1453. It was the final phase of the no-longer Eternal Empire.

Yet, although its political identity disappeared, much of its distinct cultural legacy has persisted to the present. Perhaps the wonder of the Byzantine Empire is that the new organization managed to survive both external and internal constant threats and, in the process, to preserve and transform the inheritance from antiquity. After 1453, its own legacy would continue to influence developments in the eighteenth, nineteenth, twentieth, and twenty-first centuries throughout Europe and beyond.

Separation from Rome

It is important to note that the roots of the Byzantine Empire were in Late Rome, the age of increasingly absolutist imperial power, rather than linked with republican Rome or democratic Athens. Meaningful participation by ordinary "citizens" of Classical Greece had disappeared nearly a millennium earlier and the role of "citizens" of republican Rome had ended more than half a millennium before the creation of the new empire. In addition, the necessity of strong central authority to deal with immediate threats furthered the establishment of an autocratic political form. The connection to late antiquity produced a second major characteristic: New Rome was Christian not pagan.

And a third significant heritage derived from the inclusion of Greece within the Roman sphere of power until the end of the fifth century CE. Justinian, emperor from 527 to 565, attempted to restore the boundaries of the former unified Roman domain, which was now under control from Constantinople. He had enjoyed some success in North Africa (534) and Italy (537) but at the cost of incursions on other frontiers. Consequently, the orientation of the empire would be toward the eastern Mediterranean rather than toward the center and west of that sea.

The failure to retain the core of the Roman Empire had other consequences that were important to developing an understanding of the continuity of Hellenic culture: it weakened the Roman element of the fledgling Eastern Empire. Thus while Justinian was *Imperator Caesar*, Heraclius who came to the throne in 610, was *Basileus*, a Greek title with roots extending back to the Bronze Age.

An immediate threat came from the north in the form of migratory Slavic peoples who had propelled into the Balkans after the Germanic groups previously occupying that region had moved westward. Slavic raids into northern Greece began in 530 and the forts constructed during Justinian's reign were not adequate to prevent Slavic penetration into southern Greece. At the end of the first quarter of the seventh century, Slavs were settling into a village life in Greece itself. They brought not only themselves and their culture but probably also the bubonic plague that further decimated the existing population in the region. The impact of non-Greek language and culture would bring changes to the on-going Hellenic base of the population, not only at the time of the Slavic migration but continuing into the present.[1] The same period witnessed the push of Persians into Anatolia – not the Persians of antiquity but just as serious a threat as that faced by the Greeks in the fifth century BCE. These immediate dangers, together with difficulties in the western Mediterranean, could not be simultaneously solved. Attention was drawn back to the eastern Mediterranean.

However, one increasingly strong legacy from the Late Roman Empire was the role of Christianity in imperial governance, a role that was both a force of unification and a source of sectarian debates. The result was that whatever survived in the East would be autocratic, Christian, increasingly Hellenic, and eastward-looking. The combination of these features would bring new influences to its organization and culture. We must ask whether the result was sufficiently different to break the continuity of the way of life that we have tracked to this point in time.

Justinian shored up the structure of the Eastern Empire in the mid-sixth century, wittingly or accidentally, by turning the realm of Constantinople in a new direction. Under his reign, his armies rebuilt much of the territorial sweep of the eastern territory of the old Roman Empire; he attempted to end the divisive quarrels within Christianity; and endeavored to exert control over administrative officials, great landholders, and city councillors. Much of the effort was based on his own position and authority, defined as stemming from a divine source.

One negative consequence of the Byzantine military victories was a reaction from the native peoples in the Near East in the form of the whirlwind expansion of Islam in response to contact with the empire. The force of the new religion would destroy Byzantine advances in the Near East. After the death of Mohammed in 632, his successors conquered the Fertile Crescent and, by 732, a Muslim Empire extended from Spain in the west into India in the east. Muslims looked northward as well, driving deep into Byzantine territory in Asia Minor in 647 and, seven years later, defeating the Byzantine navy to capture Cyprus, Rhodes, and Cos. A siege of Constantinople itself in 674 was turned back by the defenders, largely due to the aid of the new weapon of Greek fire (an inflammable compound, perhaps crude petroleum), which was propelled through tubes toward a target.

Confronting the Muslim advance may have provoked an internal debate about the cause of the Muslims' success. It was possible, some believed, that divine favor fell upon those who prohibited representations of sacred images. The Islamic culture of the Muslims – who were now advancing in Asia Minor and, in 674, besieging Constantinople itself – prohibited sacred images. In Byzantine culture, icons of Christ, the Virgin Mary, and the saints were deeply embedded. The quarrel over icons within Greece produced disputes between the emperor and the patriarch of the Greek Orthodox religion; when in 730 Emperor Leo III ordered the removal of icons from religious practice (known as iconoclasm, or the breaking/destruction of images) the patriarch of the Church refused to agree and was dismissed. A larger consequence of the discord was that the pope in Rome condemned iconoclasm. Discord between both the secular and spiritual heads of the Byzantine Empire and with the papacy in Rome persisted to 787 when the Council at Nicaea, in which representatives of the pope participated, denounced iconoclasm. There was a short outbreak of iconoclastic fervor from 815 to 843, perhaps fueled in part by severe military defeats on several fronts.

The Byzantine ability to deal simultaneously with yet another threat – Bulgars migrating into the eastern Balkans – was severely limited. In 680, land was ceded to the Bulgars who consolidated it as the kingdom of Bulgaria, which would eventually reach impressive dimensions. In the north, the consolidation resulted in the loss of grain and other resources derived from Thrace. Stretched also were resources to mount campaigns by land and sea and therefore to provide effective administration of the territory still under Byzantine control. The plague and invasions had decimated the population and land ownership was increasingly concentrated in the hands of virtually independent lords.

Strong central leadership was essential during such difficulties, but frequent struggles for imperial power compounded the problems. On the death of Leo IV in 780, for example, his widow, Irene, held regency for their ten-year-old son. The brother of the late emperor was not satisfied with this arrangement so with the support of much of the army, he attempted to usurp power for himself. Irene was not averse to using her own force and, when successful against the plotters, she had them executed. Her son lived to come of age, when he was made co-ruler with his mother, but the situation was not to his liking and he was able to force her to retire to a convent. Eventually, they were reconciled as co-rulers and succeeded in putting down yet another military revolt. Even though they were successful, Irene realized that her son was ineffectual, had him arrested, deposed, and blinded, which meant that he was not fit to be an emperor. In fact, blinding was often a danger for Byzantine rulers. Finally, after twenty-two turbulent years of rule, Irene herself was overthrown. In its complications, the tale is "Byzantine," a title that is often used to describe something convoluted or tortuous. It also illustrates one constant threat to the health of the empire, namely internal disputes.

In sum, the period following the death of Justinian until the last quarter of the eighth century is often termed another Dark Age of Greece, comparable to the centuries following the collapse of the Mycenaean Bronze Age. Another similarity with the earlier period is the paucity of art and literature after the reign of Justinian due, in part, to iconoclasm. However, the skill of writing did not disappear as it had in the late Bronze and early Dark Ages.

Restoration of Order

Amidst the problems, the eighth century saw some signs of recovery. An Arab attempt to take Constantinople in 718 was repulsed; repopulation of Greece was accomplished by drawing Greek immigrants from Asia Minor; and the Slavic peoples were gradually Hellenized and Christianized by contact with their Greek neighbors. For instance, the Slavic Nikitas became patriarch of the Church in 766. To contradict the view of German scholar Jakob Fallmerayer that the Hellenic culture and blood was overpowered, one could say that more Greek peoples were drawn back to Greece, and Hellenic culture enfolded people of other cultures, thus demonstrating continuity of Hellenic culture and a Greek way of life.

Such developments paved the way for the rebirth of the Byzantine Empire under the Macedonian Dynasty from 867 to 1025, a time that is designated the Golden Age of

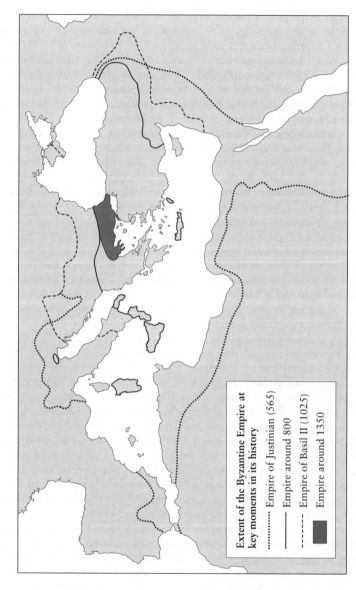

Extent of the Byzantine Empire at key moments in its history

········· Empire of Justinian (565)

——— Empire around 800

– – – Empire of Basil II (1025)

▓▓▓ Empire around 1350

Figure 7.1 Shifting dimensions of the Byzantine Empire. Source: Jason Shattuck

Byzantium. Comparison with contemporary western European cultures reveals how remarkable the creation of a strong centralized administrative structure was. Western Europe was still dealing with the impact of invasions that had continued after those incursions had collapsed the Roman Empire, and, as a result, small kingdoms were only just beginning to take shape. By contrast, the Byzantine Empire was an international power.

Rebirth came on the shoulders of re-conquest of lost territory. The kingdom of Bulgaria, now Christian, became a protectorate of the empire in 927. Less than a century later, in 1014, the Byzantine army won a massive victory over the Bulgarian force, taking some 15,000 prisoners. Four years later, Bulgaria became a subject of the Byzantine Empire and did not recover as an independent state for another two centuries. Thus the potential threat had been neutralized, at least temporarily, not unlike the neutralization of Thrace by Philip II of Macedon in order to extend his kingdom to the Black Sea and, thereby, advance against the "real" enemy, Persia.

In the east, Byzantine forces regained Asia Minor whose resources in men and products were vital to imperial strength. Crete, too, was restored to Byzantium after being captured by the Arabs in the ninth century. In fact, in the 930s and 950s, Byzantine forces penetrated to the plains of Mesopotamia. Antioch fell to Byzantine armies in 969, marking the height of the drive against the Muslim world. Russian raiders – those Vikings who turned eastward – became sometime-allies, a link marked by the marriage of a daughter of the emperor to Prince Vladimir of Kiev in 989. With such successes in the north and east, later emperors cast their eyes westward. The memory of Justinian's short-lived restoration of the Roman Empire had not disappeared from the Byzantine worldview. They established a presence at Bari on the western coast of Italy and at Tarentum in the arch of the boot of the peninsula. Now territory of the former Roman Empire was again coming under Byzantine Greek control. But the success in Italy would prove to be a costly mistake.

The strength of the empire owed much to militarization: portions of the army were organized by the districts in which they were located – called *themes*, where troops lived on land grants of imperial estates. The strong regionalism imposed by the environment continued to play a major role in the political structure of the state. This regional tie promoted a readiness to defend the region even though it might also encourage generals of the *theme* armies to seek power for themselves. Later, other regiments responsible directly to the emperor – *tagmata* – were more mobile units that could be deployed in particular hot spots anywhere in the empire. An ordered apparatus of administration also promoted centralization, which was enhanced when a succession of emperors passed in an orderly fashion, as was the case in the Comnenian Dynasty from 1081 for nearly a century. The end of iconoclasm in 843 brought another element of unity to the empire. And, finally, enlivened scholarship drawing on the deep inheritance of earlier Greek culture provided a further force of Byzantine identity.

This is not to say that the emperors lacked challenges. New enemies to the existence of the state appeared in seemingly endless succession. Pechenegs, Turkish nomads who settled in southern Ukraine, were pushed westward by a branch of Turkic peoples where they began to threaten the empire. By 1091, the Pechenegs were encamped at the walls of Constantinople. Bulgarian strength revived, the kingdom of Serbia was expanding in the western Balkans, and Russia was no longer a friendly ally. To the east, Seljuk Turks defeated the Byzantine force at Manzikert in eastern Anatolia in 1071 and then moved quickly west, reaching western Anatolia within twenty years. Resolute antagonists in the persons of western Vikings – or the Normans – were consolidating power in Sicily and southern Italy and soon would demonstrate their interest in the territory on the eastern shore of the Adriatic. In 1086 a Norman force attacked Dyrrachion on the northwest coast of Greece.

The Comnenian emperors were forced to deal with all of these threats simultaneously, using any and all tools at their disposal: military power, diplomacy, marriage alliance, the offer of trade concessions for assistance, fomentation of rivalry among their several foes, and faith in the efficacy of being a Christian realm.

External pressures sparked internal disruption as rivalry between the military aristocracy and members of the civil service mushroomed under weak emperors. The magnitude of internal strife is evident in the establishment of the Comnenian Dynasty: Isaac Comnenus, from one of the important military families, inaugurated the dynasty in 1057 but he was forced to abdicate two years later because of pressure from the leaders of both the civil service and the Church. During the next two decades several emperors held power briefly while a series of military revolts hamstrung strong central leadership. In 1081, the nephew of Isaac Comnenus, Alexius I, gathered enough support to march on Constantinople and to restore the Comnenian line. Succession passed to his son John II and grandson Manuel I, but not without struggles among members of the family and from other would-be emperors.

The line's end came at the hands of westerners, enabled by the internal dissention. The enemy that caused the fall of the Comnenian Dynasty took the form of the Crusaders, called by the pope to restore the Near East to Christian control. More often than not, Constantinople was involved in the Crusades although not by contributing Crusaders to a common goal. Rather, the location of the city made Constantinople a strategic crossing from Europe into Asia, which had been an important reason for its initial foundation as Byzantium in the seventh century BCE. The first Crusaders arrived at Constantinople in 1096, crossed into Anatolia, and marched south, reaching Jerusalem by 1099. Initial success led to the establishment of small Crusader states in the Levant, states that occupied territory once under Byzantine control. The second Crusade, too, had ramifications for Constantinople when the German contingent with its wounded leader – the German emperor, Conrad – made its way to the Byzantine capital where all were well treated and, in gratitude, Conrad promised German aid to the emperor against the Normans.

Great relief surely accompanied the decision of the third Crusade to by-pass Constantinople, but Crusaders of the fourth campaign were invited by a pretender to the Byzantine throne to stop in the city to assist his efforts. The Crusaders assembled at Venice, a city with long and strong ties to Constantinople which had begun during the reign of Justinian I in the sixth century. Venice was, in fact, an exarchate of the Byzantine Empire into the ninth century when it recovered its independence. Even when freed, Venetian aid to the Byzantines was so considerable that Venetian merchants were given extensive privileges of trading throughout the empire without payment of custom fees and port taxes. However, when the fleet of the fourth Crusade reached Constantinople, the outcome was anything but friendly: the Crusaders took the city by force in 1204.

To be sure a new ruler was installed: not a pretender or any other Byzantine candidate but rather Baldwin of Flanders who received a quarter of the imperial territory. Venice gained three-eighths of the territory and the remaining three-eighths were allotted to other Crusader lords. Only Epirus and a few pockets of resistance were still Greek. The bulk of mainland Greece remained under western European control into the fifteenth century and western Europeans generally were very involved in affairs of the eastern Mediterranean. Moreover, the Normans established earlier in Sicily and southern Italy became increasingly militant in western Greece. By the twelfth century, national states were emerging in western Europe. Kings of those states were leaders of the Crusades, anxious to enhance their own power as well as that of their realms, and Byzantium had much to offer.

Decline

With the conquest of Constantinople in 1204, Constantinople together with Thrace became a new empire directed by Baldwin of Flanders and his Venetians. The principality of Achaea, almost the entire Peloponnese, was entrusted to French barons who continued their control until it was absorbed into an Ottoman despotate in 1432. The duchy of Athens, which included Attica and Boeotia and extended into Thessaly, was also allotted to the French; it continued under non-Greek rule until it was taken by the Ottomans in the fifteenth century. In essence, most of Greece remained in the hands of western Europeans. The deposed Byzantine emperor, Alexius III, held only the region of Thessaloniki and his son-in-law held the northwest area of Byzantine Anatolia. Somewhat surprisingly, then, by 1261, a new line of Greek emperors returned to Constantinople in the person of Michael Palaeologus. Baldwin of Flanders and his Venetians fled, although Venetian control of the Aegean islands continued. The regions entrusted to the other Crusaders remained in their hands. Thus, much of Greece returned to its situation under the Roman Empire with Latin as the official language and Roman Catholic religious practice replacing Orthodox religion.

Yet, as Hellenic culture had influenced ancient Romans, the enduring Hellenic cultural heritage had a similar effect on the new lords of Greece. Three regions were not in the control of the Crusaders: Epirus; a kingdom centered on Nicaea in Anatolia; and a kingdom of the Trebizond in northeastern Anatolia. These locations were critical in the restoration of power to Greeks. In fact, many of the western lords became philhellenes; one of these rulers (the Florentine Nerio Acciaiuoli) returned Greek as the language of Athens and allowed Orthodox religious practices and officials. When he died in 1394, he left the care of the Parthenon to the city of Athens, specifying in his will funding for the care of that structure and stipulating that he be buried there (known in its present incarnation as the Santa Maria di Athene). This western link would eventually provide the assistance in another form necessary for the birth of the modern state of Greece.

The success of the Byzantine general-emperors of the thirteenth century was encouraging, demonstrating that Greek rule could be restored. Several would-be emperors operated in different spheres but they shared the common ability to face combat like a Homeric hero fighting in the forefront of battle. In a struggle with the Seljuk Turks in western Asia Minor in 1211, it was a Byzantine emperor, Theodore I Laskaris, who beheaded the sultan as he was driving toward his intended victim. The sight of the sultan's head impaled on a spear caused the Turkish army to flee. By similar physical feats, the emperor's successor, John III Doukas Vatatzes, managed to recover much of the hinterland of Macedonia and Thrace in the 1250s. His success prepared the way for the next emperor, Michael Palaeologus, to enter Constantinople in 1261 and to inaugurate the Palaeologan Dynasty. Michael prevailed against some of the Latins in Greek fiefdoms but his heirs were not so fortunate.

The story of those heirs is filled with disasters, both internal and external in origin. Division within the Byzantine Empire mounted, leading to a peasants' revolt in 1342. Nature added its own dose of poison in the form of the return of the bubonic plague in 1347. In a search for aid, Byzantium gained the support of Mongols whose defeat of an Ottoman force in 1402 spared Constantinople for another half-century. During that time, however, Byzantine territory was taken by the Ottomans until Constantinople became a virtual island in an Ottoman sea. By 1451, the city was encircled and the following year saw the construction of an Ottoman fortress on the European shore within sight of Constantinople. After refusing to surrender, Constantinople, with its 8,000 defenders, fell to an Ottoman force of 100,000 troops on May 29, 1453. From Florence came the report, "We can hardly tell you how shocked we are by the painful news, which seems to us to be such that all Christian princes should make peace with one another, and the rest of Christendom should wear mourning."[2]

As the Modern Greek poet Cavafy pictured the event:

Theophilos Palaeologus

The last year this is. The last year for
the Greek emperors. And with what grief
the many gathering round him speak.
For in his desperation and grief
Kurios Theophilos Palaeologus
says, "I wish death not life."

"Ah, Kurios Theophilos Palaeologus,"
how much sorrow for our peoples' grief
and their exhaustion from injustices and persecution
your five tragic words contain."

Die he did, along with a host of others in the once-glorious Byzantine Empire. On the other hand, much of Byzantine culture survived under Ottoman control to play a powerful role in the struggle for Greek independence 350 years later. That inheritance was the definition of Greek territory centered on the eastern peninsula of Europe, the original and enduring environment of Greece in its several manifestations. For most of the life of the Byzantine Empire, it was governed by Greeks whose language was Greek. In sum, the environment and people acting within it endured.

The Byzantine Greek World

The larger territorial configuration of the Byzantine world was in flux throughout the life of the empire, as it had been throughout history, thanks to the role of sea and the needs and opportunities that the sea provided. Generally the empire encompassed mainland Greece and many of the Aegean islands with some northern extension into the Balkans and parts of Anatolia. Constantinople, with a population of approximately half a million people, was the hinge between the portions. Its physical situation between Europe and Asia, at the entrance to the Black Sea, was strategic to both defense and trade. This city was also of great consequence in being one of the few truly urban enclaves in the empire. Thessaloniki was the second major city but other older centers, although continuing to have some economic and/or sentimental value, were of minor significance in affairs of the empire. Cities had begun to decline in size, population, and prosperity in the Late Roman Empire, and the decline continued in early Byzantine times. Consequently, the local focus of life was now the village as it had been in early antiquity. Gone, for the most part, was the city-based administrative structure of the Hellenistic and Roman Ages.

Constantinople certainly was a grand city, a hub of the medieval world. Sited on its triangular peninsula of land, the water of the Propontis offered some natural protection, enhanced by 13 miles of massive walls and a great chain guarding the entrance to the Golden Horn. Within those walls, two buildings were most significant: the palace and Hagia Sophia, the Church that was the seat of the religious leader, the patriarch. These two buildings were the physical statements of merged power between the emperor and Christianity. The palace has not survived but Hagia Sophia still stands today in all its enormity and magnificence: more than 250 feet in length, some 237 feet wide, and 104 feet in height, it was for several centuries the largest church in the world. Interior decoration featured mosaics, icons, silk hangings, and altar ornaments, which were perhaps just as impressive as the architecture of its design and size. Equally grand was the church's role as the point of departure for the emperor as the head of his army, for campaigns began with the proclamation "May God be with you!"

Other churches had a place in the city as did commercial and social centers such as *forums*. These *forums* were open structures, serving as civic institutions, and they revealed the Roman elements of the empire that continued the role of the *agora* from Classical Greek times. Most of the urban population lived either in blocks of apartments or low-rise houses. Aqueducts were an indicator of public services to the urban mass, carrying water over long distances to the cisterns of the city. While the public baths of the Roman period disappeared early in Byzantine times, the hippodrome was a successor to the arenas and coliseums of the past. More than a place for chariot racing, it became a usual venue for the emperor's public appearances and, like his imperial predecessors, he might be greeted by either ovations or angry shouts of disapproval.

Most of the inhabitants of the empire would not be familiar with the buildings of Constantinople. Rather they lived in small villages averaging between 50 and 150 inhabitants who shared common lands and worked their own smallholdings. Life consisted of farming, animal husbandry, and production of basic equipment and goods. At various periods, large estates held by powerful families would arise, appearing like nearly secluded islands in the countryside. Rural churches were smaller and less grand, sometimes converted from their function as temples. The grand Parthenon of Athens became the church of the Virgin Mary where Basil II celebrated his victory over the Bulgarians in 1018.

Composition of the population also varied over time. During the early Byzantine era, both the size and composition of the population were markedly unstable. A significant decline in numbers had occurred during the Roman Imperial Age: as early as the second century CE the Greek writer Plutarch had estimated that an army of 3,000 men was all that Greece could field. Incursions of Slavs brought a large new element to a depopulated Greece in the fifth, sixth, and seventh centuries. Later, a consequence of the fourth Crusade was the introduction of a Latin element to the Greek sphere. Accommodation with the Slavs was reached primarily through Slavic conversion to Orthodox Christianity, which permitted the survival of both peoples. In the case of the Latins, however, little intermarriage or even mingling of cultures occurred.

Administration

Byzantine society was theocentric: there were two governing authorities, secular and spiritual – the emperor and the patriarch respectively. The unifying factor was not a single individual but rather it was God who granted power to both:

> The greatest blessings of mankind are the gifts of God which have been granted us by the mercy on high: the priesthood and imperial authority. The priesthood ministers to things divine; the imperial authority is set over, and shows diligence in, things human; but both proceed from one and the same source, and both adorn the life of man.[3]

The administration of the empire had two branches: the military/civil stem whose power flowed from the emperor and the religious stem directed by the patriarch of the Church in Constantinople. The two branches met in the officer of the *synkellos*, a high cleric appointed by the emperor in agreement with the patriarch of the Orthodox Church, who acted as a liaison between the two high dignitaries of state. The civil/military service grew to great proportions: by the seventh century there were sixty bureau chiefs. Key positions included three treasury officials, a chief secretary with his large secretariat, a *de facto* foreign minister, and a supervisor of the massive imperial household.

The emperor, along with the empress, embodied good order and, it was hoped, projected that condition to all people under the royal sway. Special advantage to gain royal power in the future came to children who were "born to the purple" – that is, born to parents who were rulers at the time of their birth. Empresses could gain power in their own names as regents or even as full rulers, as the case of the formidable Irene, cited earlier, demonstrates. Anna Comnena, whose life sketch concludes this chapter, illustrates a more frequent power of women during the Byzantine Age. Avenues to power other than birth existed; the importance of military leadership in preserving the empire from its many enemies could raise a general to the position of co-emperor. A man named Lecapenus rose from being commander of the fleet to gain the role of emperor from 920–944. The hierarchical structure of Byzantium offered a built-in mechanism of patronage. Bestowal of an official post would allow its recipient to gain a livelihood while pursuing personal interests. An historian might serve as an imperial secretary while a philosopher could earn his living wage as a teacher in the patriarchal school.

The organization of imperial territory demanded a new structure, one that would encourage the reestablishment of a healthy peasantry to restore vitality to agriculture and to provide soldiers for an army that, by the ninth century, had grown to 120,000 men. A depopulated Greek mainland was incapable of providing either economic or military stability. Thus territorial units known as *themes* – mentioned earlier in this chapter – replaced the fragmented provincial structure of the Later Roman Empire. Each *theme* was under the command of a *strategos*, the ancient Greek title for general, who was responsible for both civil and military government in his territory. This altered the Roman practice which had been to divide these competencies between two officials. Soldiers were given inalienable grants of land and freed from most taxes but in return each provided a man (himself or, perhaps, an adult son), a horse, and arms when summoned. If the recipient honored this requirement, his land would pass to his eldest son while other sons could find new holdings of uncultivated lands. Each generation would bring more land under cultivation and add peasant-farmers to the ranks of the army, thus lessening the reliance on costly mercenaries, although some paid professionals remained important in the standing central army stationed in or near Constantinople. The role of the citizen in the Classical *polis* as a hoplite or rower when needed comes to mind when we consider this administrative Byzantine structure of developing a landed class of soldiers.

Law was a major ingredient in Byzantine administration from the time of the massive codification of Roman law under Justinian in the sixth century. A new, brief code of Leo VI in the eighth century served as a handbook for local judges in the belief that justice within the empire was essential to the ability to deal with enemies. Photios, one of the most renowned patriarchs appointed in 858, oversaw a new code of canon law and, perhaps, also a new legal code. Law was formally taught in Constantinople where, by the eleventh century, universities of both law and philosophy were respected institutions. But although the welfare of "the people" was of genuine concern to the emperor and his high functionaries, the political role of ordinary folk was minimal. They might draft petitions or give acclamations or even use violence, but a formal role was non-existent except at the village level.

Excessive power of the gift-devouring lords of Hesiod's village had fostered a similar recognition of the essential role of law as the bulwark of the *polis* community. Socrates drank the hemlock rather than leave Athens in an escape arranged by his friends. He explained to his friends that the Laws of Athens had chided him, asking, "Tell us, Socrates, what do you have in mind to do? Is the action that you are proposing to attempt anything other than the destruction of us, the laws, and the entire *polis*?[4]

Yet social mobility did exist in the pyramid shape of Byzantine society, which had its base in the peasantry and narrowed to the emperor and patriarch by way of the civil/military and religious orders and successful traders and craftsmen. The significance of the peasant family for military needs enhanced the status of the nuclear family and a successful career in the army was a good springboard for higher aspirations. Basil II, often regarded as the greatest figure of the Macedonian Dynasty in the Byzantine Empire, began his way to power as a groom in the imperial court. Clear rules of behavior defined relationships between equals and with inferiors and superiors. Order and proper ceremony were the backbones of imperial relations, Church liturgy, diplomacy, and religious communities. Part of the ordered society was state care for its poor and disadvantaged members. However, Byzantium society was hierarchical and lacked any pretense to be egalitarian.

The interplay between Church and state had its effect on society with the growth of Church officials, as well as the rise in numbers of holy men who preferred to withdraw from society, living apart in caves or in deserts or atop pillars. By making such a choice to withdraw from the world, the preference of these holy men was the antithesis of both the ideal citizen of the ancient world and the bulwark necessary for a healthy Byzantine state. In time, monastic communities largely replaced the solitary lives of hermetic holy men; in a list of some 2,000 names of Byzantine saints, the majority was monks. The growth of the monastery was due in part to the gain of the privileges and responsibilities that monasteries enjoyed, and which required at least three members. The largest community, Mount Athos, housed 700 men. Monasteries could be privately founded and could retain their private status but the majority seems to have been affiliated with the Church. Membership was a profession as those initiated into the body were expected to stay at their chosen monastery until death.

Economic Health

For a good portion of its life, the Byzantine Empire was healthy. An extensive system of commerce and industry rested on an agricultural foundation. As in the past, olives, grapes, and flax were important exports to which were now added sesame and cotton. The location of Constantinople was valuable in drawing trade from several directions, linking the empire to the whole Mediterranean world, as well as to Russia and even, for a time, to the Far East. Tools of managing this activity were sophisticated: all trade was regulated by treaty and foreigners were limited to certain ports. However, foreigners were protected by law. Customs dues and excise taxes produced wealth and the Byzantine gold *solidus* coin held its value for seven centuries. Shipbuilding, a lively activity for purposes of trade as well as naval warfare, drew on Hellenistic scientific knowledge, which may also have inspired the development of Greek fire, the flammable compound shot at enemy targets through a tube.

The importance of trade and industry throughout the empire is clear in the *Book of the Prefect* of Emperor Leo VI (886–912) and the sway of imperial rule was immense in its regulation of guilds and oversight of trade agreements, by identifying matters including hours of buying and selling, price control, management of industry, and rules of products that could and could not be exported.

Thus Constantinople was an entrepôt where many cultural currents came together. The Byzantines themselves would have preferred to eliminate the frequent attacks by enemies but even the lucrative trade had disastrous repercussions, such as the controversy over trade agreements. Perhaps these dangers made the emperors especially adept at diplomacy, which was highly developed. Treaties and alliances, sealed by marriage between the Byzantine royal family and the other party, were regular. Such an alliance drew Byzantium and Kiev together in the ninth century. Many emperors were skilled at playing one unfriendly power off against another. Most successful of all means, however, was missionary diplomacy. The efforts to introduce Christianity to non-Christian newcomers in the Balkans bore fruit for the Christian faith, certainly, but also enabled improved relations between now "kindred" peoples.

Byzantine Culture

Culture shows the many tensions embedded in the problems besetting the Byzantines along a continuum of seeming opposites. Major stress existed between Christian and other beliefs; between inherited traditions and new directions; between Western and Eastern influences; and between the life of the elite and that of the ordinary members of the realm. The visual arts, literature, philosophy, and the Christian religion reflect attempts to balance the pull in two quite different directions, not easy especially when foreign occupation dictated a change of direction.

Religious practice demonstrates vividly the stress between earlier pagan belief and Christianity. As early as 435, Emperor Theodosius II decreed that all pagan temples were to be destroyed. Some did survive after being converted to churches (*basilicas*). In fact, even pagan views of deity did not disappear quickly. After Justinian decreed in the sixth century that pagans could no longer teach in schools and were excluded, along with heretics, from holding any kind of office which included the military, Plato remained particularly respected, even though he was a pagan from Classical Greece. The Academy founded by Plato in the fourth century BCE still functioned in the fifth century CE. In the eleventh century, Emperor Constantine IX founded an imperial school of philosophy with the goal of training civil servants but also encouraging original research. Some Byzantine scholars, like Plethon in the fifteenth century, were avowed Platonists describing proper ordering of states after the fashion of Plato's *Laws*. But there was danger in being a Platonist or Neo-Platonist inasmuch as basic tenets of those philosophies could conflict with religious orthodoxy as Byzantine philosophers learned.

Michael Psellos, born in Constantinople in 1018, was appointed to head the school in educating future civil servants. Well trained in the work of Plato and Aristotle he combined ancient wisdom with Christian beliefs. That he was forced to resign and become a monk reveals the tension between ancient philosophy and Christianity. Yet he regained importance as an advisor to four emperors ruling between 1056 and 1078. Others such as George Gemistos (known as Plethon due to his devotion to Plato) were not as fortunate. He was exiled for heresy surely due to his liturgies in honor of Zeus and Apollo and his advice to the emperor to share the land with all members of society. Plethon took his philosophy to Italy. John Italos was also overly bold as a Platonist and was condemned for heresy in 1082. As Anna Comnena, daughter of the emperor at the time, reported, "Italos was everywhere causing trouble and leading many astray" so that he "was ordered to retract these propositions from a pulpit in the great church." He was excommunicated and later changed his ideas and "repented of his former errors."[5]

Religion was also the cause of the tension between western and eastern Christian churches. Major controversies erupted early and continued throughout the life of the empire over the relation between God the father and Christ the son. Questions about the nature of Christ drove these controversies: was Christ of like-nature to God (*homoioousios*) or of the same nature as God (*homoousios*)? This was a fight that has been described as the battle over a missing vowel. And what of the dual nature of Christ: how did his humanness relate to his divinity? Although the Council of Chalcedon in 451 determined that both natures were complete in themselves, many believed that the divine nature absorbed the human element: Christ was of one nature, the monophysites argued. An attempt to break the deadlock was proposed by Emperor Heraclius in 639 on the grounds that whatever the number or condition of Christ's nature(s), they were animated by a single will. Not only did the answer not solve the issue, but it further divided the eastern and western Christians as the explanation was denounced as heresy by the Roman pope.

In literature, too, tensions existed as the Classical tradition continued but was accompanied by new forms and purposes. Nevertheless, the legacy from the past was appreciated in its own right. The Byzantine Empire served as a store-house for much of the inherited literary tradition that was preserved and studied for its own value. Copying skills of monks were invested in inherited works as well as theological tracts; in fact, much of Classical Greek literature that has survived to the present is due to the activity of Byzantine monks. Commentaries written to explain the texts are also products of Byzantine scholarship.

During the Comnenian Dynasty of the thirteenth century a classicizing renaissance emerged in both literature and art. However, the "Classics" would not be appreciated by everyone: Orthodox Christians were likely to disapprove of pagan imagery and literature. Moreover, the scholarly discussion of texts would find few admirers in the villages. In Greek language, too, there was a growing split between popular, vernacular Greek and the Greek of scholars. It is important to remember that the language of the inherited tradition, more recent literature, and vernacular song was Greek.

Thus a blending occurred. Historical epics were of old subjects – the capture of Troy – as well as new, such as the life of the hero Digenis Akritas, which was filled with adventures and struggles between Christians and Muslims and set on the borders of those two cultures. Some accounts of reigns of emperors were written. Perhaps the best known is Anna Comnena's *Alexiad*, recounting the reign of her father, Alexius I. Another record of the decline of the empire to its fall in 1204 was composed by Nicetas Choniates. However, in general, the ancient genre of historical writing was largely replaced by chronicles. Poetry, too, was infused with Biblical allusions, but the rule of emperors and empresses also produced court poetry. Sung poetry could deal with ordinary life but it also presented liturgy for the Church.

Buildings and their architecture also had an ambivalent fate. The imperial decree that all pagan temples be destroyed was impractical in part due to their excellent, enduring construction. Consequently, many survived in modified form and were used for different purposes. Temples were converted to churches and other monumental structures became palaces or official buildings. The variety of influences from the end of the Roman Empire until the emergence of the Modern Greek nation resulted in many conversions in a wide array of styles.

The Athenian acropolis offers an excellent example of the history of structures and the multiple transitions they underwent, dating from the sixth century BCE and, in more expansive form, to fifth-century BCE Periclean Athens. The citadel itself returned to its Mycenaean function as a place of defense; eventually there would be a second wall at the base in addition to walls on its higher slopes. The grand entrance – *Propylaea* – became a palace, probably for the archbishop in Byzantine times and for the military governor under Ottoman control. The *Erechtheion* was converted to a church in the seventh century and, under Latin rule in the fourteenth century, it was home to the archbishop and, under the Ottomans, it was the governor's home.

Conversion to a church required extensive alterations. Its direction was altered to face east, a bell tower and interior walls added for the needs of Christian ritual, dedication given to Mary rather than Athena, and improper sculptures and images removed or whitewashed, then replaced with appropriate icons. Some elements were spared since they could be interpreted in more than one way: a *metope* (a square space between triglyphs in a frieze), originally identified as symbolizing the fall of Troy, was now read as the epiphany to Mary by an angel. After the taking of Athens by the Ottomans in 1456, the structure was converted again, now to serve as a mosque with a minaret added to the bell-tower.

Earlier motifs survived in new contexts as, for example, Christ depicted as Orpheus among the animals and the image of a young man in military garb in a church near Troy labeled "The Prophet Achilles." On the other hand, there was a deliberate turning aside from early artistic tradition in an effort to capture the inner person rather than the human physical form. Varying religious practices of the rulers of Greece drew on images reflecting the tenets of their faith. Iconoclasm also had a major effect on the visual arts not only in its contemporary impact but also in defacing or removing images from the past that did not agree with present views of the nature of representations. Removal of inherited portrayals by the Ottomans eradicated what they considered inappropriate images from the Byzantine past.

However, some areas of the Greek world experienced a vigorous artistic tradition that combined high Byzantine features with new influences from Italy. Crete under Venetian control until 1669 was one of these areas. The city of Candia (now Herakleion), with its mixed population of Cretans and Venetians, had a vibrant mix of Late Byzantine and Renaissance styles as well as its highly regarded icon painting. That combination produced artists such as Domenikos Theotokopoulos, better known as El Greco, born in 1541. In Candia he became an important icon painter before he left for Venice in about 1567 where his style gained new directions during the ten years of his residence before he left for Spain. When Crete came under Ottoman control, artists fled to the Ionian islands and Italy to continue the interaction of Greek and western Mediterranean art.

A different force is also important in understanding the visual arts of the Byzantine and Ottoman periods and, in fact, Modern Greek culture. A growing separation between urban life in the few large cities and village life that prevailed throughout much of the Greek world was reflected in the arts, sometimes known as "folk" or "popular" art. Utilitarian goods made from cloth, wood, stone, and metal often were decorated with techniques which did not require sophisticated technology: cloth, for example, could be woven in a pattern or decorated with embroidery; wood could be carved with a sharp tool and stone could be sculpted; painting of pottery had a long history, as did working of metal. A weaver might not always work an intricate pattern or embroider the cloth but for a wedding gown or jacket or a shroud the effort would be made (as Penelope understood). Recent attention to these arts of later Greece has demonstrated their quality and importance.

Byzantium was stationed between East and West, old and new, Christian and pagan, elite and popular, not only in location but also in mentality. And the Byzantine Empire survived those inner tensions in its formative centuries so that Constantinople became the hub of the Mediterranean, European, and western Asia worlds for more than three centuries, creating another "Golden Age" that replicated but also surpassed Athens' achievement in the fifth century BCE. That analogy also attracted others to the hub for peaceful and belligerent reasons alike. Although both states could serve as a model of culture, they could also be prizes for successful enemies.

For the Byzantine Empire, deliberate efforts included the spread of Orthodox Christianity carried by missionaries to Slavic and Turkic peoples of the Balkans. The missions brought a modified Greek alphabet as well. Byzantine diplomacy, too, was deliberate and could result in alliances cemented by marriage. The Vikings, engaged in creating their own kingdom around Kiev, were converted from being regular attackers of Constantinople to allies by the marriage of a daughter of Emperor Leo VI to Prince Vladimir of Kiev in 989. The Kievans also converted to Orthodox Christianity. It is interesting to ponder the consequences of a possible marriage alliance between Charlemagne, ruler of the Holy Roman Empire, and Irene, widow of Leo IV, who had aspirations to rule in her own name. When Irene was sent to a convent by those who opposed her rule, the marriage clearly became impossible. Other forms of influence were from the trader states, particularly Venice, which were drawn into Byzantium's far-flung network by deliberate inducement of concessions on tariffs and customs duties. The empire's coinage circulated widely as the standard of transactions.

Much of Byzantium's influence was unintended, however. Its wealth and power made it a target to be taken and employed by others. Invaders had successfully penetrated the Balkans and the Greek peninsula quite steadily since the third century; however, these newcomers had either been attracted elsewhere or had been assimilated over time. The nature of groups eyeing Constantinople from the eleventh century differed from earlier opponents. As we will see, this is true of the Seljuk and Ottoman Turks who would successively claim Anatolia as the center of their states. As important was the change in relative status of the parties: the Byzantine Kingdom was no longer the pre-eminent kingdom in the European sphere in power, culture, wealth, and numbers. And Europe was no longer a territory of shifting barbarian groups. Instead, the earlier migratory peoples had settled long before the eleventh century and had constructed their own expansive realms.

The tensions within Byzantium, as well as its perceived role, drew more and more belligerent attention from Eastern and Western powers, Christians and non-Christians, as well as would-be successors and those who would create a new form of state. Some of the tug-of-war continues to the present day.

Anna Comnena: Daughter of the Emperor and Historian of Byzantium

Known as the first woman historian, Anna Comnena had good connections for writing a history of the Byzantine Empire in the eleventh and twelfth centuries. As the daughter of Emperor Alexius Comnenus I and his empress, Irene, Anna was born in 1083 in the room set apart for an empress's confinement named the *porphyra* or the "purple" room, designating the royal/purple lineage. The honorific title served as a declaration of legitimacy for children of a Byzantine emperor and empress. "At dawn, a baby girl was born to them, who resembled her father, so they said, in all respects. When all the ceremonies usual at the birth of royal children had been faithfully performed ... there was, I am told, an unprecedented outburst of joy. After a determined interval of time my parents honored me too with a crown and imperial diadem."[6] Royal women, like the men, had to be flawless physically, a quality that was enhanced by clothing and insignia. These are the words of the firstborn of seven such children. She has given a full account of the reign of her father, the Byzantine emperor, Alexius I.

Her childhood was privileged: children of the emperor, even girls, had access to a fine education. As Anna wrote over-modestly, she was "not without some acquaintance with literature having devoted the most earnest study to the Greek language … and being not unpracticed in Rhetoric and having read through the treatises of Aristotle and the dialogues of Plato, and having fortified my mind with the Quadrivium of sciences …".[7]

It was no surprise that Anna, being of noble birth and having had the privilege of an elite education, admired nobility and beauty, the latter characteristic a remnant from the Classical Greek period or earlier. Thus she was also full of admiration for her father, for he was the highest of nobles, and although short in stature, when he "sat down on the imperial throne he reminded one of a fiery whirlwind, so overwhelming was the radiance that emanated from his countenance and his whole presence."[8] Beauty was not all, however, for mental acuity was required to survive and stay in power; she regarded her father as "sharp" in matters military, diplomatic, and governmental. These facts presumably moved her to write "an account of my father's deeds, which do not deserve to be consigned to Forgetfulness."[9]

Its value derives in part from its first-hand report of the conditions of the empire confronting Alexius when he became emperor in 1081, and of the struggles he had as emperor until his illness in 1112, and eventual death in 1118. His succession to

Figure 7.2   Anna Comnena. Source: Anne Lou Robkin

the throne came by way of a coup against the previous ruler, demonstrating serious internal issues. There were grave external threats also at a time when the empire "was weak and at the same time crushed by poverty."[10] In the *Alexiad*, Anna provides fifteen chapters or "books" of detail and, as the writer, has her father, Alexius, say, "It was my misfortune to find the empire surrounded on all sides by barbarians with no defence worthy of consideration against the enemies who threatened it.[11] On the west were Normans crossing from Italy into what is now Albania, on the east Turkic people were moving through Anatolia, while others threatened from the north.

"What then was this young emperor ... to do? Briefly, he had two courses open to him: he could either abandon all in despair and abdicate ... or, of necessity, he could call on allies wherever available, collect from whatever source he could enough money to satisfy their demands, and recall by means of largess his army now scattered to the four points of the compass."[12] In a word, he must be as skilled as a Homeric hero. Amazingly, he managed to restore a degree of stability before even worse conditions overwhelmed the kingdom following his death in 1118.

Another asset of the *Alexiad* is its demonstration of the power of women, at least imperial women, in Byzantine culture. Empresses could be regents – Alexius appointed his mother regent early in his reign. Anna remembered her grandmother Anna Dalassena who "had an exceptional grasp of public affairs, with a genius for organization and government ... she had vast experience and a wide understanding of the motives, ultimate consequences, interrelations good and bad of various courses of action ...; her intellectual powers, moreover, were paralleled by her command of language."[13]

As the eldest child of her parents, Anna hoped to have a similar status and perhaps even succeed her father. When her brother John gained the power and her husband died, she took refuge in a monastery (or was banished there) where she was able to write her account of her father's ability as a ruler, an account described by a translator as "a document more urbane, more vivid, more inspiring than any produced by her Latin contemporaries in the West."[14] Anna was likely still writing her father's history in 1148.

As a person, Anna Comnena serves as one of the rarest representatives of the complex integration of Byzantine and former Greek cultures, not only on account of her gender and her position in the empire, but because of her work, the *Alexiad*. She was a devout Christian noble, born to the highest rank, who was influenced by her studies of Greek literature from the Classical period. Perhaps embittered by the eventual loss of privilege, power, and her chance for rule (real or imagined), she realized that as an imperial princess she had been born to a life that "in spite of the good luck of her parentage, the rest has been one long series of storms and revolutions."[15] And yet, in spite of those storms, she remains extraordinary to this day because the *Alexiad*, written shortly after her father's reign, shows us a rich glimpse into the Byzantine Empire, its culture, and way of life.

Notes

1. The force of this influence poses a serious issue for the question of Hellenic continuity. In the nineteenth century, German scholar Jakob Fallmerayer asserted that no drop of unmixed Hellenic blood flowed in the veins of the Christian people of Greece in his day. His view has not been accepted and, just recently, has been further undermined by genetic evidence.

2. Quoted in N. Rubinstein, "Italy," in "The Fall of Constantinople: A Symposium Held at the School of Oriental and African Studies, 29 May 1953." School of Oriental and African Studies, University of London, 1955, 25.
3. Justinian, *Novella* VI in R. Schoell, ed., *Corpus Iuris Civilis*, vol. 3 *Novellae* (Berlin, 1912), 35–36.
4. Plato, *Crito* 50a–b.
5. Anna Comnena, *The Alexiad*, Book V, translated by E. R. A. Sewter (London: Penguin, 1969; reprinted 2003), 179–80.
6. Comnena, *Alexiad* VI, 196–197.
7. Comnena, *Alexiad* VI, 7.
8. Comnena, *Alexiad* VI, 109.
9. Comnena, *Alexiad* VI, 17.
10. Comnena, *Alexiad* VI, 157.
11. Comnena, *Alexiad* VI, 185.
12. Comnena, *Alexiad* VI, 157.
13. Comnena, *Alexiad* VI, 119.
14. Comnena, *Alexiad* VI, 16.
15. Comnena, *Alexiad* VI, 20.

Further Reading

Cavallo, Guglielmo, ed. 1977. *The Byzantines*. Chicago, IL: University of Chicago Press.
These essays are an excellent way to understand the lives of people in Byzantine society: the peasantry, soldiers, teachers, women, entrepreneurs, bishops, functionaries, emperors, and saints.

Comnena, Anna. 1969 (reprinted 2003). *The Alexiad*, translated by E. R. A. Sewter. London: Penguin.
As the daughter of a Byzantine emperor, her account reveals the life of one born into the ruling family with its advantages, such as an excellent education, and also its threats, both internal, in terms of the struggle for rule, and external from Crusaders and Ottoman Turks.

Mango, Cyril. (Ed.). 2002. *Oxford History of Byzantium*. Oxford: Oxford University Press.
The account is carefully organized to examine the several main phases of Byzantium: four major sections begin with an historical sketch of those years, which is followed by important topical discussion. For example, the period 306–641 has chapters on life in city and country, religious culture, and the rise of Islam.

Treadgold, Warren. 2001. *A Concise History of Byzantium*. New York and Basingstoke: Palgrave.
This well-organized discussion is accessible for general readers although its contents reflect the serious scholarship of its author. Chapters deal with the six periods of Byzantium with nice running commentary by the author.

Whittow, Mark. 1966. *The Making of Byzantium, 600–1025*. Berkeley: University of California Press.
The orientation of this account is useful in that it looks to the older Roman world circa 600 CE and subsequent history to 1025. Attention given to the "neighbors" of the emerging Byzantine Empire is welcome.

8

Ottoman Greece
1453–1821

The span of three and a half centuries from the capture of Constantinople by the Ottoman Turks to the raising of the flag of independence in the Peloponnese is often termed a "Dark Age" of Greece. It is akin to the "Dark Age" following the collapse of the complex culture of the Bronze Age in being a time of impoverishment for most Greeks. However, it is dissimilar in being the result of control by a foreign power rather than internal decline.

Much of the cultural legacy from the past was preserved during the period of Ottoman control, not unlike the situation in the first Dark Age. Also akin to the earlier period, preservation was not part of the daily life of the majority of the population. In fact, awareness of the rich legacy of the past came through the travelers from western European states who began to come to Greece in increasing numbers in the seventeenth and eighteenth centuries. Life in both Dark Ages was difficult both for those who lived then and, consequently, for the longer-term of history of Greece. As C. H. Woodhouse remarked, 1453 is "rightly chosen to mark the end of an era. ... [N]one of the other calamities suffered by Christendom .... could be compared in finality or dramatic intensity to the fall of Constantinople."[1] There might be a regular chorus of the words of Hesiod, who wished that he had been born not in his time but before, or after, or not at all.

The impact of the period affected not only Greece but Europe generally. However, the developments were very different: life for most Greeks returned to the Neolithic level of basic subsistence with the addition of hardships for many akin to the end of the second millennium BCE. By contrast, the last decades of the fifteenth century CE demonstrate the recognized transition from medieval to modern history in northern and western Europe. While major developments in much of the rest of Europe moved in a dramatically new and dynamic direction, inhabitants in Greece and a large portion of eastern Europe were largely untouched by those developments as subjects in the Ottoman Empire. Somewhat curiously, however, knowledge of ancient Greek culture was instrumental in the western European movement. Classical Greek culture was known through its written and material products, admired, and integrated into

Greece: A Short History of a Long Story, 7,000 BCE to the Present, First Edition.
Carol G. Thomas.
© 2014 John Wiley & Sons, Inc. Published 2014 by John Wiley & Sons, Inc.

the early modern cultures. Acquaintance with the products began to draw westerners to Greece, where they would see the great differences between present and past in Greece. Charles Perry, an English medical doctor, noted, "This nation, which in ancient times made so great a figure in literature, the polite arts and sciences, and in military prowess, is now become pretty much estranged to all those splendid virtues and accomplishments."[2] Magnificent buildings and other objects of the past were in ruins. The huge dissimilarity would eventually draw many "rescuers" to help restore an independent state. In sum, its location, as in earlier periods, drew Greece into the dissimilar spheres of the Mediterranean and the Near East.

Much of what was new in Europe can be described through maps of territories. Early European consolidation took the form of vast territorial states created by forceful, complex powers over groups of less developed peoples, thus continuing the tendency of the ancient world. As we have seen, Rome extended control over a vast array of different peoples. Some of those people, like the Gauls and Germans, were divided even among themselves, living in small villages or still leading a migratory way of life. Others were sophisticated kingdoms of the Hellenistic East that had weakened through relentless warfare or mismanagement of resources. The Byzantine Empire rose out of similar conditions, drawing upon both newcomers to Greece and the Balkans as well as on the remnants of the Eastern Roman Empire.

In its sudden, successful expansion from Spain to India, Islam also gathered disparate elements into a sweeping empire. At the same time, the Carolingian kings in Europe created a new Roman Empire, officially recognized with the coronation by the pope of Charlemagne as Holy Roman Emperor in 800 and continuing to the defeat of its imperial army in 1268.

It is worth mentioning that the victorious army was that of France, one of the new forms of state emerging throughout Europe from the tenth century onwards. National states, not fledgling empires, were consolidating their borders. Some, like the city-states of Italy, were relatively small; others – England, France, Poland, Sweden, and Norway – grew to larger dimensions yet they still were of more limited expanse than the empires of the past or present.

Pressure from other states partially explains the shrinking size. Another factor was a growing sense of the common elements uniting the population of the region, a burgeoning nationalism. In such states, an emperor was an outsider and viewed in that light. Kings rather than emperors were leaders of the emerging states. Even though they were smaller, kingdoms could play a major role in the increasingly interconnected European sphere. The Normans in southern Italy and Sicily were one of the most worrisome enemies of the later Byzantine rulers and the Norman states were able to hold out against Ottoman expansion. In the north of Italy, too, city-states like Venice and Genoa were key partners in the widespread trade centered on Constantinople.

Links between Venice and Constantinople were especially significant since, according to fifteenth-century scholars like Bessarion, Venice had become a "new" Rome only slightly later than Constantinople had been re-founded as a Christian capital by Constantine the Great. Romans fleeing the advance of the Ostrogoths into Italy had taken refuge in the island realm of Venice in 421. In Justinian's attempt to recreate the boundaries of the Roman Empire (527–565), Venice became an exarchate of the Byzantine Empire. That status was broken when iconoclasm was adopted by the Byzantine emperor in the eighth century but the rising commercial entrepreneurship of the Venetians forged another strong bond, one that produced favorable tax conditions for the Venetians in their trade with the Byzantines. The Venetian fleet could also carry armies which it did in response to the Byzantine request for aid against enemies and also in transporting crusaders to the East. The most memorable occasion that residents of Constantinople experienced was the arrival of soldiers of the fourth Crusade in 1204, a visit that resulted in the capture of the Byzantine capital by the Latin leaders with Venice gaining three-eighths of the territory of the empire.

Conceptual changes also distinguished the new states: as early as 1215 the Magna Carta stated that "No free man shall be taken, or imprisoned, or dispossessed, or outlawed, or banished, or in any way injured … except by the legal judgment of his peers, or by the law of the land." Moreover, often the religion of an empire was found to be inadequate for many of the subject peoples. It is not surprising to note that Christianity assumed new guises in early modern Europe since the specific form of religious practice was one means of defining the particular identity of a state.

While the nation-state was taking root in the West, the Ottoman Empire was extending its reach: its sweep extended from all of Asia Minor, Constantinople, and Greece into Europe by 1471. During the reign of Suleiman the Magnificent (1520–1564), Ottoman armies reached Belgrade in southern Hungary in 1521 and nine years later arrived at Buda in the north of Hungary. From there they crossed into the Habsburg Empire but were stopped at Vienna. For Europe, the Ottoman success was a threat not only in sheer military terms but to a new order of political organization.

The Ottomans also presented a challenge; in addition to being feared, they were disliked for severing the access to trade with the East. Western Europeans had been ever more drawn into this activity from the thirteenth century and, until 1453, Constantinople had served as link between west and east, north and south. The value of such contact with Asia was significant enough to spur western Europeans to search for new routes once Constantinople fell to the Ottomans, who could and did restrict access to others. The quickness of beginning the search is evident in a handful of dates: the cape of Africa was rounded in 1488; Columbus crossed the Atlantic in 1492; and in 1498 Vasco de Gama reached India. While the early ventures were largely confined to luxury items, the ramifications of these new routes would explode in the sixteenth century, increasing the differences between the European states and the Ottoman Empire. For our understanding of Greece, it is significant to note that certain tools of seafaring developed in the Greek world now passed into western hands and that Greeks, especially those who emigrated westward, participated in the ventures.

Apart from adventurous individual Greeks, Greece itself had virtually no role in this explosion. Being cut off from the larger world of trade was disastrous for the internal well-being of Greece. Hesiod would have recognized the hardships of village, self-sufficient life as being akin to his own circa 700 BCE when things were "never good." An anonymous poem has a distinctly Hesiodic tone:

> Alas for our trouble, Krima[3] for our druggery
> We build all the day, night destroys it.

Yet Greece was becoming better known to the larger world not only to visitors to Greece but also through Greeks who left their homeland in search of a better life. Moreover, the transmission of its preserved legacy of scholarship now flowed to the west at the end of Byzantine days in the form of scholars and preserved knowledge. Leonardo Bruni of the city-state of Florence gave eloquent testimony to the impact of Greek scholars and scholarship.

> At this time I was studying the Civil Law, though I was not an ignoramus in other studies and I had devoted no little effort to dialetic and rhetoric. Thus, I was actually of two minds when Chrysoloras (a Greek scholar from Constantinople) arrived, as I thought it shameful to abandon the study of the law, and at the same time a sort of crime to miss such an opportunity to learn Greek. So, in a youthful spirit, I would often ask myself:

> When you had a chance to see and converse with Homer and Plato and Demosthenes and the other poets and philosophers and orators, about whom such wonderful things are said, and to acquire the wonderful education that comes with their study, will you leave yourself in the lurch and deprive yourself of it? Will you pass up this god-given opportunity? For seven hundred years now, no one in Italy has been able to read Greek, and yet we admit that it is from the Greeks that we get all our systems of knowledge. What a contribution to your knowledge, then, and what an opportunity to establish your reputation, and what an abundance of pleasure will the knowledge of this language bring you! There are plenty of teachers of the Civil Law; so you will always be able to study that, but this is the one and only teacher of Greek; if he should disappear, there would then be nobody from whom you can learn.

> Overcome by such arguments, I took myself to Chrysoloras, which such an ardor to study that what I learned in my waking hours during the day, I would be working over at night even in my sleep.[4]

Bruni went on to translate into Latin many Greek works for the edification of men like Cosimo de'Medici, founder of the line of rulers of the important city-state of Florence, and the pope. He also wrote treatises of his own embodying Greek principles and philosophies. He was not alone.

Thus Greece could be – and came to be – viewed as a victim worthy of saving. What is more, the crusading spirit persisted; Christian Greece should be rescued from Muslim control just as Crusaders had endeavored to rescue other parts of the East from non-Christian control.

Ottoman Control of Greece

The rescue would be delayed for more than 350 years. Even an anonymous folk song, "The Last Mass in Santa Sophia," recognizes the likely duration of rule by the Ottoman Turks.

> God rings the bells, the earth rings the bells, the sky rings the bells, and Santa Sophia, the great church rings the bells: 400 sounding boards and 62 bells, a priest for each bell and a deacon for each priest. To the left the emperor was chanting, to the right the patriarch, and from the volume of the chant the pillars were shaking. When they were about to sing the hymn of the Cherubim and the emperor was about to appear, they heard a voice from the sky and from the mouth of the Archangel: "Stop the Cherubic hymn, and let the holy elements bow in mourning. The priests must take the sacred vessels away

and your candles must be extinguished, for it is the will of God that the City fall to the Turks. But send a message to the West asking for three ships to come; one to take the Cross away, another, the Holy Bible, the third, the best of the three, our holy Altar, lest the dogs seize it from us and defile it." The Virgin was distressed and the holy icons wept. "Hush, Lady, do not weep so profusely; after years and after centuries they will be yours again.[5]

The fall of *the* city was predictable in light of the rapid extension of control of the Ottomans. From their nomadic origins to settlement as a small frontier principality, the Ottomans were propelled by Mongol migration in central Asia into Anatolia where they expanded their holdings. Their numbers grew rapidly from the original 40,000 "tents" of followers of Othman. Another momentous development was conversion to Islam.

While the fertile lands and resources of Anatolia would remain the economic base of the eventual empire, Ottoman armies soon pushed westward into Europe and their expansion was facilitated by internal rivalries within the Byzantine Empire. As early as 1352, Suleiman Pasha crossed the Dardanelles at the urging of John Cantacuzenus – a major official to the emperor – hopeful that Ottoman arms would establish him as Byzantine emperor.

Capture of Constantinople was delayed by a century but, by then, virtually all except the territory immediately surrounding Constantinople was in Ottoman hands. In 1365, Andrianople in eastern Thrace was taken, by 1372 Bulgaria was a vassal of the Ottomans, and, six years later, Serbia had the same status. From 1391 to 1398 most of Greece was conquered but, although besieged, Constantinople did not fall to Ottoman forces. Within another thirty years, Thessaloniki – the second city of the Byzantine Empire – was joined to the Ottoman Empire and most of the northern Aegean islands were also added to its expanding territory. Thus it was only a matter of time before Turkish guns would crack the defenses of the city of Constantine.

Fully aware of the imminent fall of Constantinople the last emperors sought western aid. In 1438 Emperor John VIII traveled to Italy where, at a council of Ferrara and Florence, representatives agreed to terms for reunion of the Orthodox and Roman churches, an agreement that produced a new Crusade in 1440. The Crusaders did defeat the Turkish force twice before they themselves were defeated in 1444. When John VIII died in 1448, his successor, Constantine XI, also made efforts to gain western aid but only one western ruler – the king of Aragon and Naples – sent a force that was soon withdrawn. On the other hand, volunteers from many lands came to the aid of the besieged city: Greek defenders were joined by Italians, Germans, Hungarians, Serbs, Castilians, Catalans, and even some Turks.

Their efforts were in vain: Constantinople was taken and sacked, albeit not completely. After this victory in 1453, Ottoman forces took control of Athens three years later and added the Peloponnese by 1460. Control in the Balkans tightened as well. In the sixteenth century, under the reign of Suleiman the Magnificent, Ottoman forces marched through Hungary into the Habsburg Empire where they were finally halted at Vienna. At the same time, the southern Aegean islands were joined to the Ottoman sphere of control; only Crete held out until 1669. Until the twentieth century, Ottoman rule encompassed Anatolia, the Balkans, North Africa, and Arabia.

From its creation, the basis of the Ottoman Empire was military. The nomadic origins of the Turcomans created an understanding of the necessity of physical strength for mere survival while conversion to Islam introduced the realization that warfare was a means for extending the realm of followers of Mohammed. War was thus holy, a *Jihad*, on the part of the soldiers of Allah, the *Gazis*. Another legacy of their nomadic origins was the term for subjected people, *Rayah* or "cattle." As territorial boundaries were stabilized, a continual military presence was essential to control the conquered.

In addition to military readiness, a centralized administrative structure emerged to define the roles of both the rulers and the ruled. Its basis rested in the sacred law of Islam, or *Sheri*, with additions over time of new decrees and other appendages of that law. Sultans, the highest figures in this structure, were subject to divine law as well as being its dispensers. Thus, the Ottoman state was a theocracy, with temporal and religious rule united. However, Islamic law pertained only to Muslims. One solution was to convert subjected peoples to Islam. For peoples who did not convert, another solution was found in allowing the law of non-Muslim religions to provide the foundation of their governance. Four religious groupings – or *millets* – were the means of organizing the collective lives of the Jewish, Armenian, Catholic, and Greek Orthodox populations. *Millets* were not firmly fixed as bounded territories although both historical developments and a tendency to live among people of similar beliefs fostered something of a geographical division of religious groups by region. Greeks were the *Millet-I Rum* – that is, the *Rum millet*,[6] which contained all the Orthodox Christian inhabitants of the Ottoman Empire.

The religious head of each *millet* became an "officer" of the Ottoman Empire with rights to govern members of that faith. Consequently, the religious role of the heads of each religion was expanded to include civil responsibilities. For the Orthodox *millet*, the patriarch of Constantinople stood at the apex of a pyramid that descended through bishops and priests to the village level.

Formal territorial division did exist. The capital was Constantinople. (The city's name changed to Istanbul with the establishment of the modern Turkish State in 1930. The derivation of the name is interesting in revealing the reason it was chosen as the capital: "Istanbul" is a product of the words "to the *polis* [*eis ton polin*]" – that city had been *the polis* in size and importance of the entire empire since Late Roman times.) The vast territory perpetuated the provincial system in place since Roman times; now each province was a *bey* governed by a *beylerbey*. Initially two, the number of provinces rose to thirty as Ottoman territorial control expanded. The *beylerbey* of mainland Greece resided in Sophia. These large territories were subdivided into small units called *sanjaks*. Originally Greece was divided into six *sanjaks*; over time five more were added. Each *sanjak* was under the control of a *sanjakbey* who held military and fiscal responsibility through the chain of command reaching to the sultan in Constantinople. The *sanjakbeys* provided military control in their *sanjak* through their retinues and were, in turn, supported by a living from non-hereditary lands and resources. Smaller local units were *pashaliks*, each governed by a *pasha*.

An umbrella over the entire domain was the imperial structure headed by the sultan from Constantinople. His palace was designated the "Porte." Due to the importance of law, he was aided by a host of interpreters, learned *mufti*, as well as

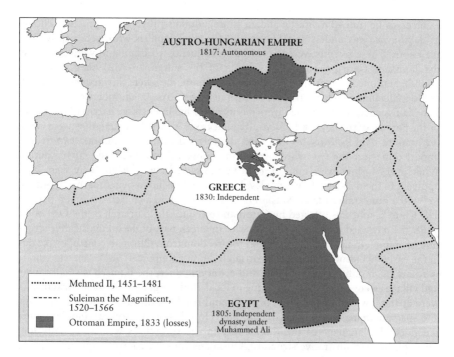

Figure 8.1 Greece within the Ottoman Empire. Source: Jason Shattuck

two chief justices and many local judges. In practice, the Grand Vizier was the lieutenant of the sultan in the administration of legal matters. A vast bureaucracy of something like 20–25,000 functionaries developed as the empire achieved its immense size. Major officials were true Ottomans whose sons inherited the status and positions of their fathers. An advisory council, or *divan*, was composed of representatives of all aspects of Ottoman rule.

Some Greeks played important administrative roles: the patriarch and descending levels of religious figures in the Orthodox Church were especially powerful but certain Greek families in Constantinople made themselves valuable through trade and commerce and were increasingly drafted into official positions. These privileged families tended to reside near the patriarch in the lighthouse district of the city – the *Phanar* – and hence are known as Phanariots. Although they were relatively few in numbers, their importance in events of the late eighteenth and nineteenth centuries would be enormous. Their location in Constantinople, their knowledge of the governance of the sultan, and their economic status raised them far above the status of the majority of Greeks in the empire. These qualities would play an essential role in the struggle to gain independence in the late eighteenth and early nineteenth centuries.

A military presence was an integral part of the governing apparatus and it was provided by troops that were stationed throughout the empire and supported on feudal fiefs. Enrollment from families within the empire fueled the numbers of troops. In Greece, one of each forty households provided a son between the ages of eight and eighteen to be trained militarily and, at times, administratively. The practice, known as *devshirme*, was understandably painful for most families who were deprived of their sons. These recruits were converted subsequently to Islam and were known as the Janissary Corps, the infantry soldiers of the sultan. In 1527 they numbered 28,000. Stationed to regions throughout the empire, they were directed by generals.

Non-Muslims also felt Ottoman control in other ways. In addition to sons trained to be Janissaries, young women were recruited for life in the large harem of the sultan or the harems of the *beys* and *pashas*. Regular taxes were substantial; they were twice the amount paid by Muslims and took the form of head and land tax, export and import duties for the few who engaged in commerce and trade, and curvée duties. While non-Muslims were not governed by the sacred law of Islam there were laws applying to them as well. It was not legal for a non-Muslim to own firearms or horses, to build a home taller than a Muslim home, or to rebuild a church without a permit. The Church, too, was affected by Ottoman rule since the patriarch of the Orthodox *millet*, who resided in Constantinople, was, in effect, part of the administrative structure of empire. In fact, when revolution for freedom from Ottoman control broke out in the early nineteenth century, the patriarch did not support it.

Apart from military surveillance and economic dues, the numerous small towns and villages were largely self-governing in local affairs; village elders and local priests were at the low end of the chain of command reaching through provincial bishops and metropolitans to the Patriarchate and Holy Synod in Constantinople. Greek remained the language of the *Rum millet* in the Church as well as in daily life. Through the administrative structure, Ottomans came to control large amounts of land in the regions of their empire but, generally, Turkish residents lived apart from their subjects. As the traveler Bernard Randolph noted in his report of 1689:

> The Turks for the most part live in, or under the Command of Castles, and at their Farms in the Country (where they sometimes are); they have Towers built about Thirty Foot high, the Door of which is about ten Foot from the ground. ... [S]ome have only a Ladder, which they take up into the Tower.[7]

Each group of subjects tended to live in its own towns and villages. Communication between them was, consequently, difficult. Personal relations between the rulers and the ruled were often unfriendly. A later traveler, Nicholas Biddle, witnessed the despicable treatment "which a common [Turkish] soldier dared to give to an old man, a respectable man and an officer. Until this moment I had never known the meanness of tyranny."[8]

Life for most of the Greek population was rural since, apart from Constantinople and Thessaloniki, few true cities remained. Even Athens had a small population both in its urban core and larger territory of Attica. During the Periclean Age, Attica had a population of some 300,000 – admittedly huge compared with other *poleis* – and half of that number resided in or near Athens. At the time of its capture by the Ottomans, the whole of Attica contained about 35,000 people, a mixture of Greeks and Turks. For a picture of life for most Greeks under Ottoman reign, a useful comparison is the life of the majority of Greeks during the Bronze Age: they were controlled from a citadel center whose power extended to the bulk of the population living in small towns and even smaller villages throughout the realm.

Basic agriculture and household industry defined the work of most people. A report from 1689 lists basic products such as olive oil, raw silk, wax, honey, soap, skins, butter, cheese, raisins, currants, figs, melons, gourds, wines, wheat, barley, rye, oats, dried acorns, fustick wood, pernocke seed, and the fruit of orange, lemon, citron, pomegranate, apricot, peach, plum, cherry, apple, pear, and walnut trees. Sun-dried bricks resting on foundations of stone were the materials of their homes and other buildings.[9] In their worldview, most Greeks resembled the bishop of a small town discovered by an intrepid American traveler in 1806: "Of the world he knew little except from the report of passing strangers" even though he was now in his seventieth year and was, as the traveler described him, "one of the most amiable men I have ever seen."[10] We might now cast our minds back to the Neolithic Age and the basic nature of gaining subsistence from the environment that defined the life of a community.

This way of life is also reminiscent of Hesiod's description of his back-breaking round of labor each year at the end of the eighth century BCE or of the lot of many peasants under Roman rule. That it was felt to be far more repressive under Ottoman control than in Hesiod's age is evidenced by the contrast in settlements of the non-Muslims and those of the Turks. Small villages with some larger towns defined the Greek communities. By contrast, the Turkish residents of Greece lived in locations similar to that at Coron: "on a point of land which runs out about half a mile having walls above forty foot high, a round tower above sixty foot high, about seventy good guns about the wall."[11] In the eighth and seventh centuries BCE no such grand structures existed.

The capital of empire had grown from 10,000 in the aftermath of the siege in 1453 to some 700,000 inhabitants. More than 250 tons of wheat were needed daily to feed the huge population of the city of Constantinople. Industry, commerce, and trade flourished here, in stark contrast to most of the conquered lands of the empire.

Unhappiness produced localized revolts but perhaps more significant was the emergence of local leaders, called *klephts*, who lived in isolated regions where they increasingly took control of affairs themselves. In their position as subjects of *beys* and of the sultan they were outlaws who took advantage of local non-Muslims as well as their Muslim overlords. Initially they were an irritant to Ottoman officials; eventually, they would be a major source of overthrow of Ottoman rule.

Eighteenth Century

During the eighteenth century, conditions for the ruled worsened further and quickly. It was progressively more evident to peoples both within the empire and outside its reach that the Ottoman Empire was unhealthy. The explosion of European trade had damaged the Ottoman monetary system as early as the sixteenth century and, although the economy had recovered by the eighteenth century, its resources were strained. The vastness of the empire made control difficult. At its height, the empire reached the size of 2 million square miles. While administration was centered on Constantinople, more direct control of smaller regions was essential: the largest (provinces) grew to 32 while smaller regions (*sanjaks*) numbered roughly 400. Local officials often were forced by emergencies to act independently without awaiting orders from the distant sultan, while ambition drove others to expand their own sphere of power. One of those local officials, Ali Pasha, had succeeded in establishing a virtually independent realm of his own stretching further and further from its core in Epirus in northwestern Greece. His life is useful for understanding conditions throughout Greece, and indeed throughout the empire when we consider the scope for independent governance based on 432 potential challenges by the sultan's own "officials."

A son born to an Albanian Muslim chieftain of Epirus in the 1740s had grim prospects. Epirus was splintered by mountains and was not rich in natural resources. By the mid-eighteenth century, steady control from Constantinople was weakening, allowing – and, in fact, demanding – local leaders to assert their own management. In addition, the late eighteenth century saw the increasing role of foreign powers in furthering the empire's decline. The life of this son, Ali, was both a symptom and a cause of the decline.

Ali also had serious personal difficulties for his father died young and life was precarious for young widows. Fortunately, Ali's mother was related to a powerful chieftain who took the young Ali into his service as a guard in his force to preserve the territory of the chief from competitors. From that position, he became a minor chieftain in his own right and, eventually, the sultan's official – *pasha* – of most of Greece, from Thessaly south to the Gulf of Corinth, with authority over one and a half million people. Consequently, he is known as Ali Pasha.

His path was steady. Initially, Epirus was divided among three *pashas*, one of whom was suspected of disloyalty by the sultan. Ali was appointed to observe the suspect and given a *firman* (a mandate from the sultan) for his death should disloyalty be demonstrated. After ingratiating himself with the suspect, Ali waited for an opportunity to exercise the *firman* and received a *pashalik* of his own. By 1787 his authority included Thessaly and Ioannina, which became a major capital within the full Ottoman Empire due to its power and culture.

Lord Byron visited the *pasha* in his country palace which reminded Byron of an English castle. In front of the palace were troops of Albanians, Tartars, and Turks in their splendid finery – "the most magnificent in the world" – together with slaves, couriers, and 200 steeds "ready caparisoned to move in a moment," all accompanied by kettle drums beating. Then he was shown to "a very handsome apartment" and given "a full suit of Staff uniform with a very magnificent saber." He discovered that Ali Pasha was "to me indeed a father" and they conversed of traveling, politics, and England as well as war. On the other hand, as "a mighty warrior, [he] is as barbarous as he is successful, roasting rebels etc." Byron soon learned that Ali Pasha was "only nominally dependent on The Porte."[12]

Not fully satisfied with his extensive territory, Ali undertook further acquisitions, especially of the Ionian islands, which were declared autonomous in 1800 although foreign powers retained unofficial power, power that Ali coveted for himself. Eventually the sultan became alarmed and sought to limit Ali's power indirectly by demoting the position of Ali's son and finally by ordering another *pasha* to lead an army against Ali himself. Ali Pasha was besieged within the fortifications of Ioannina in 1821 and in 1822 was killed in negotiations with the besiegers. The sultan demanded that Ali's head be sent to Constantinople where it was exposed at the gate of the *serai* (palace). Four other heads of *pashas* soon joined that of Ali: the heads of Ali's three sons and his grandson.

Similar histories can be told of much of the empire. The account of Ali is important to Greece, according to George Finlay, since his career "with all his power and
wickedness, would hardly have merited a place in history had circumstances not
rendered him the herald of the Greek Revolution." [13]

Conditions of disorder throughout the empire enhanced the role of the Janissaries.
Reflecting their high status, fiefs became heritable. Taxes rose on subjects of the empire
as the costs of administration increased but higher rates of taxation brought no
corresponding services. Flight away from the reach of tax officials, banditry, and revolts
were symptomatic of rising despair on the part of the peasantry. The division by *millets*
also brought problems that fostered rancor between the four *millets*: the *Rum millet* was
believed by the others to be favored by the Ottomans, as it indeed was in certain respects.
One important indication was the gain of greater power by the heads of Phanariot families not only in Constantinople but through connections with other powerful states,
particularly Russia, France, and England. In the Danubian regions of Moldavia and
Wallachia bordering the Black Sea, Phanariot Greeks held a privileged position in
commerce within the Ottoman Empire. Thus they could be a threat to Ottoman power
as well as raising the hackles of members of the other *millets*. Other less fortunate
Greeks viewed the Phanariots' role as one of despicable cooperation with the enemy.

The power of the Patriarchate created tensions of another sort. On the one hand,
the importance of the office made it much sought after: during the seventh century,
fifty-eight people held the position. As the representative of all Orthodox Greeks, the
patriarch should offer a continuous sense of his role; thus a change of holder every
other year could perhaps undermine such continuity. Moreover, affiliation with the
Ottoman regime, coupled with control of orthodox belief, fueled anti-clericalism,
especially among the educated but it was also apparent at the popular level of society.
Anger at the condition seen as corrupt focused on the cause of that condition: sub-
jection to the Ottoman Empire.

Difficult in other ways to the Ottomans were the great powers of the age; in the last
four decades of the century Russia, under Catherine the Great from 1762 to 1796, was
the greatest threat to the integrity of their empire. In her plan to divide the Ottoman
Empire, Catherine believed that one part would be a new Greek Empire with
Constantinople as its capital. Her grandson, named Constantine III in the line of
Constantine the Great, could be a re-founder of that city as a Christian Rome. To facilitate that plan, she promoted a rising in the Peloponnese in 1769–1770 that did capture
the important fort and harbor site of Navarino but had no further success. However,
it did plant seeds for the future and the Russians enjoyed successes in Ottoman territory
in the Aegean. Then they took control of Crimea in 1783, thereby collapsing the circuit
of the Turkish "lake" – the Black Sea. Although the plan for a new Greek Empire did
not materialize, the vulnerability of the Ottomans was demonstrated to others who
had an interest in the defeat of the Ottoman Empire for different reasons.

Western Europeans had strong interests in Greece. The city-state of Venice just
across the Adriatic Sea had become a major trading power by the eleventh century
and, after the taking of Constantinople by the Crusaders in 1204, gained control in
Crete, Attica, Euboea, and other Aegean islands. By the fifteenth century, Corfu and
Dalmatia were also under Venetian rule. As Venice had profited from special dispen-
sations of the Byzantine emperors earlier, so the state also hoped to make inroads
into Ottoman territory.

Other players in Greek territory were the Normans who had taken or created king-doms in southern Italy and Sicily. Adventurous descendants of Robert Guiscard (the "cunning") were drawn eastward across the Adriatic, as the Romans had been earlier, to become serious foes of the later Byzantine emperors, as noted in the previous chapter. Other peoples complicated the safety of the seas through piratical activities: the Barbary corsairs of North Africa, the Slavic Uskoks along the northeastern coast of the Adriatic, and the Knights of Malta were the most numerous and troublesome.

Increasingly diverse populations within Greece itself were producing a multi-cul-tural social order by the fifteenth century. Trade brought an increasing Jewish element, especially in the larger cities of Constantinople and Thessaloniki. An Albanian element, present since the seventh century, was also significant. Dissatisfaction with Ottoman control, therefore, was not limited to the Greek Orthodox *millet*. Albanians, for instance, would be among non-Greek freedom fighters in the 1820s.

Greece became the means to take advantage of Ottoman vulnerability as Greeks and western Europeans learned more about one another. Foreigners were now com-ing to Greece in official capacities. More Greeks were living in Europe as merchants and officials in the service of other states. Knowledge of events in America in the 1770s and in France between 1789 and 1793 revealed that revolution from what was perceived as a cruel tyranny of power was possible. Greeks abroad were telling others of the situation at home as well as experiencing the level of culture in many eighteenth-century European states.

In addition to Greeks who left Ottoman Greece to experience the very different conditions in other parts of Europe, Greeks who remained began to learn from visi-tors to their land of those same conditions. Nicholas Biddle (1786–1844) was secre-tary of the American minister to France and used his stay to visit Greece where he traveled widely. He kept two journals (one of which is quoted earlier in this chapter) about conditions in Greece during the early nineteenth century. In a village near Delphi, he met the bishop, the chief official of the Greek people in his bishopric, who said, "of the world he knew little except from the report of passing strangers," and he "loved to hear of [it] at a distance. From him I learnt in my turn something with regard to the state of the country which is cruelly oppressed by the Turks."[14] Learning personally of life in Greece allowed Biddle to compare the actual situation with his earlier view of the brilliance of Greek civilization.

The growing understanding of life in Greece compared with that in other parts of Europe and America produced military reaction against Ottoman control. Thus, rather than using a single person to embody Greece under Ottoman control, our account presents a variety of people, some of whom left and some of whom remained, but all of whom said "no," in different ways, to the status of Greece in the eighteenth century.

Those Who Said "No"

Theodore Kolokotronis

The nature of Greek territory assisted many who would become leaders in the revolt. Mountains rendered many areas of Greece difficult to access and even more difficult to control. Those conditions favored the rise of local loyalties and local

Figure 8.2 "Those who said no." Sources: Kolokotronis: lithography by Karl Krazeisen/ Wikimedia; Korais: Wikimedia; Feraios: painting by A. Kriezis, Benaki Museum, Athens. Composite by Jason Shattuck

leaders to advance their causes. Theodore Kolokotronis is one of those local leaders who have been especially praised:

> Of all those who have been called upon to aid the Greek cause, Colocotroni deserves most particular notice. This chief had never submitted to the Ottomans, but like his ancestors, had almost from his cradle carried on a petty warfare against them, spreading alarm throughout his native province, at the head of a band of faithful and determined followers.[15]

Born in 1770, he was raised in Arcadia, the central territory of the Peloponnese ringed by sheer mountains and, thus, a land difficult for Ottomans to control. Theodore's father, a local leader and a *klepht* endeavoring to limit Ottoman control, had participated in the earlier revolt fostered by Catherine the Great of Russia and he was killed in 1780 by the Turks. Theodore and his two brothers continued their father's efforts within the Peloponnese. Theodore expanded his skills serving on Russian ships and joining the Greek infantry in the newly freed Ionian islands that were now under British rule. He rose to become an officer in the British Army. Returning to the mainland in 1821, he was a major figure in the four revolts against the Ottomans raised in 1821. In 1822, he commanded a force of some 2,300 Greek troops to a victory over an Ottoman force estimated to have been 30,000 strong. If the disproportion is astonishing, the nature of the two forces is even more striking. As Kolokotronis described in his own memoirs, "it was not until our rising that all the Greeks were brought into communication. There were men who knew of no place beyond a mile of their own locality. They thought of Zante [Greek Zakynthos in the Ionian islands] as we now speak of the most distant parts of the world. They said it was in France."[16]

There were as many *klephts* as there were regions in Greece. Each might unify the Greek peasants in his immediate territory but coordination of activity was essential to success over the entrenched Ottoman garrisons and officials. As news of uprisings trickled into the mountains, a growing sense of common cause could spur connected activity and it did just that. It is interesting that the four uprisings in 1821 occurred within a period of ten days. The *klephts* continued to be an essential force in the developments after 1821.

Adamantios Korais

Greeks in some areas of the Ottoman Empire were more fortunate in the nature of their communities. The coast of Anatolia has been integral to Greeks from the Bronze Age and even earlier if we remember the expansion of farming and farmers out of Anatolia in the Neolithic Age. The Aegean coast of Anatolia and the off-shore islands were now the center of the vast trading network centered on Constantinople. The city of Izmir (ancient Smyrna) was an especially important trade center in the empire. It was not isolated by high mountains and was carefully controlled by Ottoman authority. The life of Adamantios Korais (1748–1833) illustrates the possibilities of a very different life for a Greek inhabitant of Izmir than for a son of an Arcadian *klepht*.

Merchants from other parts of the world were welcomed in the Ottoman Empire and the Dutch merchant community in Izmir was particularly strong. The chaplain of the community recognized in young Adamantios an innate intelligence that deserved nourishing and, consequently, instructed him in French, Italian, German, and Latin in return for instruction in Greek from his student. Languages and the link with the Dutch, which brought training in business dealings, eventually took Korais to Amsterdam as a merchant for six years. His command of French led him to Montpellier in France to study medicine, focusing on Hippocrates; his thesis and later publications commanded high respect from others. His own interests and knowledge of earlier Greek literature encouraged Korais to promote the publication of the works of Classical Greece. Those intents took him to Paris in 1788 where he became an editor and publisher of texts. Korais' appreciation of the power of learning is nicely demonstrated in his practice of providing free copies of published texts to poor and orphaned students and to teachers.

His writing served another purpose in frequently comparing ancient and contemporary Greece, which revealed the differences between conditions of Greeks in the two ages. Of the contemporary condition, Korais described the "thousand evils" of his enslaved fellow countrymen. His 1803 "Memoir on the Present State of Civilization in Greece" broadcast that situation in learned, compelling prose.

Korais was not alone and, in fact, societies were being formed for precisely the purpose of drawing foreign friends to the cause of Greece. These societies, or *hetairiai*, had the overt aim of creating friends of Hellenism; their tacit goal was to influence others to come to the assistance of Greek independence. And the cause of philhellenism increasingly drew support – political, personal, and financial. In fact, westerners began to travel to Greece deliberately, not accidentally, as earlier sailors had done when blown off course in the eastern Mediterranean. Surviving reports become increasingly full and accurate. Initially visitors to Greek locations were surprised to find that Greece was still inhabited by Greeks.

They were drawn to Greece for various reasons. Trade was one magnet and political relations with the sultan were a second strong force bringing ambassadors from foreign states to Constantinople; Thomas Bruce, the seventh earl of Elgin, was the British ambassador to the sultan from 1798 to 1802. While there, Lord Elgin received permission from the sultan himself to study and remove what were described as stones from the ancient Temple of Idols. Those stones, in Athens and elsewhere, were in themselves a reason to travel to Greece: some travelers sketched the remains – Jacques Spon and Sir George Wheler did so in 1676 – and purchased certain pieces of "rubble" to take home as souvenirs. Others were seeking the identity of famous ancient sites, a search that two members of Elgin's entourage undertook in 1801. Conflict, too, drew others to Greece as hostilities between the Ottomans and other states increasingly brought ships and forces into Greek waters. In short, Greece was becoming familiar through first-hand observation.

Rigas Velestinlis (Pheraios)

Yet another vital element for the uprising rests in the connection of the privileged Phanariot families who were essential to the coordination between the central government of the sultan and the subject peoples. Some were Greek families with deep roots in the past; others were of Hellenized Albanian or Romanian families. They connected their ethnic communities with the sultan in three primary capacities: as mediators between the patriarch and the sultan; in business matters of the empire such as tax collection; and as commercial officials in the extensive territory of the Ottomans. In this last capacity, they were rewarded with the title of *hospodar*, essentially prince, of the rich territories hugging the west of the Black Sea – Wallachia and Moldavia (now Romania).

A Hellenized Vlach from Thessaly, Rigas Velestinlis (1757–1798), had fought locally for independence, akin to Theodore Kolokotronis. But on killing an important Ottoman, he fled from Thessaly, initially to the holy community of Mount Athos but then to assist the prince of Wallachia. While there, he may have become a member of an emerging organization of secret societies (*Philiki Etairia*, or group of friends) of individuals gathering force for Greek independence. Next he was drawn to aid the French consul in Bucharest where he learned much more about the French Revolution and hoped that it might serve as a model for Greece. On to Vienna where he published his own *Declaration of the Rights of Man* as well as other political tracts. He hoped to secure the aid of Napoleon Bonaparte for Greece. In his subsequent travels in search of outside aid for a Greek revolution he was betrayed to the Ottomans and put to death in 1798. His "War Hymn" of 1797 has been called the "Greek *Marseillaise*."[17]

> How long, my heroes, shall we live in bondage,
> alone like lions on ridges, on peaks?
> Living in caves, seeing our children
> turned from the world to bitter enslavement?
> Losing our land, brothers, and parents,
> our friends, our children and all our relations?
> Better an hour of life that is free
> than forty years in slavery!
>
> In the east, west, south and north,
> let all have one heart for one land.
> Let each worship God in the fashion he pleases,
> let us hasten together to the glory of war,
> let each whom tyranny has exiled
> now return to his own.
> Bulgarians, Albanians, Armenians, Greeks,

> black and white, let us belt the sword
> all together in a surge for freedom,
> so the world will know that we are the brave!
> How did our forefathers surge like lions,
> leaping for liberty into the fire?
> So we, brothers too, must seize our arms
> and cast off at once this bitter slavery,
> to slay the wolves who impose the yoke,
> and cruelly torture Christian and Turk.
> Let the Cross shine on land and sea,
> let justice make the enemy kneel,
> let the world be healed of this grievous wound,
> and let us live on earth as brothers – free.[18]

Countless other Greeks were leaving Greece beginning in the sixteenth century and accelerating in the eighteenth both in numbers and in destinations. Many were drawn to Italy especially Venice, Florence, and Naples. They were eminent scholars, artists, soldiers, rowers in huge fleets. Greek merchants were engaged in major European centers and ordinary skilled laborers were also sought: for instance, the silk workers recruited to France. Some Greeks who had held political positions outside of Greece were now returning to the recently freed Ionian islands. All were learning and practicing skills of which they were essentially deprived in Greece itself. And should they return to their homeland, they would be equipped to confront the securing of independence and, then, the rebuilding of an independent state.

Notes

1. C. H. Woodhouse, *Modern Greece: A Short History* (London: Faber and Faber, 1968), 97.
2. Charles Perry, *A View of the Levant, Particularly of Constantinople, Syria, Egypt, and Greece* (London: T. Woodward, 1743), 514.
3. "Krima" can be translated as "pity" or "crime."
4. Leonardo Bruni, *Rerum suo tempore gestarum Commentarius, Rerum Italicarum Scriptores,* t. 19 (Bologna, 1926), Part 3, 431–432. Cited in translation in Gordon Griffiths, "Classical Greece and the Italian Renaissance," in C. Thomas, ed., *Paths from Ancient Greece* (Leiden: E. J. Brill, 1988), 92–117; 95–96.
5. "The Last Mass in Santa Sophia," in Constantine A. Trypanis, ed., *The Penguin Book of Greek Verse* (Harmondsworth: Penguin, 1971), 469–470. It contains both Greek texts and English translations.
6. The Greek population was identified by its inclusion in the Roman Empire and by its survival after the fall of Rome itself as the Eastern Roman Empire.
7. Bernard Randolph, *The Present State of the Morea, Called Anciently Peloponnesus Together with a Description of the City of Athens and the Islands of Zante, Strafades and Sergio* (London: printed for the author, 1686), 15.
8. R. A. McNeal, ed., *Nicholas Biddle in Greece: The Journals and Letters of 1806* (University Park: Pennsylvania State University Press, 1993), 102.
9. Randolph, *Present State of the Morea,* 17.
10. McNeal, *Nicholas Biddle in Greece,* 99.
11. Randolph, *Present State of the Morea,* 6–7.

12. L. A. Marchard, ed., *Lord Byron: Selected Letters and Journals* (Cambridge, MA: Harvard University Press, 1973), 30–31.

13. George Finlay, *A History of the Greek Revolution* (Edinburgh and London: W. Blackwood and Sons, 1861), 87.

14. McNeal, *Nicholas Biddle in Greece*, 99–100.

15. Edward Blaquière, *The Greek Revolution, Its Origin and Progress* (London: General Books, 1823, reprinted 2009), 65.

16. E. M. Edmonds, ed. and tr., *Kolokotronis the Klepht and the Warrior: Sixty Years of Peril and Daring: An Autobiography* (London: T. Fisher Unwin, 1893), 123.

17. Thomas W. Gallant, *Modern Greece* (London: Arnold, 2001), 12.

18. Rae Dalven, ed. and tr., *Modern Greek Poetry* (New York: Russell and Russell, 1949), 65–67.

Further Reading

Brewer, David. 2010. *Greece, the Hidden Centuries: Turkish Rule from the Fall of Constantinople to Greek Independence*. London: I. B. Tauris.
The author provides a readable account of the wider international context to the condition of Greece under Ottoman rule.

Chaconas, Stephen G. 1942. *Adamantios Korais: A Study in Greek Nationalism*. New York: Columbia University Press.
Korais typifies the Greeks who left Ottoman Greece for western Europe where his intellectual skills made him a leading figure, refuting the prevalent view that the Greek population was composed of simple, uneducated subjects to the Ottomans.

Davenport, R. 1822. *The Life of Ali Pacha, of Janina*. London: Lupton Relfe.
Ali Pacha eked out a small role within the Ottoman governance of Greece from which he expanded his power to become a threat to the Ottoman sultan himself. His life demonstrates clearly how Ottoman rule affected the Greeks. A more recent account is that of K. E. Fleming. 1991. *The Muslim Bonaparte*. Princeton, NJ: Princeton University Press.

Faroghi, Suraiya. 2009. *The Ottoman Empire: A Short History*, translated by Shelley Frisch. Princeton, NJ: Markus Wiener Publishers.
This compact account of the nature of the Ottoman Empire in which Greece was embedded for nearly four centuries is excellent. Although there were differences between regions of the empire, the basic structure of Ottoman rule was similar.

King, Dorothy. 2006. *The Elgin Marbles*. London: Hutchinson.
Discovery of the earlier culture of Greece was a major factor in the support of Europeans in the Greek struggle for independence. One of the more famous Europeans is Lord Elgin (Thomas Bruce, the seventh earl of Elgin) who entered the service of the Ottoman sultan as an ambassador. Knowing the existence of antiquities, he received a permit to excavate and export them. Most notable are the marbles of the Parthenon.

Manthos, Dimitri A. 2008. *Black Was the Night: The Greek Nation as Seen by Foreign Travellers* (1453–1821). Athens: K. Spanos Editions.
An excellent picture of the lives of most Greeks during the Ottoman occupation is shown through the eyes of foreigners who saw those conditions at first hand. This amazing account tracks the identities and reasons for their travels in Greece.

McNeal, R. A., ed. 1993. *Nicholas Biddle in Greece: The Journals and Letters of 1806*. University Park: Pennsylvania State University Press.
One visitor, Nicholas Biddle, traveled through much of Greece during the later period of Ottoman occupation. His account brings the reader into the way of life he encountered – from that of Ali Pasha to Greek villagers.

Randolph, Bernard. 1686. *The Present State of the Morea, Called Anciently Peloponnesus Together with a Description of the City of Athens and the Islands of Zante, Strafades and Sergio*. London: printed by the author and sold by Tho. Basset, John Penn, and John Hill.
This seventeenth-century account is a "photograph" in words. Particularly interesting is the contrast between the Ottoman centers of control and the villages of those controlled.

Vacalopoulos, Apostolos E. 1976. *The Greek Nation, 1453–1669: The Cultural and Economic Background of Modern Greek Society*, translated by Ian and Phania Moles. New Brunswick, NJ: Rutgers University Press.
The period examined is important in demonstrating the increasing role of western Europeans in Greece during the "Dark Ages." The author emphasizes the importance of the Church and local communities as well as the increasing interest of other Europeans in preserving Greece.

9

Building a New State
1821–1935

March of 1821 marked the outbreak of revolt with uprisings in the Balkans and in the Peloponnese. Widespread anguish of living under Ottoman rule drew together all levels of Greek society from the successful Phanariots, to intellectuals who held important positions outside of Greece, to leaders in remote regions of Greece where village families daily felt the brunt of foreign control. The northern effort was led by Alexandros Ypsilantis whose Phanariot family held important commercial positions in Wallachia and Moldavia (united as Romania in 1862). Alexandros, a general in Russian service, raised a force to fight for Greek freedom in the wake of Romanian unrest. While the effort failed – in fact, it was denounced by the Ecumenical Patriarch, Gregory V – it was an impetus for regional revolts that erupted later in March in the Peloponnese. Their leaders included Alexandros's brother, Demetrios, one of the *klephts* who were originally bandits in remote areas contending with the official government but were now freedom fighters. Their numbers included other powerful chiefs like Petrobey Mavromichalis and Theodoros Kolokotronis who, following the revolts, would convene a congress to draft a constitution and establish a government.

While the four sites of revolt were separated by location in the North and the South, their timing indicates coordination. At Areopolis in the south Peloponnese, revolt began on March 17; on March 23, Kalamata in the Mani (the central peninsula of the southern Peloponnese) fell to the Greeks and at Vostitsa along the Gulf of Corinth attackers forced Turkish occupiers to flee that site. Three days later, Ottomans surrendered Kalavrita in the hills where sieges continued for months accompanied by indiscriminate killing on both sides in the Peloponnese and more distant regions. Ottoman reprisals ensued, often in larger communities of Greeks living in Constantinople, Thessaloniki, and Asia Minor. Perhaps as many as 50,000 people, primarily civilians, died in the first years of the struggle.

However, the success in the Peloponnese was a powerful impetus to the Greeks and a National Congress was convened in December of 1821 to plan the future of the new state. The result was a constitution modeled on the French constitution of 1795 and the election of a president, Alexandros Mavrokordatos, a member of one

Greece: A Short History of a Long Story, 7,000 BCE to the Present, First Edition.
Carol G. Thomas.
© 2014 John Wiley & Sons, Inc. Published 2014 by John Wiley & Sons, Inc.

of the important Phanariot families in Constantinople. The new "state" of Greece was minuscule. Defining the territory of the final state remained an issue partly solved in 1947 but, in a sense, the boundaries of Greece remain an issue today.

The following years brought additional military victories for the Greeks: in 1822 the Ottoman flagship was sunk and by 1823 the push for independence was carried into central Greece. Such successes began to draw the attention and help of Europeans, both individuals and states. Outside assistance was critical to the on-going success of establishing an independent state: not only were Turkish garrisons strongly fortified but Ottoman rules forbade subjects to own guns and, generally, Greek technology was extremely limited.

Perhaps the most familiar example of an individual who gave aid is George Gordon, better known as Lord Byron. He had become enamored of Greece during a visit lasting from 1809 to 1811, which produced the words, "If I am a poet, the air of Greece has made me one." The prominence of Greece in his poetry and letters written while he was in Greece reflects the correctness of these words but even greater proof lies in his return to Greece to participate in the War of Independence.

Encamped at Missolonghi on the north coast of the Gulf of Corinth, he led a force of 600 Souliots[1] from Epirus and a remnant of 26 Germans from a larger force. His private funds paid for much of their upkeep and equipment and his leadership was so crucial that he was offered the governor-generalship of all Greece. Spring of that year was exceptionally wet and Byron fell ill with fever and pains; he died on April 19, 1824, fulfilling the vision in his poem entitled "On this day I complete my thirty-sixth year," written in Missolonghi on January 22, 1824. The concluding stanza of the poem shows how Byron viewed fighting for Greece.

> Seek out—less often sought than found—
> A soldier's grave, for thee the best;
> Then look around, and choose thy ground,
> And take thy rest.

His own decision to fight for Greece and his death in that effort symbolize the mounting Philhellenism in the Western world. Britain supported the war effort with a loan of 500,000 pounds. From America, relief supplies valued at some 140,000 dollars were sent to Greece during an eighteen-month period in the late 1820s. In addition to funds and supplies, people set off to follow Byron's example. As this aid demonstrates, Greece had not been forgotten by other foreign powers during the centuries of the Ottomans.

Although the Turkish garrison at Athens had capitulated in 1822, Athens was retaken by the Ottomans in 1826. An effort to free it drew many non-Greek volunteers and a number of them have left accounts of their experiences. Participants described are a veritable example of the vital importance of Philhellenes in the creation of an independent Greece. When Charles Fabvier, a French diplomat and general, came to Greece he was entrusted with the organization of a regular Greek army – 500 regulars and 40 Philhellenes. His countryman Jean Philippe Paul Jourdain, a retired frigate captain in the French navy, volunteered to aid the cause of Athens along with volunteers from Germany. The British held major commands in the campaign: Sir Richard Church as general, Thomas Cochrane, earl of

Dundonald, as high admiral. Ordinary combatants, such as Italian Giovanni Macchia, came from a wide range of Western countries. And there were doctors a-plenty: from America came Samuel Gridley Howe and John James Gerry, from Switzerland Louis André Gosse, and Britain's examples were Henry Joseph Stelle Bradfield and Heinrich Treiber who stayed for the remaining sixty years of his life. His account of the struggle describes 102 Germans as well as 59 Philhellenes from elsewhere who died in Greece. Medical aid was sorely needed as the campaign failed. Athens was finally freed from Ottoman control in 1833, through negotiation rather than battle. Foreign supporters were essential, especially in the early years of conflict, but why were they there? Might another form of outside control continue after the expulsion of the Ottomans?

Military defeat was accompanied by political failure in the first decade of independence. At the second National Congress in 1823, quarrels raged, resulting in two rival governments headed by two rival presidents. The division was especially dangerous since, by 1826, an Ottoman force of approximately 20,000 trained in the techniques of contemporary European warfare pushed hard to recapture Greece. The initial success of the Ottomans drew another form of Western intervention by means of a treaty between Great Britain, France, and Russia – the Treaty of London – for the purpose of aiding the Greeks. A fleet of the outside powers was dispatched to Greek waters. An ultimatum to the Ottoman forces to relinquish the Peloponnese was ignored.

Two British officers, who were invited to command the Greek army and navy, imposed the requirement that their military leadership was contingent on the creation of a single government under a single president. The Greeks agreed and joined the fleet of Britain, France, and Russia, engaging the Ottomans at the Battle of Navarino on October 20, 1827. The Ottoman fleet was almost totally destroyed and 10,000 lives were lost. Greece was freed and recognized as a state although it was not until 1829 that the sultan was compelled by foreign powers to recognize the autonomy of Greece. The territory of the fledgling state included the Peloponnese, a few islands, and, from 1833, Athens. Five years later it would encompass central Greece to the Arta-Volos line. Even though free, the new state owed its existence to the intervention of outside powers and it would require their protection well into the twentieth century.

The necessity of on-going outside support was immediately demonstrated by the first attempt to create a governing structure for Greece. Selected as president to begin this process was Ioannis Kapodistrias. Born on the island of Corcyra (Corfu), he had enjoyed a career in the foreign service of Russia, residing in Paris during the years leading to, and extending into, the war for independence. From his foreign connections, he had been influential in gaining support for outside intervention and, as something of an outsider himself, he had not been involved in the factionalism that had spoiled the second National Assembly and fractured the third National Assembly in 1826. Following the success at Navarino and the agreement made with the British officers who had demanded unity as a condition for their support, the third National Assembly reconvened in 1827. The agenda was two-fold: in addition to the drafting of a new constitution, Kapodistrias was elected to serve as president for seven years.

When Kapodistrias returned to become president with extraordinary power in 1828 he was confronted by monumental problems: the Ottomans remained an immediate military threat and Ottoman Turks were still living in parts of Greece. No formal civil administrative structure existed inasmuch as Ottoman rule had relied on the religious structures of the four *millets* to manage local affairs of its subjects. Consequently, educational, legal, and ecclesiastical systems had to be established. Centuries of Ottoman control and the fighting during the past seven years had left the country unable to provide revenues for governance. Agriculture, the mainstay of the economy, was in a sad condition; fighting had destroyed two-thirds of the olive trees, three-quarters of the vineyards, and nine-tenths of the flocks of sheep and goats. Since olives, grapes, and secondary products of sheep and goats comprised a large proportion of Greek exports, the basis of trade was severely damaged. More than 650 villages had been destroyed, producing masses of refugees. And when revenues did exist, local senates were loath to turn them over to a central government whose structure had yet to be determined and, therefore, was often a suspect institution. Kapodistrias struggled to grant land and provide loans but, not surprisingly, failed to effect solutions that satisfied everyone.

Other would-be presidents were a second major issue. Many who had been directly involved in the fighting were unhappy with the presidency of Kapodistrias on personal grounds. Leaders of local armed contingents, like Kanellos Deliyannis, admitted that, "None of us chiefs of the districts was prepared to place himself under a chief who lacked an armed following of his own. None of us could impose himself on the rest. Everyone was therefore independent of everyone else, since everyone had his own armed men who had joined the struggle from the beginning."[2] His words give a vivid image of the conditions. Kapodistrias was not one of these chiefs; rather, he came from the diaspora Greeks who, while instrumental in gaining aid for the struggle, had not participated in the actual fighting.

A third element was the non-elite, the people who might create a participatory democracy. But what did these peasants know of self-rule after more than a millennium of monarchical governance? Kings and sultans were familiar but there was little if any comprehension of the doctrine of the "inalienable rights of man." Consequently, the leader of the First Republic of Greece had to reckon with more than the nearly insurmountable difficulties of creating a central government. In fact, most of the issues would remain unsolved well into the twentieth century. Moreover, Kapodistrias' earlier career continued to make him suspect in the eyes of many of the now-free people of Greece. He was born on Corfu, which was never under Ottoman control; much of his early career was in the Russian diplomatic service; he had not fought in the mainland revolts but cautioned patience for gaining independence. The Great Powers also had serious concerns about the First Republic: in 1829 Russia, France, and Britain proposed at the Conference of London that Greece should be governed by a king selected by those three nations. Kapodistrias reacted as expected to that decision, fueling tension with the victors of the Battle of Navarino. Internal discord continued, driven both by the natural regionalism of Greece and the slow progress in gaining freedom throughout the territory. Kapodistrias was assassinated in 1831 by chiefs from the Mani and anarchy flourished. The proposal of 1829 by the Great Powers for establishing a monarchy would become fact in 1832.

The urgency of creating a stable government to deal with the strong threat posed by the Ottoman Empire was obvious. Equally evident was the incapacity of Greece to design a participatory form of governance. For more than 2,000 years, Greece had been controlled by a foreign sovereign: from the second century BCE, by the Senate and officials of the Roman Republic and, from the late first century BCE, Rome's emperor and his officials. With the collapse of the Western Roman Empire, Greece did gain self-rule under its own Byzantine emperor but, in 1453, another foreign sovereign, the Ottoman Empire's sultan, was empowered. How, then, could an independent Greece develop a government akin to that of Classical Athens or the modern European states?

The process of constructing a strong structure of government is one of five major issues that were at the core of Greek development for the next 125 years, with even more recent echoes. The monarchy proposed in 1829 was established in 1832; however, reconciliation of monarchy and democracy was not a simple matter. In retrospect it appears to have been impossible. Conflict within the dual government impacted domestic and foreign affairs from 1832 to 1947. And even today a Greek king lives on, albeit in London, perhaps hoping to return to Greece.

Closely related was a second issue that persists today: the role of outside powers in matters that should be the concern of Greeks. In the early nineteenth century, outside powers intervened in the creation of an independent Greek state for several reasons. One strong force was Philhellenism grounded in admiration for earlier Greek accomplishments, while another was their own hostility toward the Ottoman Empire, and recognition that a westward-turning Greece could be a strategic ally.

Another impetus stemmed from a realization that Greece had virtually no infrastructure on which to build a strong state. There was no civil administration or legal code; the Orthodox Church had filled some of the void created by the Ottoman system of control through the *millets* but the Church was not free to enact edicts or laws. Public education was virtually non-existent; the economic base was severely damaged; land ownership had to be defined, especially since the removal of Ottomans from their large estates freed land for reallocation. Greece had not been part of the industrial revolution but, to compete with those states that had felt the results of that revolution, the new state had to be pushed into the modern era. Building this infrastructure is the third persistent issue in the story of modern Greece and outside support was an essential element to its construction.

The identity of countries with powerful influence in Greece has changed over time: other powers than the original *troika* of Britain, France, and Russia became closely drawn into Greek affairs. Different, too, were the natures of their involvement and the impact of their influence. Clearly the influence of Italy, Germany, and Bulgaria during the Second World War was catastrophic. On the other hand, the aid of the Marshall Plan following that war was critically important to the recovery of Greece.

Creation of an infrastructure presupposes a centralized state. However, as we have seen in the force of the environment on human life within it, Greece has been characterized by regionalism rather than a strong central authority over the whole of the territory throughout its long history. Even in Golden Age of the fifth century BCE, the role of Athens in flouting its authority roused the ire of a coalition of other independent *poleis*. The success of those *poleis* in the Peloponnesian War led to the defeat of Athens. Similar localism had been fostered under Ottoman rule, which gave rise to the powerful chiefs who refused to relinquish their local power to a central authority. Overcoming regionalism that has persisted through Greece's long history is a fourth issue that stems from and impacts the other critical concerns.

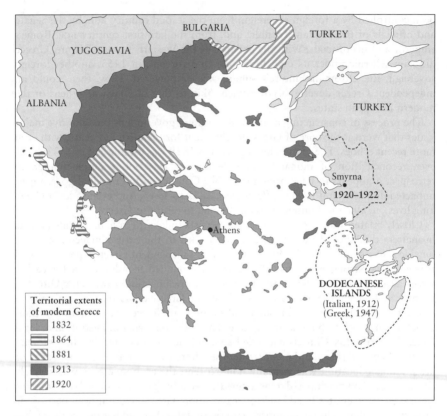

Figure 9.1   Territorial expansion, 1832–1930. Source: Jason Shattuck

And what territory was to be centralized? Definition of the territory constituting the modern state has been a fifth abiding issue since 1821, an issue still not fully settled today. As a result of the victory over the Ottomans, only 50 percent of Greek speakers were included in the new state. Athens was not freed from its Ottoman garrison until 1833. Northern Greek lands, Crete, and many of the islands were controlled by others into the twentieth century. A drive for *enosis*, or the reunion of these various regions, has determined policy from the first half of the nineteenth century to the present. Bringing all the Greek population in the Aegean sphere into a single state became the *Megali Idea* – or Great Idea – driving much of subsequent Greek history.

These five interconnected issues give rise to an encompassing issue: how is Greek identity to be defined? Does the solution exist in territory or ethnicity? How significant are roots to the past by comparison to new developments in more recent times? This chapter and the next will follow these critical issues with the goal of describing the nature of the Greek culture created by the interaction of people with their environment in the five aspects of that interaction.

Enter Otto I

The outside powers who had aided Greece in gaining independence now took a strong role in the creation of a functional state. Its form was to be a monarchy and a king was found in Prince Otto of Bavaria, the son of the ruling Bavarian monarch. Together with 3,500 Bavarian troops to help quell the turmoil and a loan of 60 million francs, Otto arrived in the provisional capital of Nauplion in the eastern Peloponnese in 1833. The king and his government moved to Athens in 1834. However, since the king was still a minor, actual governance rested with a three-man regency, only one of whom had personal experience of Greece through his participation in the struggle for Athens in 1827. The king's father, a practicing monarch, acted as his son's advisor.

Abundant difficulties were apparent from the outset. Although a Philhellene himself, Otto was a Catholic rather than Orthodox Christian. Religion had been the decisive element in one's identity during Ottoman control and it continued to define Greek identity. A Greek king might be expected to follow the Greek Orthodox religion. Nor was the plan for governance likely to engender stability: quarreling that arose between the three regents over their respective powers did not foster stability at the highest level of government. Friction also existed among the supporting allies which, in turn, created factions within Greece as each faction favored one of the three powers. Greeks themselves had a minimal role in their governance (the first Greek prime minister was selected only in 1837), a situation that provoked increasing anger. Volatility was great due to the presence of thousands of armed, former freedom fighters in many parts of the country.

Nor had deep inroads been made into solving the serious economic and social problems confronting Kapodistrias. Destruction of hundreds of villages had produced countless refugees without food or shelter or livelihood since a solution to land distribution had not been found. Although considerable land, formerly in Ottoman hands, was available the plan for its redistribution was inadequate. All Greeks and non-Greeks who had fought in the war, or widows of those fighters, were given credit certificates for the purchase of this national land but conditions were not generous: the amount of credit was adequate to purchase only inferior land, a tax of 3 percent of the value was due in cash at the time of purchase, and the new owner received a thirty-six year mortgage at 6 percent. Moreover, most parcels were too small to provide basic subsistence and vital sources of livelihood had also been destroyed: olive trees, vineyards, and animals. None of these conditions promised strong results for the resuscitation of agriculture and animal husbandry which remained the primary form of livelihood throughout Greece.

No more successful was the plan for creating a national army which was to consist of the existing Bavarian force and a newly constituted Greek force trained and commanded by German officers. "Better to sleep on the mountains in a goatskin cloak as a *Kleft* than to wear the hated Bavarian uniform," was the verdict of the freedom fighter Mavrokordatos. The irregular forces – men who had fought in the initial struggles for independence – were disbanded and a law declared that possession of firearms demanded a license. In spite of the law, armed gangs persisted in raising serious insurrections under way as early as 1834 and 1836.

Organization of civil administration was equally unpopular. Greece was divided into three categories according to size: the largest were 10 *nomarchies*, subdivided into 59 *eparchies*, which, in turn, contained 468 *demes*. The result was more subdivisions than had existed under Ottoman control. *Nomarchs* and *eparchs* were nominated by the king while *demarchs* were appointed by the king from a list of three candidates selected by the wealthiest men in each *deme*. In a land where the tradition of local rule had always been stronger than centralized control, the "management" of local politics from above was hated. Obviously this organization fostered the regionalism due to natural territorial division rather than promoting centralization.

Equally intolerable was the situation of the Orthodox Church. When the Greek Church was severed from the patriarch in Constantinople, King Otto became its head. However, he remained a Catholic, which put him at odds with the majority of the Greek people who were accustomed to following a religious leader who was a major power in the administrative structure of the Ottoman *millets*.

All these tensions collectively were producing growing hostility to the power of the Bavarian (*Bavarokratia*), finally resulting in a coup in 1843 led by the cavalry commander of the garrison of Athens. Although the coup was bloodless, it forced the calling of a National Assembly to draft another constitution. In fact, King Otto had governed without a constitution for ten years. The promulgation of that constitution in March of 1844 produced a constitutional monarchy in which power was shared between the king and his ministers and a bicameral legislature. While members of the lower house, the *Vouli*, were elected on the basis of mass enfranchisement, successful candidates would need the support of the local pyramids of personal power. Members of the Senate, or *Gerousia*, were appointed by the king. It is interesting that both terms had ancient roots: *Vouli* reaching back to the council or *Boule* of Athens and *Gerousia* to the Spartan advisory council. Perhaps those roots meant little to most Greeks of the early nineteenth century but they were one sign of the abiding link between past and present and some hoped to restore more involvement of citizens in their rule. The powers of the king were somewhat restricted and another of his concessions was a promise that his successor would be Greek Orthodox.

The start of the next decade, if not calm, was less fraught with imminent storms. The issue of Otto as head of the Church in Greece was solved in 1850 with the designation of the archbishop of Athens as head of the Church in Greece. In spite of this resolution of one major issue, Otto made his own position more precarious, oddly, by attempting to foster another issue – the goal of bringing all Greeks into the territory of the modern nation. Surely this was a goal of Greeks as well as their Bavarian king. And Greek territory had been more precisely defined by Ioannis Kolettis, a Vlach[3] from northwest Greece who became an increasingly major politician, serving as prime minister from 1844 until his death in 1847. In the struggle between Russia and the Ottoman Empire in the Crimean War, King Otto saw a good opportunity for a new "Crusade" against the Ottomans. France and Britain, concerned about the growing strength of Russia, intervened on behalf of the Ottomans and, in 1854, occupied the Piraeus and ordered Otto to stand down. Rather than gaining higher stature in the eyes of his subjects, he was belittled. Nor had he named a successor. The thundercloud building against *Bavarokratia* burst in the 1860s: an attempt against the life of Queen Amalia in 1861 nearly succeeded; a massive revolt broke out in the port city of Nauplion in 1862; and, shortly thereafter, another bloodless coup forced Otto's abdication.

The extent of territory under the new governance had grown in the decade after the initial revolutions but remained essentially unchanged from 1832 to 1861. And everyday life for most Greeks was little changed since 1821. The land that had been in Ottoman control could be redistributed to Greeks but that land and its resources had been devastated. The population was increasing modestly from roughly 770,000 to 1.1 million and the majority was the class whose subsistence remained working the land with tools that Hesiod would have recognized; the industrial revolution would arrive in Greece only later in the century. Even by 1875, there was little real improvement in the Greek economic sphere.

Reconstruction demanded a territory-wide scheme but regional ties for the Greeks were stronger than national bonds. Contact with the even larger world was non-existent for most of the Greek population. Indirect knowledge as well was limited by lack of formal education. Travelers in many regions of Greece in the late eighteenth and early nineteenth centuries discovered very little formal education. Description of two schools in Athens reported that they had a few books; another account noted a venerable man who sat in front of the door of his home instructing a few boys; and many noted the role of monks and priests as teachers. Yet, proper formal education did exist, often in locations with important political or commercial status. Ali Pasha's important capital of Epirus at Ioannina had two academies; Amphilochia and Pelion, both seaports, possessed considerable Greek schools; Chios, a major island of production and trade, could boast that Chios-town had a large school for 200 boys with a library of 2,000 volumes. Smyrna in Asia Minor was an international city, as the life of Adamantios Korais attests. As described in the previous chapter, his instruction by the chaplain of the Dutch merchant community prepared him for his future career of study in France. Constantinople, with its large and important Phanariot community, was able to educate its young Greek sons. As the life of El Greco demonstrates, Candia on the island of Crete had a flourishing school of painting while that city was under Venetian control. Thus, formal education did exist in major cities but was not widespread throughout Greece.

By contrast, brigandry fostered by poverty was extensive even in populous parts of Greece as English visitors learned in 1870. During an excursion on the plain of Athens the carriages in which the visitors were seated and protected by two cavalrymen were surrounded by twenty-one armed men. Shooting the guards and sending two ladies and a girl back to Athens to collect a ransom, they took the others into the mountains. The capture occurred less than 10 miles from the center of Athens, the nation's capital![4] The brigands – and the reactions of the British and Greek governments – caused an international incident that became known as the Dilessi Affair.

In sum, the interplay of the features stemming from the efforts of humans within their environment had not moved toward greater command but rather suffered decline. In the early attempt to create a modern nation, the nature of the control of central authority was ricocheting throughout every other aspect of life in Greece. The system was responding negatively as the issue of central authority impacted the other aspects of Greek culture. Regionalism was stronger than central authority which also suffered by division between the roles of foreign and Greek powers. The base of subsistence remained agriculture and animal husbandry and there was little stimulus to technological improvement.

1862–1913

The following fifty years of independence brought positive change to the young nation especially in serious attention to the infrastructure. While the five major issues persisted and continued to be intertwined, the greatest strides occurred in improvements to the social and economic conditions which were gradually redressed as an infrastructure was shaped. In the process, centralization made progress in the tug–of–war with local interests. The power of the monarchy persisted in the person of a new king but now the position of the monarch was defined in a constitution. Thus under the new constitution, the state was called a democratic monarchy. To be sure, the two elements continued to clash but the role of the prime minister, now held by a Greek, grew stronger and confrontation between a prime minister and a king could result in the exile of a king. Definition of the territorial configuration of the state became a burning issue but the *Megali Idea* did move forward. Finally, the great powers continued to direct Greek affairs, but the nature of their relationships with Greece altered as the period progressed: Greeks were drawn into larger affairs of their "benefactors" and they now participated successfully as soldiers and statesmen.

After the abdication of King Otto in 1862 a National Assembly was convened to draft a new constitution which was broadcast in 1864. Although far more democratic in character, the government continued to be divided between a king and a parliament. The powers of the monarch were more restricted than they had been during the rule of Otto but still consisted of the power to appoint ministers, dissolve parliament, declare war, and make treaties. Parliament became more democratic with a single body, the *Vouli*, elected by direct, secret ballot from Greek males age twenty-one and older who were property owners or practiced a trade. This body had full legislative powers. Greek citizens also hoped to decide the question of their next king; a plebiscite cast 95 percent of the vote for a son of Queen Victoria of Great Britain. Inasmuch as this would tip the balance of power between the three great powers to Britain, the solution was not acceptable to France and Russia. This and other grounds for disagreement revealed problems associated with the intervention of several major powers: they spoke with three different "voices." Moreover, they attracted differing supporters within Greece: the French "party" attracted military warlords and island ship-owners while the English "party" appealed to urban elements, intellectuals, and Western progressives, and Russian support came from conservatives and small landowners.

An alternative monarch was found in the son of the future king of Denmark, Prince Christian William Ferdinand Adolphus George. Though young, he avoided the mistakes of Otto in matters of religion through his marriage to a Greek Orthodox wife (although he was Protestant), and by agreeing that his successor would be Greek Orthodox. His rule continued from 1863 to 1913. However, even with the new constitution and a more modern monarchy, the political situation remained volatile. In fact, direct election to a single legislative body seemed to increase the play of regional factions: clubs and guilds with roots reaching to a home constituency caused a breathless change of governments. In the decade between 1865 and 1875, eighteen administrations took turns on the carousel of power. An article entitled "Who is to Blame?," referring to this constant revolution of those in power, answered the question boldly by laying blame on the right of the king to dissolve parliament. Each dissolution, it was argued, would cause a rush on the part of many interested parties to create new governments. The author of the article, Harilaos Trikoupis, maintained that only the leader of a majority of members of parliament should be asked to form a new government. King George agreed, albeit reluctantly, and the wisdom of the new provision was demonstrated by greater stability and continuity of policy; only seven general elections occurred through the remainder of the century.

Trikoupis himself directed policy for more than a decade, concentrating on building the infrastructure of the state. He was of a new generation of leaders: not of an age to have been a freedom fighter, rather he studied law in Athens and Paris and then entered diplomatic service in 1856. While serving in Britain he was elected representative of London's Greek community in the Hellenic Parliament and he also aided in the accession of the Ionian islands. Returning to Greece in 1866, he was elected representative of his home, Missolonghi (where Lord Byron had fought for Greek independence), becoming foreign minister then prime minister in 1880.

Inasmuch as agriculture remained the base of the economy, strengthening that base was a key concern, not only to provide for basic subsistence but to support trade in those products. To weld Greece into a cohesive state demanded an investment in the means of more distant communication: roads, trains, harbors, steam ships to replace sailing vessels, and special projects such as the completion of the Corinthian canal in 1893. In the decade of the 1880s the number of roads for wheeled vehicles tripled. In 1869 Greece had less than 9 kilometers of railway – from Athens to the harbor of Piraeus. By 1896 it had expanded to roughly 1,000 kilometers. The rail system was extended to the Greek/Turkish border in 1909 and, in 1916, it linked to Europe.

Public education was another ingredient in the construction of a modern state; local public schools were increased as more boys and girls received a primary education while, simultaneously, opportunities for higher education expanded. It is noteworthy that the University of Athens had been founded in 1837 but far more schools of all levels throughout Greece were needed. Between 1860 and 1900 the number of boys in primary school quadrupled and the number of girls rose ten-fold. University enrollment subsequently tripled.

By the end of the century the population also had tripled, massive social and industrial legislation had been enacted, a legal code promulgated, and participation in the political process included more of the population, even if only loosely through the rise of groups of men in both urban and rural areas who held similar views. These "groups" were the ancestors of official parties. Social and economic distinctions abiding from the Ottoman period had been lessened. Investment in roads and railways served to tie the regions of the nation more tightly together, while ship construction and harbor improvements produced a five-fold growth in maritime trade. Naturally, this construction was costly. Without a strong economy, the main source of revenue came from taxes. As they rose, Trikoupis fell from favor in 1885. Nonetheless, an impressive start had been made and its tempo would increase in the early twentieth century.

Trikoupis' failure to gain re-election was also due to differences of opinion on priorities. By focusing on internal developments, less immediate attention had been given to the question of *enosis* although Britain had ceded the Ionian islands to Greece in 1864. The issue of fuller recovery of territory became more fervent in the last decade and a half of the nineteenth century and the first two decades of the twentieth. Revolutionary societies emerged to achieve this goal. Both the northern boundary, reaching from Arta on the Adriatic to Volos on the Aegean, and Crete were areas of ferment. In 1881, Thessaly and southern Epirus were ceded to Greece by the sultan through the intervention of Britain and Austria, adding nearly 300,000 people and 132,000 square miles to the Greek state.

Although they were impressive additions, they fueled revolutionary hopes in other regions, particularly Crete and Macedonia. Crete's petition for union with the new state in 1839 had been rejected by the great powers and, following that rejection, uprisings on the island occurred sporadically. Those in 1866 and 1896 were particularly serious, resulting in great loss of lives and intense internal division over strategy. After the struggle in 1896, a solution was found in the appointment of the son of King George (also named George) as high commissioner nominally under Ottoman sovereignty. It was not satisfying to the predominantly Greek population of the island as the revolt of 1905 demonstrated, and unrest continued until formal unification occurred in 1913.

Just as much turmoil existed in the North where the northern boundary of Greece now touched Macedonia and northern Epirus, and in both regions conditions were fraught with multiple tensions. These regions were neither unified states nor inhabited by largely single-population groups. In addition, they were claimed by Serbia, Bulgaria, and the Ottomans as well as by the Greeks. Almost continuous conflict prevailed through the late nineteenth and early twentieth centuries. A final effort known as the Balkan Wars found the surprising alliance of Bulgaria, Serbia, and Greece, which produced a combined force of 1.29 million soldiers against the Ottomans. Success went to the allies. In a rush for Thessaloniki, the capital of Macedonia, the crown prince of Greece led the first division to arrive to accept surrender from the Ottoman commander. The Treaty of Bucharest in August of 1913 gave Macedonia to Greece whose territory had now expanded 90 percent since 1880. The *Megali Idea* – the main goal of the young nation – was moving forward. However, the expansion of territory would increasingly involve Greece in more distant relationships with other nations. Developments in both territorial expansion and consequences of outside interests in Greek affairs are encapsulated in the life of Eleftherios Venizelos.

Eleftherios Venizelos, 1864–1936

Eleftherios Venizelos has been described as "the most dynamic figure in modern Greek history" by C. M. Woodhouse.[5] Cecil Woodhouse knew Greece and Greeks well, first as a Classics scholar winning honors at Oxford, later leading in the Greek resistance forces in the Second World War, and, finally, devoting the majority of his writing to Greece. His praise of Venizelos, consequently, has a solid, deep base.

For our purposes, Venizelos' life provides an exceptional picture of the five major issues confronting the young state of Greece. His birth on Crete in 1864 demonstrates why the issue of *enosis* of the Greek territory was a major driving force in his career. Entangled with that effort was the on-going regionalism produced by the physical character of Greece, which regularly resulted in differing opinions about priorities. That division also inhibited the efforts to create a centralized structure governing the entire territory of Greece, whatever its physical extent may have been at particular times. Governance was fraught with conflicts between the two quite different players in determining policy: the monarch provided by the great powers and the Greek arenas of participation. In addition to the role of France, Britain, and Russia in Greek affairs, other great powers were becoming important players. Surely of momental significance was the issue of building and/or rebuilding the infrastructure of Greece: its economy and its social bases of life gravely needed the support of a strong infrastructure, which had improved but then was delayed.

Some progress in strengthening the economic and social structure had been achieved even in Crete in the later nineteenth century. Venizelos was born in the city of Khania, which had been a lively city under Venetian control until 1669. As a member of a professional family, he had a good education completing a degree in law at the University of Athens. His education directed him toward a career as a lawyer and journalist, success now possible for young men but not widespread.

His return to Crete placed him in the increasingly heated struggle for Cretan liberty from Ottoman control. In the uprisings in 1889 and 1896–1897 he became a leading player, arguing for the use of guns *and* negotiations. Following a thirty-day war between Greece and Turkey, conditions for Cretan status improved with the grant of autonomous status albeit still under Ottoman control. Now, however, the king's son, Prince George, was appointed as high commissioner. Venizelos' role in that effort had given him a wide reputation for effective leadership: he became leader of the liberal bloc, participated in drawing up a constitution, and was appointed the first Minister of Justice. However, when little progress toward unification was evident under the direction of Prince George, Venizelos resigned his ministry and, with like-minded followers, raised a revolt in 1905 establishing a "provisional" government in the mountains under his leadership. The critical situation demanded the attention of the Great Powers who forced Venizelos and his followers to yield but they were given promising terms for Cretan independence in the near future. Prince George resigned as commissioner.

Unrest was not limited to Crete. A military coup in Athens in 1909, coupled with violent demonstrations by members of guilds and uprisings by peasants, a fiscal crisis, and loss in faith in King George, produced chaos in the Greek government. In 1910, Venizelos was invited to come to Athens as an advisor. His demonstrated leadership was clear and his anti-monarchical stance was evident; he appreciated the importance of "blocs" of like-minded people. Continuing the *enosis* of Greece was surely predicable during his role of authority in Athens.

More than advisor for the current crisis, he proved to be a powerful, albeit challenged, leader for two decades. Immediately urging the call for a National Assembly to revise the constitution, he remained in Athens and, in the elections in December, was elected prime minister. His new liberal party, called *Fileleftheron* ("freedom-loving"), gained a majority of 300 to 64. His goal of *enosis* was rewarded with Crete

Figure 9.2   Constantine II and Eleftherios Venizelos. Source: K. Kerofilas, Venizelos, 1915/
Wikimedia

and Macedonia being added to the nation under his guidance. As a populist, he turned attention back to the infrastructure that Trikoupis had sought to rebuild: land reform, a national health system, reform of the tax structure, and expansion of education were major issues of his administrations. Knowing that Greece must defend itself, he urged strengthening both the army and navy through compulsory national service as well as by formal training of officers. The successes were not easy due to differing priorities of the king. Venizelos' experience in Crete with the son of the king had been hostile and, in Athens, his relations with the king were even more volatile, especially after 1913, when Constantine succeeded his father, George I, who was assassinated in Thessaloniki.

That city figured prominently in the larger events of the century when Greece, Serbia, and Bulgaria allied to form the Balkan League to take action against the Ottomans. The decision drew in the three European states involved in Greece: Russia played a role in the establishment of the League; the British encouraged Greek participation; and France, initially neutral, joined Russia and Britain in the struggle that flared in 1913. When the Balkan League was successful in March 1913, only constantinople and a single site in Albania remained in Ottoman control within Europe.

The new situation affected most of Europe where, by 1914, two alliances had been formed among the major powers. The Austro-Hungarian Empire shared common interests with Germany while France, Britain, and Russia retained similar perspectives. These new alliances drew members of the Balkan League into a far more extensive sphere of interaction. When forces of the empire of Austria and Hungary responded to the outcome of the victory of the Balkan League by invading Serbia in 1914, the response of other major European powers culminated in First World War. The great powers divided into two alliances; the Triple Alliance of Germany, the Austro-Hungarian Empire, and Turkey; and the Triple Entente of Britain, France, and Russia. Much of the ensuing warfare occurred in the Balkans; the Entente established a front around Thessaloniki extending north and stretching from western Thrace to the Adriatic. Consequently fighting was on-going in this part of Greece until success was achieved by Britain and France (Russia had withdrawn in 1917), accompanied by Greek troops in September 1918.

How and why did these events affect Greece? Internally, they heightened the counter-active roles between the king and the prime minister that became explosive on the question of Greek participation in the First World War. King Constantine had strong views about proper alliances with the greater powers. His brother-in-law was Kaiser Wilhelm II, who pressed Constantine to bring Greece into the alliance with Germany, the Austro-Hungarian Empire, and Turkey. These views did not agree with those of Prime Minister Venizelos and his party who firmly maintained that Greece must ally with its traditional friends: Great Britain, France, and Russia. In the stalemate, Constantine dissolved parliament and Venizelos returned to Crete where he established a provisional government that continued to deal with the powers of the Entente. The crisis was known as the *ethnikos dichasmos*, or National Schism. The years between 1915 and 1923 were a whirlwind of exits and returns of Prime Minister Venizelos and King Constantine and his successors. Often Greece had two governments operating simultaneously from different locations. While conflict between the king and his prime minister was a regular and unsettling occurrence in the young nation, this whirlwind occurred in a far larger context as the Greeks were being mobilized to participate with the Entente along the Macedonian front.

Moreover, the outcome of Greek military participation almost solved the issue of the *Megali Idea*. Nine Greek divisions participated in the victory and, in company of their allies, they entered Constantinople on November 11, 1918. As a consequence of their participation, the Treaty of Sevres of 1920 granted to Greece Thrace, the Gallipoli peninsula, the northern coast of the Propontis, most of the Aegean islands, Smyrna, and northern Epirus. Greece was actually to achieve its full territory. But because of the factionalism at home the prize was lost. Venizelos was defeated in the next election and would no longer play the same strong role in governmental affairs. King Constantine, who had left Greece in 1917, returned, claiming that he had never formally abdicated.

To regain favor, King Constantine pressed for even greater expansion into Anatolia in a massive campaign of 1921–1922. While there were initial Greek successes, quickly the reinvigorated Turkish forces under the leadership of Mustapha Kemal gained an overwhelming victory in Smyrna where, within only a few days, 25,000 Greeks and Armenians were killed and some 200,000 refugees sought safety. Ernest Hemingway reported to the *Toronto Star Weekly* the scene that he had witnessed in Thrace:

All day I have been passing them, dirty, tired, unshaven, wind-bitten soldiers hiking along the trails across the brown, rolling, barren Thracian countryside. No bands, no relief organizations, no leave areas, nothing but lice, dirty blankets, and mosquitoes at night. They are the last of the glory that was Greece. This is the end of their second siege of Troy.[6]

The Treaty of Lausanne of 1923 decided the actual disposition of territory as a result of the conclusion of the First World War and the outcome of Constantine's Turkish campaign. Greece kept only western Thrace, thus virtually defining Greek territory to the present day; only the Dodecanese islands would be included later. Internal consequences of the war were equally traumatic.

1922–1935

The impact of the Anatolian disaster would be long-lasting. With the end of the dream of the *Megali Idea* – at least for many people – Greeks had to seek a different means of fashioning a strong modern state. An answer would only begin to emerge at the end of the century in looking westward into Europe rather than eastward toward Anatolia. However, in the short term, the defeat in 1922 led to another method of uniting Greeks: a compulsory exchange of population brought 1.3 million Greeks to Greece while some 380,000 Turkish residents of Greece were moved to Turkey.

The movement disrupted the lives of those huge numbers of people who were taken from the lands in which their roots were often deep to be were resettled in areas foreign to them. For those who had farmed the fertile soil of Anatolia, settlement in the rocky soil of Greece was gravely disappointing. Some of the Turkish population had become Greek-speakers while many of the Greeks were more conversant with the Turkish language.

At another level, the relocation presented massive problems to the state. With an additional 300,000 refugees from Bulgaria and Russia, the central government was faced with the care of more than 1.5 million new residents, many of whom were both despondent and desperately poor. Greece, too, was desperately poor but relief efforts brought new forms of outside power to alleviate the situation: aid of the Red Cross brought 3 million dollars in the eight months between October 1922 and June of 1923. The League of National Refugee Treasury Fund was also a major humanitarian contributor to deal with the displaced people. The settlement of the refugees produced a change in demography as certain areas – Athens especially – experienced rapid growth in population where many refugees were initially housed in quickly constructed structures. A project of the International Refugee Settlement Commission provided rural land for some of the refugees. However, many were unable to produce sufficient crops and/or animals to remain independent and, consequently, were reduced to the status of sharecroppers. In addition, whole regions witnessed a change in the make-up of population; Macedonia, for example, was heavily settled by the incoming Greeks from Anatolia.

The magnitude of solving basic issues immediately worsened the already fractious nature of the current government which was divided between the royalist supporters of King Constantine and the adherents of Venizelos. In the immediate aftermath of the catastrophe in Asia Minor, eight politicians and soldiers were court-martialed for their "high treason" and six, including the commander of the Asia Minor force, were executed. The Venizelist Party, headed not by Venizelos but by Colonel Nikolaos Plastiras, gained power. King Constantine was forced into exile in 1922 and was succeeded by his son, George II. After a failed royalist coup, King George also fled in the following year. As a result, the divisive interplay between king and prime minister was eliminated for some years. In fact, a plebiscite re-established the republic in 1924.

Although the following year brought a military dictatorship that lasted eighteen months, in 1927 the republic was again re-established and 1928 inaugurated the last Venizelos government, which until 1933, returned a brief period of stability including an agreement with Turkey on respective boundaries. Again a series of attempted coups exploded in 1933 and 1934. Venizelos took self-exile in 1935, first to Rhodes and then to Paris where he died in the following year. Not surprisingly, King George II returned to Greece. The next stage of state formation – and all its turmoil – would then begin.

Notes

1. Souli is located in Epirus. People of this mountainous region are notable for their fighting skills and were often drawn into Greek affairs including this time of struggle for independence.
2. Kanellos Deliyannis, quoted in J. Koliopoulos and T. Veremis, *Greece: The Modern Sequel* (New York: New York University Press, 2002), 13–14.
3. The origin and history of the Vlachs is uncertain. Their language is akin to Romanian and has affinities with Latin. Vlachs have led essentially a pastoral life in northern Greece and the Balkans. The location has produced adoption of Greek language and culture.
4. Denton Snider, *A Walk in Hellas* (Boston: James R. Osgood, 1883), 51. The author notes that, "Clearly brigandage has become a power, a Great Power."
5. C. M. Woodhouse, *Modern Greece: A Short History* (London: Faber and Faber, 1977), 187.
6. Ernest Hemingway, *Toronto Star Weekly*, November 17, 1923.

Further Reading

General Accounts of Modern Greek History

Clogg, Richard. 2002. *A Concise History of Greece*, 2nd ed. Cambridge: Cambridge University Press.
> Excellent, relatively brief account (238 pages) embedded with useful illustrations and discussion of their significance; 19 pages of brief biographies of major individuals; 16 pages of useful documentation.

Gallant, Thomas. 2001. *Modern Greece*. New York: Arnold/Oxford University Press.
> The author follows the themes of Greek identity, the diaspora, relations with great powers, and modernization of society. Specific information on subjects such as demographic and social changes that affected the local populations of Greece is essential for a full understanding of changing conditions.

Koliopoulos, John S. and Thanos M. Vermis. 2010. *Greece: The Modern Sequel from 1831 to the Present*. New York: New York University Press.
> The date of publication allows discussion of more recent events than Clogg's 2002 account. An important element is its setting of Greek history into its larger political and economic environment.

Mylonas, George E. 1946. *The Balkan States: An Introduction to Their History*. St Louis, MO: Eden Publishing House.
> This account of the long and complicated history of the Balkans by a notable archaeologist and art historian of Greece is balanced and clear.

Woodhouse, C. M. 1977. *Modern Greece: A Short History*. London: Faber and Faber.
This British scholar knew Greece well and was a prolific writer on Greek history, primarily in more recent periods. His short history begins with the foundation of Constantinople.

The Struggle for Independence

Dakin, Douglas. 1973. *The Greek Struggle for Independence, 1821–1833*. London: Batsford/ Berkeley and Los Angeles: University of California Press.
The author provides a clear account of the factors that led to the war for independence and developments following the initial revolts in 1821 to the establishment of the governance of outside powers over the recently freed "state."
Finlay, George. 1861. *A History of the Greek Revolution*. Edinburgh and London: W. Blackwood and Sons.
An excellent source that provides accounts written from the perspective of the time of their occurrence.

10

A Player in the Modern World
1935 to Present

The year that brought the self-exile of Venizelos saw the return of King George II after a twelve-year absence during the constant changes of government. His return, however, did not solve the differences with the prime minister who was head of the elected government. The royalist and liberal parties were deadlocked in the election of 1936, with a fledgling Communist Party holding the balance of power. Unable to solve the issues, the king responded in what would become a significant departure, entrusting the power of prime minister to General Ioannis Metaxas whose credentials included a background in an aristocratic family long established in the Ionian islands. His route of advancement had been through the Greek military, after he had trained with the Prussian Guard. That training fostered close links with the royal family which had ties with Kaiser Wilhelm II through marriage. Metaxas rose through the ranks of the Greek army and became acting chief of staff for the royal family. In the whirlwind of the schism between the king and Venizelos, Metaxas resigned that post as well as his military command. He continued to play a political role, albeit minor, until King George returned and soon looked to the loyal royalist Metaxas as his prime minister. In 1936, that title would change to Dictator Metaxas.

The nature of national governance drove events from 1936 to 1941. On-going coups, divided parliaments, a great number of political parties, massive unrest in the army, and great depression through the country had provoked insurgency. In the face of large revolts and the expectation of a massive general strike planned for August 5, King George named Metaxas Secretary of War and then on August 4 declared him dictator. His dictatorship lasted from 1936 to January of 1941.

What level of progress can occur in the major issues of building a functioning modern state in conditions like these? The territorial state had suffered the loss of physical gains in the early twentieth century and faced the necessity to fit more than a million refugees into its boundaries. Assistance of outside powers continued not only by furnishing a king and settling coups but also in financial support for the victims of the population exchange. These demands were immediate; consequently the efforts of the late nineteenth century to build the basic infrastructure would take

Greece: A Short History of a Long Story, 7,000 BCE to the Present, First Edition.
Carol G. Thomas.
© 2014 John Wiley & Sons, Inc. Published 2014 by John Wiley & Sons, Inc.

second, or third, or fourth place. Not only had monarchy not been reconciled with participatory government, but now the existing dysfunctional combination of a monarchy with participatory governance was replaced by a dictatorship. Lacking a strong government, regionalism fostered by the physical nature of Greece would be intensified by lack of support of the administration from Athens. In addition, the role of far greater powers would have terrifying results for Greece in a second world war. Already in 1936, the prospects were glum; and they would decline to the point that the future of a modern state of Greece was doubtful.

An admiration for the fascist regimes of Germany and Italy, fostered in part by Metaxas' military training in Germany, translated into regimentation of both a political and social nature. Parliament was dismissed, the constitution was suspended, political parties and unions were banned, and the communists were actively persecuted with some 30,000 members of the party arrested. On the model of Germany, Metaxas organized associations of young people who would build the third Greek civilization by combining the best of the ancient legacy with Byzantine religion. Economic growth would be simulated through trade with Germany as well as with Britain.

The attachment to Germany and Britain placed Greece in a struggle between the new alliances of powerful states: the Axis powers were initially Germany, Italy, and Japan with other states, including Bulgaria, drawn in later. Opposed were the Allied powers that initially were Britain, France, and Poland with other states, including Russia and the United States, joining soon. This was a repetition of the alignments of First World War with more and new participants. The expansion of players deserved the name – Second World War. Mussolini's goal of recreating the *mare nostrum* of the Roman Empire brought increasing aircraft and submarine activity in Greek waters that hastened Greek efforts of re-armament. On October 28, 1940, Mussolini delivered an ultimatum through his minister to Metaxas that would allow Italian forces to occupy locations in Greece. Metaxas' answer was the famous "Ohi" ("No") to joining the triple alliance between Germany, Austria-Hungary, and Italy. He had received assurance from France and Britain that if Greece resisted the Axis power aggression, then they would provide as much assistance as possible and, in fact, a British expeditionary force arrived in 1940.

Italian forces began to invade through Albania in October of 1940, possessing the advantages of initiative, arms, and troops – ten divisions compared to three Greek divisions. On the other hand, Greeks had the advantage of knowledge of the mountainous environment and it allowed them to achieve a "military miracle," leaving 12,000 Italians dead or wounded and 23,000 taken as prisoners. Greeks suffered 1,200 deaths and 4,000 wounded. Mussolini, who was present to witness the disaster for the Italians, is claimed to have said, "It's absurd, grotesque, but that is how it is. I shall have to ask Hitler to arrange an armistice."

Hitler was less than pleased. No armistice was arranged; rather, German troops marched into Yugoslavia and Greece in April of the following year. Metaxas had died in January of 1941; thus he did not witness occupation of most of the Greek mainland and Crete. German forces held the urban centers of Athens and Thessaloniki, eastern Thrace, and western Crete; Bulgarians controlled much of northern Greece; and Italians held the Peloponnese, Attica, northern Greece, Euboea and other southern Aegean islands, and eastern Crete. Against their combined strength, the combined British/Greek armed forces fell in April 1941.

Figure 10.1   Modern Greece, 1930 to the present. Source: Jason Shattuck

Black Was the Night – D. A. Manthos' account of the conditions during occupation – captures the wretched lives of the Greeks with fearful starkness. Fighting was deadly, with some 870,000 people killed and another 175,000 imprisoned. Some 300,000 Greeks died of the widespread starvation that existed during the occupation. The Nazi solution to the Jewish question resulted in another category of death: from Thessaloniki alone some 50,000 members of the Jewish community were deported to Auschwitz. It is estimated that 87 percent of the total Jewish population lost their lives. About 200 villages with their animals and crops were destroyed as were thousands of buildings; roads, bridges, and 90 percent of the transport system were wiped out; 74 percent of the Greek ships were obliterated. Rebuilding the infrastructure would require a new beginning for whoever governed the region in the future. Missing too was the true Greek government, which was in exile in Egypt while a quisling government cooperated with the occupying powers.

Yet Greeks continued to fight; throughout Greece, most men of military age retreated to mountain eyries as resistance fighters. Elderly and very young men remained in place but they too formed makeshift units, armed with whatever weapons were at hand such as pikes and ancient muskets. Greek forces remained elsewhere: the Greek Navy continued to serve in the Mediterranean while other troops participated in other theaters: for example, the First Greek Infantry Brigade Group was engaged in the Battle of El-Alamein in Egypt where two battles were fought in 1942.

Resistance Fighters

Especially prominent in the resistance were the communists who were growing in number and who were devoted to their mission of expelling the occupying armies. Among their numbers were women who fought alongside men. The role of women not only demonstrated the urgent need for combatants but also pointed to a major future change in the role of women in Greek society. Women had impressive roles in earlier Greek history; some scholars believe that it was a woman who ruled over Knossos in the Bronze Age and Cleopatra VII retained the independence of Hellenistic Egypt after the other successor kingdoms of Alexander had been conquered. However, that level of status had been diminished under Roman control, during the Byzantine Empire, and even more so under Ottoman control.

Severity of the foreign occupation demanded the participation of every able body, female as well as male, and much earlier history provided examples of women's ability to fight for their state. In ancient Sparta women were physically prepared to defend their *polis* and it was even one of their responsibilities. Similar perspectives emerged during the occupation of the Second World War; one fighter reported that she joined the resistance because "there were the conquerors in our country" and "we also had fascism on our soil ... and that had to change." But another motive was "the development of us personally ... as I told you, for women, it was a chance to make things better."[1]

In the longer term, the most dismal circumstances can have positive consequences for the future. At the time, however, the situation throughout all of Greece was hellish. Louis de Bernières in his novel *Corelli's Mandolin* captures vividly the conditions in small villages between troops of Allied powers. By the end of the occupation

> The Germans had killed perhaps four thousand Italian boys, including one hundred medical orderlies with Red Cross armbands, burning their bodies or sinking them at sea in ballasted barges. But another four thousand had survived, and, exactly as in Corfu, the British had bombed the ships that were taking them away to labour camps. Most drowned in the hulls, but those who managed to leap into the sea were machine-gunned by the Germans, and once again their bodies left to float.[2]

By 1943, the Axis powers were not as successful in their Greek campaign due in part to new participants in the conflict and the attacks on German territory by those same participants. America had joined the Allies and American bombing on Germany began in January. In May when the Allies took Tunis, the Germany and Italian armies there surrendered. The Allies then advanced to Sicily in July and their presence compelled the Germans to evacuate in August. The Russian army was advancing into central Europe and the Balkans by the end of the year and by January 1944 the Allies were in Italy. June of that year saw the D-Day landings in Normandy followed by the gradual liberation of France and, thereafter, of other nations under German control.

Confronted by these reversals, the Italians retreated from Greece in 1943 and the Germans withdrew in 1944. In April of 1944 Mussolini was hanged and Hitler committed suicide. In May, the unconditional surrender of all German forces was celebrated and, in October, Athens was liberated. Through the post-war settlements, the Dodecanese islands were integrated into Greece by the Paris Convention of 1947, a positive development for the *Megali Idea* but not a final solution to territorial claims.

Jeanne Tsatsos lived through the occupation of Athens and kept a diary from which she later wrote an account. Her own experience and excellent description allow a reader to sense the mood of Greeks during the war years and, finally, at the time when the enemy suddenly disappeared. On October 10, 1944, she reported that "The whole world is in the streets – how strange! What do they expect to hear? What do they expect to see? The Germans are still here." Two days later, her words virtually shouted "Greece is once more our own." Sadly, however, she worried as early as April: "The war will surely end, and the Allies win. But what will become of Greece?"[3]

1944–1952

When the occupiers withdrew, the Greeks battled one another. Instead of combat with a foreign enemy, factionalism among Greeks produced devastating civil war for the rest of the decade. It arose quickly on the heels of liberation from occupation. Dictatorship disappeared immediately and with its extinction as many as forty-four parties contended for positions of political power. These were not only the traditional conflicts between regional and central authority but were embedded in strikingly different political ideologies introduced from other cultures. Especially significant was the communist ideology, which argued that socialism would provide far better conditions for ordinary people. The communist perspective would appeal to those many ordinary people who, on the heels of the occupation, were in atrocious straits.

Two established parties emerged when the on-going struggle between royal and democratic governance resumed: a royalist/populist party that regularly collided with the liberal/centrist party which had been created by Venizelos. The more recent additions were the socialist and communist parties: the first Marxist socialist party was founded in 1918 and it became known as the KKE (*Kommounistiko Komma Elladas*) three years later. Impoverished elements of the population had been drawn to the KKE early in its history in Greece and numbers were swollen during the occupation. In September of 1941, the National Liberation Front (EAM) was founded and December of that year saw the creation of its military arm (ELAS); both were largely communist. Young men and women secreting themselves in inaccessible mountainous regions had been the major resistance force against the Italians and Germans and they expected to play a role in the restoration of the Greek national state after 1944.

A bid by EAM and ELAS to either absorb or suppress other organizations that had also been active in the resistance was a sensible plan to organize a unified front but, predictably, it was met by opposition from the royalists and centrists. Large-scale conscription by the KKE resulted in even greater fear among royalists and centrists which was sufficient to produce a national government headed by the Liberal Party leader, George Papandreou, who had returned to Athens in October of 1944. There was no king in Athens since King George II had not yet returned to Greece.

Concern about the motivation of EAM and ELAS led the Liberal Party in power to the decision to demand the demobilization of the ELAS forces. Not surprisingly, reaction from the KKE to the new government took the form of an uprising in Athens in December of 1944, critical enough to bring one of the major outside powers to Greece as mediator, in the person of Winston Churchill. An agreement in February of 1945 persuaded the communists to turn over their weapons in return for an amnesty. Although fighting was suppressed for a time, open civil war broke out again in 1946 following the elections in March that gave a victory to the royalists with the Left abstaining. In addition, King George II returned in 1946.

The return of monarchy did not prove to be the stabilizing force expected by the British but rather compounded the difficulties of political fragmentation. Thus it was an element in a third round of fighting that lasted until 1949. Goals were to disband the ELAS force and recreate a Greek National Army under the hero of the Albanian War against Italy in 1940–1941, Alexandros Papagos. That plan produced brutal civil war resulting in the deaths of 160,000 people. In addition, the civil war compelled large numbers of Greeks to emigrate; Australia, Canada, West Germany, and Britain were principal destinations. Also leaving Greece were many of the communists who were pushed by the National Army further and further northward into communist countries between 1949 and 1952.

In addition to removing dissident communists from Greece, either by voluntary or forced means, the government initiated a program of re-educating communists and other left-wing citizens. Some were sent to live on Makronisos, a small, uninhabited island off the west coast of Attica that had served earlier as a place to detain war prisoners. Camps opened in 1947 and continued through August 1950. This solution to political violence was described as purification:

> Like Hera, who according to the ancient legend, by
>   immersing herself
> in the waters of the Kanathos, used to acquire virginal
>   strength and beauty
> in the same way the entrants in the national school of
>   Makronisos are
> cleansed from any spiritual pollution and rust of the soul,
>   and acquire new strength.[4]

Another perspective was reported by Yannis Hamilakis who visited the island in 2004 in the company of a survivor of a Makronisos prison camp. The survivor said that the experience "is something that cannot be described and narrated." Hamilakis continued, "As if to compensate for the fact that he could not describe to me his experience ... he promised to take me to the 'haradra' (ravine) where the barbed wire isolation ward for the 'unredeemable' was, and where he spent much of his time."[5]

The intervention of outside parties, in the form of military support, financial aid, and monitoring of conditions rather than as direct intercession, was essential to the return of a degree of stability under a moderately democratic government in the 1950s. Of immediate relief was the creation of a special commission of investigation within the United Nations to collect information on the trans-border movement of Greek guerrillas. The 767 page report led to the formation within the United Nations of a Special Committee on the Balkans that met from December 1, 1947, to June 1948. Subsequently, an Observer Mission studied and reported the situation on the northern borders through July 1950, noting improvement.

However, the direct role of major powers in Greek affairs continued to be strong and, by mid-century, a new "great" power was assuming management in the place of the earlier "mentors" of Greece, all of whom had been seriously damaged by the Second World War. Britain, whose military and economic aid had been crucial to Greece, announced in March of 1946 that it must end all aid to Greece, given the magnitude of its own problems. Conditions in France were equally desperate following German occupation of that country. Russia had also been invaded by the Germans. In 1947, American president Truman announced the Truman Doctrine to contain communism and the Marshall Plan was initiated to provide aid to war-stricken countries of Europe. That plan brought to Greece 1.7 billion dollars in economic aid and 1.3 billion in military aid between 1947 and 1960. Greece was viewed as a test case for democracy in the struggle between Russia and the United States in the Cold War. As it had been in the past, the location of Greece between East and West made it a pivotal player in the contest of foreign powers. Walter Lippmann stated candidly in the *New York Herald Tribune* of April 1, 1947, that, "We have selected Turkey and Greece not because they are especially in need of relief, not because they are shining examples of democracy and the four freedoms, but because they are the strategic gateway to the Black Sea and the heart of the Soviet Union."

1952 to Present

Whatever the true intent of the aid, Greeks were desperately in need of relief. And the aid began an economic miracle: the country's gross national product gained 7–8 percent annually between 1952 and 1972. That improvement benefited the country in various other major ways as increasing stability allowed for the adoption of a new constitution in 1952. The weak infrastructure was not only repaired but expanded under the guidance of Constantine Karamanlis (1907–1998), first elected as a deputy of the People's Party from Macedonia in 1936, then advancing through significant ministries: Public Works, Social Welfare, Transport, and finally serving as both prime minister and president of the republic. His path to political success was significant for his attention to repairing the damaged, divided infrastructure that had the result of tightening centralization of political authority. Availability of aid from new foreign powers opened fresh avenues of potential growth. The combination of new opportunities and success in utilizing the natural beauty of Greece and its legacy from the past began to draw more and more visitors to the land of Odysseus, Pericles, Socrates, and Alexander of Macedon. Just as travelers to Ottoman Greece were a significant factor in the struggle for independence, visitors in the later twentieth century became a major economic stimulus. In 1987, for example, 6.5 million foreign tourists visited the country – two-thirds of the resident Greek population!

Long-standing problems did continue; it is important to remember the depth of their roots. Vindictive memories from the civil wars of the previous decade, especially directed toward members of the communist parties, were extremely divisive to national unity. And the appointment to governmental positions based on clientship demonstrated the abiding power of regional concerns. Another serious issue was the role that the United States expected to assume in return for its aid. Allying with the monarchy and the right wing, American ambassadors felt free to request resignations of Greek ministers whom they found to be less than pliant to US policy. In other words, it was a newer version of the weight of outside powers' involvement in the rebuilding of Greece since the early nineteenth century.

Karamanlis' success in the Ministry of Public Works, as well as the fact that he had not participated in the disastrous civil war, led to his election as prime minister in 1955; he was reelected in 1956, 1958, and 1961. A new party of his creation – New Democracy (*Nea Demokratia*) – was established on his return to Greece following the fall of the military junta in 1974. The party advocated a pro-western alliance and was opposed to strong royal power. Such advocacy led to another round in the battle between the royalists and the moderates, pitting Karamanlis against, first, King Paul who ruled from 1947 to 1964, and then against his successor, Constantine II.

A different source of conflict arose from the proliferation of political parties stemming from a combination of regional interests and political ideologies. During the reign of King Otto there had been three parties: the English Party, the French Party, and the Russian Party. Under King George I, there were also three parties: the Liberal Party, the Nationalist Party, and the Modernist Party. That same number continued during the reign of Constantine I and George II: the Freethinkers' Party, Liberal Party, and the People's Party. However, from 1924 to 1935 there were sixteen parties, from 1936 to 1946 the number rose to eighteen, up to twenty-eight from 1947 to 1973, and from 1974 it increased to thirty.

While Karamanlis was prime minister the communist and socialist parties had agendas that differed significantly from those of New Democracy. They would be powerfully articulated by Andreas Papandreou who began his career as professor of economics at major universities in the United States on completion of his PhD at Harvard University. Karamanlis' interest in the economic health of Greece led him to invite Papandreou to become head of the Centre of Economic Studies in Athens, a position Papandreou assumed in 1961. But as the Classical Greek philosopher Aristotle knew, a Greek man is a political animal and Andreas Papandreou was no exception to the axiom: he was elected deputy in the parliament in 1964 and was a minister in the government that his father, George, led as prime minister. Karamanlis, in turn, left Greece to live for the next eleven years in Paris.

Although George Papandreou had secured a victory in the 1963 election, governments endured for very short periods of time due to the clash of parties and the seemingly perpetual discord between the prime minister and the king. That clash rose to boiling point in George Papandreou's conflict with the king over the issue of control of the military – did control belong to the prime minister or the king? When the king refused to give matters of defense to the prime minister, Papandreou resigned in 1965. Weak central control coupled with the constant party rivalries severely diminished the efficacy of parliamentary institutions during the next three years as caretaker governments ebbed and flowed quickly. The situation opened a door to other forms of control and, as so often in crises, the military entered that door.

A military coup rendered existing government powerless as a junta of right-wing army officers seized power in April 1967. The young King Constantine II, who had succeeded his father only three years earlier, attempted a counter-coup which failed and he departed the country. Tanks moved through Athens to the main square where their weapons were trained on the parliament building. Major government leaders were arrested or placed under house arrest; the number reached approximately 10,000 people in the coming days. George and Andreas Papandreou were among those arrested.

The ostensible reason for the action was to prevent a communist takeover of the government, a fear which most believe was groundless although the one-time leader of the National Liberation Party was now part of the government. After the new government initially announced popular reforms, including price fixing, increased pensions, and redistribution of land, the colonels soon established a dictatorship whose harsh rule led to a suspension of civil liberties: trade unions were forbidden to meet; newspapers were censored; and alleged communists were arrested. The colonels enjoyed little popularity either internally or internationally – in fact, charges of the violation of human rights were investigated by the European Commission of Human Rights – but even so they retained power in Greece for seven years.

Economic conditions suffered gravely with rocketing inflation and cancellation of foreign investment in Greek projects. These conditions, combined with increasing severity of control, produced the likely reactions. The year 1973 saw a mutiny in the navy, which was suppressed. When students who were protesting at the University Polytechnic were fired on in November of 1973, causing more than twenty deaths, the junta's hold was seriously undermined but not eliminated.

It was the failure of further *enosis* of Greek territory that brought the *coup de grace* to the junta of colonels and drew the intervention of outside powers. The junta planned to dislodge Archbishop Makarios, who had become president of Cyprus when the island won its independence from Britain in 1959. In the plot, the archbishop was to be assassinated and replaced by a sympathizer of the junta who would then proclaim union of Cyprus with Greece. The plot was revealed and Makarios escaped but in the confusion Turkish forces invaded the northern coast of the island. The outcome was the division of Cyprus horizontally into a northern Turkish zone and a southern Greek zone, a situation that still exists today.

The Cypriot crisis ended any legitimacy of the colonels, who agreed to step aside. Karamanlis was asked to return from Paris – where he was said to have been reading Thucydides on the Peloponnesian War of the fifth century BCE – to head a government in 1974. His arrival was greeted by huge crowds of Greeks shouting "*Ephete!*" ("He is coming!"). Soon after his return, a plebiscite decisively rejected the return of the king thereby eliminating one of the perennial issues of Greek political life. King Constantine remained in London. In the restored constitution (that of 1952) the wording "the king" was replaced by "the president." Andreas Papandreou also returned to play an important role in Greek affairs until 1995. Others who had left during the dictatorship came back, bringing with them both the knowledge and skills they had received in other countries that were free from dictatorial rule and the fervor to restore a participatory government.

The leadership of Karamanlis in building the Third Hellenic Republic was judicious; the First Republic was under the leadership of Kapodistrias and the Second that of Venizelos. There was to be no vengeance against the members of the junta; rather, they were tried in official courts and jailed. To dampen the violent factionalism, parties were encouraged to unite in a common effort; many earlier parties joined the New Democratic Party formed by Karamanlis in 1974. Even the Communist Party (KKE) was now recognized as a legitimate participant while the Socialist Party was led by Andreas Papandreou. Its name, even in translation, identifies twin goals: to include all Greeks, especially the previously non-privileged population of Greece, and to end dependency on foreign powers. This legalization opened the door to political participation to a large, previously excluded element of Greek society.

The governing structure of the Third Republic gained a more formal configuration with the separation of powers linked by the coordination of the president. The legislative branch consisted of a parliament of deputies elected by universal, secret ballot by citizens age eighteen and older. The deputies had to be at least twenty-five years of age. The parliament elected the president who had to be at least forty years of age, a citizen for at least five years, and the child of a Greek father or mother. The executive branch consisted of the president of the republic, the government under the prime minister, and the ministerial cadre of specific ministers. The third branch, the judicial, presided over civil and criminal law and, as of 1997, an ombudsman heads a professional staff of more than 100 people that investigate cases presented on signed, written complaints, travel to various cities, and also investigate international cases. These developments laid the foundation for future political refinement. In a new constitution of 1985, the army was prohibited from direction of policy.

Unhappily, party agendas continued to produce far too many elections and swings in policy during the last two decades of the twentieth century. Major players were the New Democratic Party under the leadership of Karamanlis and the Panhellenic Socialist Movement (PASOK) under the guidance of Andreas Papandreou. PASOK would hold power, with Andreas Papandreou as prime minister, from 1981 to 1989 and then, again, from 1993 to 1996. The fluctuating leaders would be forced to deal with all but a single issue that we have been following in this story of Greek continuity; when King Constantine did not return to Greece, the tension between king and prime minister disappeared. However, it was replaced by tension between would-be prime ministers. Conflict of politics provides a continuous theme in Greece throughout the ages.

Although political parties were increasing, the New Democratic Party of Karamanlis and PASOK, under the influence of Andreas Papandreou, were prominent forces. Strong tensions resulting from their differences in policy were intensified by the fact that Karamanlis held the presidency during much of period following the collapse of the junta. While Karamanlis had promoted an official alliance with the European Union (EU), Papandreou was ambivalent, at best. Internal economic practice also differed: Karamanlis counseled cautious expansion and fiscal discipline while Papandreou's governments pursued a highly redistributive policy driven by the goals of PASOK. Clearly the two practices appealed to different sectors of the population and, with many other parties also winning constituents, several elections resulted in no party gaining a sufficient majority. In June 1989, for example, lack of a majority forced the president to declare rotation between leaders of the three main parties and, in 1990, three national elections occurred within a single year.

The internal policy differences were tightly linked to international relations. Karamanlis had been instrumental in the initial association agreement with the European Common Market in 1961 and he later guided Greece toward permanent alliance with the EU in 1981. His New Democracy party sought to work collaboratively with outside powers while the policy under Papandreou was initially adamantly set against alliance. Yet, a grant of 8 million dollars from European Community funds following the inclusion of Greece in the EU reversed Papandreou's opinion at least about certain advantages of alliance with other European states inasmuch as foreign aid from various sources remained essential to the Greek economy, especially in relief programs for the under-privileged. On the other hand, Papandreou was firmly opposed to the direct role of the United States in Greek affairs, even though he had American citizenship and had served in its navy.

Initial progress in economic improvement took a down-turn as inflation rose to more than 20 percent, currency was devalued, and bankruptcy figures grew. Borrowing was essential to raise capital in order to deal with existing fiscal difficulties; with a low public debt in 1981 and membership in the EU, borrowing was not difficult. Initially, membership produced an economic stimulus which, in turn, brought some concord between the two major parties. PASOK and New Democracy maintained their dominant roles in Greek politics, with Costas Simitis becoming leader of PASOK when Andreas Papandreou died in 1996 and, in 2004, with the leadership returning to the Papandreou family through George, son of Andreas. Leadership of New Democracy was assumed first by other seasoned players and, in 2007, fell to Costas Karamanlis, the nephew of Constantine Karamanlis.

Responsibilities of political leaders in the first decade of the twenty-first century were tied to membership in the EU. In 2002 Greece met the requirements for joining the European Monetary Union by reducing its fiscal deficit, increasing labor productivity, and promoting fixed investment under the leadership of Costas Simitis. Akin to Karamanlis before him, Simitis had promoted the alliance with the EU. Sometimes known as the "accountant," he accomplished the conditions for admission to the Eurozone during his eight years as prime minister. From a 10 percent general government deficit in the GDP in 1994, the figure fell to 4 percent in 2000 and in 2006 was at 2.6 percent, under the mandated 3.0 percent of the EU. The economy grew at nearly 4 percent a year from 2003 to 2007 and unemployment fell from 11.4 percent in 2000 to 8.9 percent in 2006. Greece was an increasingly active participant in the world market; it held first place in ship ownership through the importance of its maritime trade. Exports increased: in billions of euros they were 12.9 in 2001 and 16.6 in 2006. Its Standard and Poor's rating rose to A. And, the lure of Greece continued to make tourism one of the major compounds of the Greek economy.

Unfortunately, one outcome of Greece's role in the EU was more borrowing, for debt-funded spending such as the magnificent, and magnificently expensive, 2004 Olympics. The current result of such expenses is the EU bailout of 111 billion euros/147 billion dollars for its most troubled member – Greece. To replay this loan as well as earlier loans required cutting the deficit to less than 3 percent in 2012. That goal was not achieved but the deficit fell to 2.4% in 2013 and 2.3% in May 2014.

Greece in the New World Order

The development of a Modern Greek state posed five colossal issues. It had no defined territory, although it did have a drive to recover what it considered to be its true territorial identity. A "national" Greek governance structure did not exist apart from the *millet* headed by the patriarch of the Greek Orthodox Church. Sense of an infrastructure in the form of physical connections between regions or realization of common qualities other than religion was absent. Centralization resided in a foreign capital that was unknown to most Greeks. An effort to create these new conditions was dependent on the aid of more powerful allies. An assessment of the outcome by the second decade of the twenty first century demonstrates that the solution (perhaps near-solution) of these issues has resulted in a new type of relationship with outside powers. Membership in the European Common Market and then the EU might be that solution but it has created momentous problems for Greece as well as causing an "international crisis." However, membership has included Greece in a new *world* order.[6]

It is tempting to justify and defend Greece because of her long history. Although a powerful player at points in its 9,000 years, the country has been at the mercy of stronger states for much of that time. The most recent of those many phases continued into the last decades of the twentieth century. In 1981, Greece had been freed of the dictatorship of the junta for seven years; a foreign monarch still lived and the possibility of his return existed; foreign kings had come and left and returned often in the nineteenth and twentieth centuries. Foreign aid remained essential to recover from the destruction of the Second World War and the civil war on the heels of the Second World War. Although older foreign powers had largely disappeared from Greek affairs, new powers replaced them by providing assistance along with requirements. The larger world continued to orchestrate the affairs of Greece while Greece had minimal experience of participation in that larger world. Some Greeks realized the need to work with the new circumstances but many did not. Constantine Karamanlis was surprisingly active and effective in his outreach.

By comparison the search for common ties to promote peace and avoid war among European states reached back to the early twentieth century: an alternative to warfare was sought at the end of the First World War but not realized. Subsequently the League of Nations emerged as a force to make war impossible, another goal that did not succeed. Following the devastation of the Second World War, several European countries revived the search for an alternative to war; a direction was identified in economic cooperation. A meeting of the Council of Europe took place in 1949 with representatives from six western European countries. In the following year, the need for deeper cooperation was argued and the European Coal and Steel Committee emerged in 1951. Six years later the European Economic Community was founded to provide a common market that allowed free movement of goods, people, services, and capital among its members. Its objective of developing common policies was accomplished by 1968. From its original northern European orientation, membership included southern European states in the 1980s while central and eastern European states began to join in the 1990s. By 1992, the territory of members was without borders – a new identification of "Europe," although not all states are members even in the twenty-first century. The year 1999 brought a common currency, the euro.

Comparison between the original northern European members and the later southern European members is critical in understanding the current crisis. In the north, industrialization had been expanding since the beginning of the eighteenth century when empires were transformed into national states and there was internal emergence of the role of "common" people in their own governance. Large portions of Greek territory remained within the Ottoman Empire far later than the four initial uprisings in 1821 and the *Megali Idea* still has not been solved. Industrialization in Greece had some momentum toward the end of the nineteenth century but it was interrupted by internal disorder and external war.

The 1947 agreement to return the Dodecanese islands to Greek control virtually ended attempts at expansion – virtually but not entirely. Disputes continue with Turkey over Cyprus and the Aegean islands; with Albania over boundaries; with Balkan states over the new state of "Macedonia." Membership in the EU brings a non-military means of confronting those issues; as of 1975, peaceful settlement of border disputes became a criterion of membership. Prime ministers have actively followed this mandate in pursuing diplomatic relations with potential enemies. However, it is essential to remember how recently diplomacy has been in the hands of Greek statesmen.

For Greece – the poor man of Europe – EU membership has produced an "economic miracle" in part by facilitating technological modernization and by fostering trade without customs for all of its members. Both avenues are essential for a "backward" country to compete with countries far more advanced in the knowledge and diversity of modern economy. For Greece, this ability to compete on equal terms is further impacted by the regionalism that determines the nature of economic production.

Membership in the EU also influences many aspects of infrastructure. Democratization was a goal of the 2007 Treaty of Lisbon and, in light of the empowerment of women in other European countries, Greek women have been drawn more fully into the modern culture through education, professional employment, and as participatory citizens; as a result, their status has risen dramatically. More generally, education is a program of the Council of Europe. A nearly illiterate general population in the late eighteenth and early nineteenth centuries had been a key area for change before EU membership was possible but the growth in public education in the early twentieth century virtually ceased during the Second World War and would not begin to recover for a decade following the withdrawal of the Axis powers.

All of these requirements have expanded the political structure of EU member states. In Greece, the expansion has created an overgrown bureaucracy with, for example, 14,000 separate budget lines by 2009. Greece is also prone to clientism, driven by natural regionalism and the vacillation between political parties and their agendas. The Lisbon Strategy for Growth – launched in 2000 and re-launched in

2005 – provides funds to reform public finance, research and development, the business environment, and labor markets with EU direction. An ability to borrow money and, initially, good credit ratings led Greek politicians to borrow heavily to carry out these reforms. Borrowing was enormous (debt rose to circa 400 billion dollars in 2011) with conditions for repayment. Careful recording and timely repayment is obviously essential. The report of an International Monetary Fund official who was monitoring the Greek records reported, "They knew how much they had agreed to spend, but no one was keeping track of what he had actually spent. It wasn't even what you would call an emerging economy. It was a third world country."[7]

In short, the brief history of the EU has not been without problems either for the collective alliance or for its individual members. Yet its accomplishment is striking. In the view of Robert Kagan,

> The new Europe is indeed a blessed miracle and a reason for enormous celebration. ... For Europeans, it is the realization of a long and improbable dream: a continent free from nationalist strife and blood feuds. ... War between the major European powers is almost unimaginable. ... It is something to be cherished and guarded ...".[8]

The pattern of 9,000 years of its history makes such praise particularly appropriate for Greece. A review of the major periods of that long history reveals the constancy of warfare and its dire consequences for Greece. The end of the heroic Bronze Age is reflected in the Trojan War, now seen to describe the hostilities of the late second millennium BCE rather than a tale of a fictional world. The result was the Dark Age. Recovery led to the glorious Classical Age, nearly destroyed by internal warfare that weakened the *polis* world until it fell to Macedonian control. Alexander's conquest created another age – the Hellenistic – that preserved Hellenic elements albeit in a new form. It succumbed to the Roman legions in increasing warfare in the eastern Mediterranean until the whole of the Hellenistic sphere was incorporated by 30 BCE. Rome's empire attracted others from beyond its borders whose force ended the empire in the West in 476 CE and nearly collapsed the Eastern Empire. The region of Greece was resuscitated with immense effort to become the Byzantine Empire. Its emperors constantly waged war on all fronts and finally failed against the Ottoman armies in 1453. Military cooperation between Greeks and outside powers was the means to revolution to create the modern state of Greece and then to preserve it.

How many of the millions involved in the unending warfare might have wondered, with Achilles, why he was fighting against the Trojans who had never wronged him in any way?[9] The decision to unify with others in the EU was made by an independent government. Momentum to meet the criteria of full membership was steadfast and successful. After 1981, the Greek status of poor man of Europe began to move toward a growing economic presence. That condition has been challenged so that exceptional assistance from the EU has been – and remains – critical. It may not be too late in the present day for participants both in Greece and in other countries, particularly but not exclusively in Europe, to understand that Greece requires deeper education in being modern due to her long history of remarkable achievements in the context of unending struggles.

Constantine and Costas Karamanlis

The careers of two men describe the dilemma of inclusion of Greece in the larger world in the twentieth and twenty-first centuries. The men are related by blood and they represent the pace of their country's role during the past two generations. Constantine Karamanlis was born in 1907 and died ninety-one years later in 1998. His nephew, Costas Karamanlis, was born in 1956 and continues to play a major role in Greek politics. Constantine remains a hero; Costas, as prime minister from 2004 to 2009, struggled with massive issues of debt, natural disasters, and unrest. As prime minister, Costas was the "lightning rod" which brought a plot on his life in April 2008. Members of the same family can be very different from one another in their goals, personalities, and opportunities but the striking differences between this uncle and nephew illustrate nicely the impact of participating in a supra-national organization for a member that has not fully identified its own national structure.

Constantine was born in a village in eastern Macedonia, which was still under Ottoman control. When his schoolmaster father was dismissed from his position in 1904 by the Ottoman officials, his father turned to tobacco production. Constantine's early education was in the single primary school in the village; for secondary education he was sent to live with family friends in a larger village. A move to Athens allowed him to take a law degree at the University of Athens and to practice law for an Italian insurance company. Returning to northern Greece, he opened his own office and engaged in local politics. The 1935 victory of the political party in which he was a member brought him back to Athens as a member of parliament. Immediately, he was introduced to the difficulties of parliamentary procedure when the exiled King George II returned to Athens, dismissed the government, and dissolved Parliament. This pattern would be replayed over the next thirty-nine years of Constantine's political career.

Figure 10.2   Constantine and Costas Karamanlis. Sources: Constantine: Natsinas Family Archive Scanned Photograph/Wikimedia; Costas: EPP Congress Warsaw/Wikimedia. Composite by Jason Shattuck

Events of 1935 led to the chaos that produced the dictatorship of Metaxas followed by the occupation during the Second World War. Normal political participation was impossible for everyone during the next decade. In 1946, the restored Greek government offered Karamanlis the Ministry of Labor. Rebuilding would be long and difficult since the entire country was devastated. However, assets were available through the Truman Doctrine, the Marshall Plan, and the United Nations and Karamanlis accepted the appointment. He rose quickly through several ministries: in 1948, he became Minister of Social Welfare with the responsibility of dealing with 12 million refugees and in 1950 he was appointed Minister of Defense. By 1952, he assumed the Ministry of Public Works. And, in 1954, the Ministry of Communication was added to his positions. In all of these roles, Karamanlis did not sit in an office in Athens devising plans. Rather he traveled the country to learn existing conditions and to fashion an on-going plan for rebuilding the entire infrastructure of the country. By the creation of new roads, massive road improvements, repair of bridges, and development of hydroelectric power to facilitate industrial development, modernization of harbor and airline facilities, his efforts would do much more than repair the devastation of war; they would foster centralization of the hundreds of separate regions that constituted the nation. A newspaper article in *Eleutheria* on October 6, 1953, reported that, "motorists believe he is the only member of the government who actually works."

Karamanlis traveled extensively not only within Greece: for example, to the United States on invitation of the State Department in 1951 and to Istanbul to talk with his Turkish counterpart in the Ministry of Public Works. The results drew the attention of many in Greece. In 1955 when the current prime minister, Papagos, was dying, the king asked Karamanlis whether he would accept the position if the current prime minister would resign. Karamanlis' answer was "no." He would remain loyal to Papagos as long as he lived. Papagos did die in October of 1955 and Karamanlis became prime minister as well as one of a five-member committee of leaders of the successful party. During his first term, 1955–1963, he continued to travel through the country to sustain efforts to strengthen both the infrastructure and, thus, centralization. His early supporters continued to work with him. Yet the jousting between the prime minister and the king became enflamed by 1963. Karamanlis exiled himself in Paris from 1963 to 1974. The outcome for Greece of the political strife was the military junta of 1967 which led to the exile of King Constantine.

With the collapse of the junta in 1974, Karamanlis was asked to return to restore order. He arrived to find thousands of Greeks awaiting his flight at the airport. The king was not invited to return. As prime minister Karamanlis shepherded the creation of a new constitution without a king but with the addition of a president. Karamanlis was elected to his first term of presidency in 1980, continuing into 1985. He played a major role in the 1981 entrance of Greece into the European Community as its tenth member. That achievement, however, roused a constitutional crisis between the two major parties in the 1985 elections. Karamanlis resigned. He was reelected to a second term as president in the 1990 elections.

His nephew Costas Karamanlis followed the political path of his uncle although his route was different in many respects. He was born in 1956 in Athens, which had been freed from Ottoman control early in the nineteenth century, rather than in northern Greece, which remained under the Ottomans into the twentieth century. He too studied law at the University of Athens but then did postgraduate study at the Fletcher School of Law and Justice in the United States. His doctoral degree focused on political science, international relations, and diplomatic history. Like his uncle, Costas was active in a political party – the New Democracy party of his uncle – and in 1989 was elected a member of parliament for New Democracy representing Thessaloniki. His rise in the party was steady: he became a member of its central committee in 1994, president of the party in 1997, and, in the election of 2004, was given the mandate to form a government as prime minister of the victorious party, New Democracy.

That was a bad year: the cost of the Olympic Games in Greece was huge, and the debt stood at 112 percent of GDP. His government inherited bad statistics from the previous government. The educational infrastructure was in jeopardy. *The Economist* of September 11, 2008, reported on "Greece's Government: School for Scandal." The prime minister was the known target; a charge of corruption was brought against Karamanlis.

The comparison of the two men has meaning for the larger issue of the long history of Greece. By tracking the interaction between the people of Greece with their environment over 9,000 years, the difficulty of overcoming physical regionalism to forge a unified state has been prominent. In his chapter on the current Greek crisis ("And They Invented Math") Michael Lewis concludes that "the place does not behave as a collective; …. It behaves as a collection of atomized particles, each of which has grown accustomed to pursuing its own interest at the expense of the common good."[10]

Constantine Karamanlis understood this condition from his earliest years in a Greek village under Ottoman control. The drive for *enosis* was powerful throughout Greece but especially so in regions not yet freed from Ottoman control. He also understood the significance of centralization at a single capital but, at the same time, knew that links from all regions to that capital were essential. Equally important was the direct involvement of central officials throughout all of the country: the government in Athens must not be remote and other. Karamanlis also realized that foreign aid was essential for repair of the devastated country and encouraged association with the concord of European states formed initially to create an alternative to war. Greece, as well as other Mediterranean countries, had not achieved the economic and political level of northern members of the European Community by 1981, a fact so well illustrated by events of the first decade of the twentieth-first century. Costas Karamanlis, sadly, is an example of the consequences on a personal and national and international level.

Attention must be focused on all aspects of the infrastructure and, while organization must be coordinated through a central government, it must be an efficient node of the national structure rather than an unstable behemoth. And it must be led by a person whose interests are determined by the needs of Greece rather than the special interests of a political party. That person should be a Greek citizen; the need for foreign "kings" has disappeared. Perhaps the hope is the same as that of a peasant who lived in Anatolia in ancient times who was asked why he was digging into the ground. His reply was that he was seeking for Antigonus, the companion of Alexander the Great who was given the task of unifying the empire conquered, but not organized, by Alexander.[11] Antigonus nearly succeeded. A modern citizen of Greece might change the name from Antigonus to Constantine Karamanlis.

Notes

1. J. Hart, *New Voices in the Nation: Women and the Greek Resistance, 1941–1964* (Ithaca, NY: Cornell University Press, 1996), 104.
2. Louis de Bernières, *Corelli's Mandolin* (London: Seeker and Warburg, 1994/ New York: Random House, 1994), 359–360.
3. Jeanne Tsatsos, *From the Terrible Edge of the Sword*, translated by Jean Demos (Nashville, TN: Vanderbilt University Press, 1969), 123–124, 99.
4. Cited in Yannis Hamilakis, *The Nation and Its Ruins: Antiquity, Archaeology and National Imagination in Greece* (Oxford University Press, 2007), 215. His source is N. Margaris, *History of Makronisos, Vol 1* (Athens: self-published, 1966), 102.
5. Hamilakis, *Nation and Its Ruins*, 238.
6. Robert Kagan, *Of Paradise and Power: America and Europe in the New World Order* (New York: Alfred A. Knopf, 2003.)
7. Quoted but not referenced in Michael Lewis, *Boomerang: Travels in the New Third World* (New York and London: W. W. Norton, 2011), 44.
8. Kagan, *Of Paradise and Power*, 97–98.
9. Homer, *Iliad* I. 152–155.
10. Lewis, *Boomerang*, 82.
11. Plutarch, *Life of Phocion* 29.2.

Further Reading

Greek history expanded remarkably under the assistance, initially, of England, France, and Russia and, subsequently, by inclusion in even fuller affairs. In addition to gaining a sense of the course and consequences of the expansion, it is useful to see the developments through the participants over time.

A freedom fighter who survived to participate in the formation of a nation:
Kolokotrones, Theodoros. 1969. *Memoirs from the Greek War of Independence, 1821–1833*, edited and translated by Georgios Tertsetes. Chicago, IL: Argonaut.

A Vlach who argued the rights of man, especially the Greeks under Ottoman control:
Woodhouse, C. M. 1995. *Rhigas Velestinlis: The Proto-Martyr of the Greek Revolution.* Evia, Greece: Denise Harvey.

A fortunate and brilliant young man in Smyrna, who was first aided by foreigners who provided the foundation of an extraordinary life in Europe:
Chaconas, Stephen G. 1942. *Adamantios Korais: A Study in Greek Nationalism.* New York: Columbia University Press.

The first president of Greece:
Woodhouse, C. M. 1973. *Capodistria: The Founder of Greek Independence.* Oxford: Oxford University Press.

Replacement by a foreign king:
First attempt: Bower, L. and G. Bolitho, 1939. *Otho I, King of Greece.* London: Selwyn and Blount.
Second attempt: Christmas, W. 1914. *King George of Greece.* New York: McBride, Nast & Co.

A powerful Greek statesman:
Alastos, D. 1942. *Venizelos: Partier, Statesman, Revolutionary.* London: Percy Lund Humphries & Co.

A Greek dictator:
Vatikiotis, P. J., 1998. *Popular Autocracy in Greece, 1936–1941: A Political Biography of General Ioannis Metaxas.* London: Routledge.

The civil war:
>Woodhouse, C. M. 1985. *The Rise and Fall of the Greek Colonels*. London: Grafton.

The restoration of democracy:
>Woodhouse, C. M. 1982. *Karamanlis: The Restorer of Greek Democracy*. Oxford: Clarendon.

Leaving Greece:
>Clogg, R., ed. 1999. *The Greek Diaspora in the Twentieth Century*. Basingstoke: Macmillan.

Looking forward:
>Constas, D. and T. G. Stavrou, eds. 1995. *Greece Prepares for the Twenty-First Century*. Baltimore, MD: Johns Hopkins University Press.

Membership in the European Union: from solution for economic health to crisis:
>Lewis, Michael. 2011. *Boomerang: Travels in the New Third World*. New York and London: W. W. Norton & Company.
>This product of first-hand investigation into the outcome of membership in the EU for Iceland, Greece, and Ireland is clear and sadly engaging. While signs of problems in Greece were visible as early as 1993, they have now reached crisis stage. The situation changes rapidly so one of the best sources of weekly information is *The Economist*.

11

Conclusion
Past and Present

In a "letter from Europe" in 1982, Jane Kramer wrote that "The Greeks have been nearly done in by their history. They have taken cover as folklore caricatures of themselves – a grunting Zorba; a singing, swilling taverna fisherman; a peasant pulling his donkey up the cliff of some pristine Cycladic island; a crone in black, furiously mourning."[1] There is some truth to the assertion since this is the way in which Greek people are often portrayed to others. But it is incorrect to believe that Greeks "have taken cover as folklore caricatures of themselves" as the author of the letter writes. A proper view entails the understanding that a strong sense of the past runs through all of Greek history and permeates modern Greece both physically and ideologically. Reminders of the past are everywhere visible, not only in museums but throughout the country. Supervisors of construction projects know this only too well as when construction of a subway system brought to light thousands of artifacts that had to be "rescued" before the project could be resumed. Such finds may be problematic but they are a source of immense pride. And their care is the responsibility of a major official organization, the Greek Archaeological Service. Their worth is reflected also in national income: millions of visitors come to Greece each year to see the land and its treasures. Among those treasures are the discoveries made in creating the subway system, proudly displayed in the underground reaches of modern technology.

In addition to the force of visible reminders of the past, the essential features of Greek life and culture have persisted from antiquity to the present. A culture – any culture – can be described as a system that has two fundamental parameters: its environment and its human population. This study of the interaction of the people within their physical environment has focused on six major areas: the form of subsistence; technology; social structure; political organization; trade and communication with others; and symbolic aspects. These features constantly interact with one another. Innovation in one area of an existing system can affect and alter all other areas, thus producing a new form of culture.

Consideration of these parameters of Greece is a clear index of the on-going role of the past in subsequent periods of history. The location has remained essentially

Greece: A Short History of a Long Story, 7,000 BCE to the Present, First Edition.
Carol G. Thomas.
© 2014 John Wiley & Sons, Inc. Published 2014 by John Wiley & Sons, Inc.

Figure 11.1   A subway image in Athens. Source: Carol Thomas

the same: a peninsula between the Adriatic and Aegean seas where mountains that comprise 75 percent of the land effectively divide lower plains from one another. In the pattern of autonomy and foreign domination in its long history, recovery of autonomy will reconstitute virtually the earlier territory of an independent Greece. The *Megali Idea* of early modern Greece is the most recent example. The people are recognizably descendants of their ancestors. Recent DNA evidence has given strong proof of continuity.[2] Two common indicators of ethnic types are language and religion. Greeks can look at an ancient inscription and recognize the writing. While the nature of their religious beliefs has changed over time, modern Greeks understand the force of the Athenian words to the Spartans during the Persian invasion of Greece. They ask, how could they betray the Hellenic cause united as they are by kinship, language, and the gods? In the twentieth century, Metaxas – the general who became dictator – identified Hellenism with common language and common religion in much the same way that Herodotus had defined it in the fifth century BCE. Today Greek Orthodox religion is interwoven into the fabric of life of Greeks as worship of the ancient gods was for more than a millennium. Continuity of the sacred nature of particular places even while the religion has changed is a strong feature of Greek culture. Apollo's Delphi often produces awe in visitors of quite different faiths.

Inasmuch as a way of life emerges from the interplay between people and territory, continuity in aspects of life is more likely when there is an on-going bond between the same people within the same space. This continuity in Greece is pronounced in basic subsistence which is grounded in animal husbandry and cultivation of the soil. Both industrialization and urbanization are very recent in Greece. As a result, the traditional way of peasant life has been a feature of much of Greek history. The surrounding presence of the sea – the coastline of Modern Greek territory is between 8,500 and 9,500 miles – turned Greeks toward sailing early in their history and Greek shipping remains a strong feature of its present economy. Resulting contact with other regions has led to Greek influence on other cultures alternating with expanded interest of others in controlling this key location. The prominence of mountains has exercised its force in the political organization of Greece from the ancient past to the present. Regionalism has been difficult, often impossible, to overcome in an attempt to create a centralized state.

Persistence of these characteristics allows us to reinterpret the words of Jane Kramer. The land in which Greek history has been centered tends to produce fishermen as well as conditions in which peasants must aid their heavily laden donkeys to climb the steep mountainsides. Music and song spring almost spontaneously from the Greek language. A sense of the value of life has produced intense mourning in every age of Greek history. The words of Hesiod in his *Works and Days* (circa 700 BCE) would be all too familiar to Greeks under Ottoman control or during much of the modern period. Fifty percent of the poem deals directly with farming and animal husbandry. His advice is to work, then work harder and harder to fill the granary.

The accomplishments of their ancestors were strong motivation to subsequent generations. Hesiod remembered the past ages and he sorely wished to have been born in one of the earlier, glorious times. When Alexander of Macedon led his army of Macedonians and Greeks against the powerful Persian Empire, he was fired by his ancestor Achilles and, in fact, began his campaign at Troy where he is said to have been the first to leap from his ship, copying Protesilaus who had sailed with the Greeks in the Age of Heroes to do battle with the Trojans. Byzantium, a colony settled in the Archaic Age, reclaimed the glory of ancient, independent Greece under its new name of Constantinople, which became the center of governance and religion of Medieval Greece for more than a millennium. The legacy of earlier Greek culture also served as an impetus to Greeks to struggle for freedom from Ottoman control as well as to win aid from foreign powers in that struggle. The full heritage is incorporated into Greece of the present day.

Nikos Kazantzakis shows clearly how the life of one of the most powerful writers in twentieth-century Greece was shaped by the environment and heritage of his country. He was born in Crete in 1883 into a peasant family whose livelihood came from working a small farm, the way of life of the majority of Greeks throughout its long history; only in the past three decades have more people resided in cities than in the countryside. Crete itself was one of the first areas of settled agricultural life in the Neolithic Age and the island produced the first brilliant Aegean civilization in the Bronze Age on the basis of agriculture and stock rearing combined with a strong command of seafaring. The island has been integral to Greece from that time to the present, although it has often been controlled by outsiders drawn to it by its strategic location as well as its resources. Regaining unification with the mainland has been fraught with struggle and death.

One extended struggle took Nikos Kazantzakis from Crete in 1897, the year of a massive uprising against Ottoman authority, to the island of Naxos to study in a school run by Franciscan monks. He continued his education, receiving his degree from the University of Athens. This education began his less formal but enduring study with a number of major figures in various parts of the world. His pursuit of knowledge signifies more than an idiosyncratic personal orientation; the need for cleverness and an ability to make wise decisions runs through Greek history. Odysseus comes quickly to mind: he was not the greatest warrior at Troy but was regarded by many as the cleverest man of the Greek force, even in planning action against the enemy. Athena, famous among all the gods for wisdom, recognized Odysseus as the man preeminent for his counsel. Cultivation of the life of the mind has regularly been a characteristic of Greek culture. Thales, resident of Miletus in Greek Asia Minor, is remembered as the father of philosophy, asking questions about the nature of the world. His effort to understand the nature of the universe inaugurated a stream of inquiries that took something like canonical form in the works of Plato and Aristotle in the fourth century BCE. Plato was especially respected by intellectuals throughout the Byzantine Age – in the fourteenth century Plethon celebrated his role as a neo-Platonist – and Aristotle's legacy was so valued that it penetrated Islamic thought which had rejected much else of Hellenic culture.

Odysseus and Plato and a great many other ancient Greeks traveled to learn and to instruct. Kazantzakis continued this habit, traveling through most of Europe, to Palestine, Egypt, and Russia on several occasions, and, in the last year of life, to China. Greeks have been impelled beyond the Aegean, primarily by sea travel, for a host of reasons. Trade is one, colonization another, and curiosity an important third. Herodotus, the father of history, journeyed far to learn the cause of the conflict between the Persians and Greeks and he learned a great deal more in the process. Alexander the Great and his forces marched to India and back to lay the foundation for the Hellenistic states. While the main driving force of the campaign was conquest, his entourage included philosophers, writers, musicians, actors, and technical experts. It is interesting to remember that specimens of unusual fauna and animals were collected for Aristotle who remained in Greece. When authority passed from Rome to Byzantium, renamed Constantinople, the sea furnished the basis of a lively trade and a means of extension of power. The sea, however, was also an entrance into Greece as the Byzantine emperors learned to their distress from the Normans, Venetians, and the constituents of Crusader parties. Knowledge of, and strength over, the sea is essential to Hellenic independence and integrity as members of the more privileged Greek families who resided in Constantinople under Ottoman rule understood. Their activities in commerce and trade led them to other countries as well as to an important role in Ottoman governance.

To return to Kazantzakis: following his education under the direction of Franciscan monks he spent six months in the isolation of the Mount Athos monastery. Religion was a strong fiber in his being, as his work *The Last Temptation of Christ* shows well. But religious fervor is typical of all periods of Greek culture and, although it has taken different forms, the process of change has been cumulative. Deities familiar from the Classical Age are listed on the Mycenaean tablets that record rich offerings to the gods; religion was woven into the texture of life in the Classical *poleis*; new divinities entered the pantheon of gods in the Hellenistic Age and under Roman control but did not displace earlier deities; the Byzantine Empire was a theocentric Christian state, and during Ottoman control, authority of the Orthodox Church remained the core of Greek culture. Today that same Church is an active presence in the lives of Greek people wherever they may live.

Nevertheless, religious devotion does not prevent active participation in civil governance. Kazantzakis served as a Minister of National Education during the Greek civil war just as priests of Classical deities participated fully in the broader lives of their communities. In the world of the *polis*, being a "political" man entailed participation in every aspect of the community's well-being. Although participation in the politics of monarchy during the Byzantine and Ottoman realms was restricted, local politics at the village level would have been familiar to Hesiod, even though he complained about the politicians of his time as people do today.

The list of Kazantzakis's publications reveals a breadth of interest. His most famous work, *Zorba the Greek*, is set in the time of the First World War although the larger-than-life qualities of Zorba are reminiscent of heroes of the deep past. Akin to the figures of Greek tragedy, Zorba knows that he must confront his world directly – heroically – whatever fate may set in his path. Kazantzakis spent thirteen years writing *The Odyssey: A Modern Sequel* (published in 1938). Past and present intertwine in his works as they do in Greek culture generally.

The enduring power of the Homeric poems is clear. Their creator was, in Plato's estimation, *the* poet.[3] Establishing and preserving the texts of the poems was a major endeavor of Alexandrian scholars, and for many Romans, the *Iliad* and *Odyssey* were sources for their own literature beginning in the third century BCE. Survival in a Christian world required careful reading of Christian sources but Homeric figures were examples of virtues; Byzantine scholars edited and wrote commentaries on their literary inheritance. With the emergence of printing, the first printed edition of Homer, edited by a Greek scholar at Florence, appeared in 1488. Today Homer's poems can be read in scores of languages. An electronic search for references to the *Iliad* produced 4.22 million entries, the *Odyssey* 81.9 million.[4]

From the time of Herodotus to the present, language – both spoken and written – is a major indicator of Greek identity. The language of speech and its written products has been continuous. To be sure, the regionalism of the environment led to a variety of dialects of the language but it was the same mother language. And the purpose of written materials has produced different forms – public/private, religious/secular – and also serious debates. On the other hand, continuity of language produced a continuity of preserved culture reaching back even to that war for the sake of Helen, a "story which is its own excuse for being; so never mind about the history ...".[5] Trust in that "story" has led to a new understanding of its historical validity.

The power of both Homer's and Kazantzakis' *Odyssey* demonstrates the reason for the resilience of Greek culture even when Greek status as a political entity was weak or even non-existent. In the time of troubles in the fourth century BCE, the Athenian Isocrates declared:

> So far has our city distanced the rest of mankind in thought and in speech that her pupils have become the teachers of the rest of the world; and she has brought it about that the name "Hellenes" suggests no longer a race but an intelligence, and that the title "Hellenes" is applied rather to those who share our culture than to those who share a common blood.[6]

The potency of earlier accomplishments affected both Greeks and non-Greeks. In fact, many of the early visitors to Greece while it was under Ottoman control were so stirred by the legacy that they carried elements of its culture home with them, both physically in the form of finds from early archaeological sites and figuratively as influences to be incorporated into their own cultures. Many also returned to aid the Greeks in their revolution against the Ottomans. A dynamic example of the force of Hellenism was joyfully expressed in the modern Olympic Games of 1896 when the Marathon race of 40 kilometers was the sole remaining contest in which a Greek might win. As the Australian runner was moving convincingly toward the finish, a stocky Greek – Spyros Louis, whose "training" had been his job as a water carrier – began to close on the leader. As he ran into Athens, his speed increased and when he entered the stadium, two men joined him: King George and Crown Prince Constantine ran with him to the finish line. We must remember that the king and crown prince were Bavarian!

The modern Greeks are not caricatures of their ancestors; they are products of a deep, enduring tradition. Some years ago I asked a friend – Elena Korakianitou – to

Plate 1   Painting by Elena Korakianitou. Source: reproduced courtesy of the artist. For color details, please see the plate section.

paint a picture that embodied her perception of the country of her birth as well as my perception as a confirmed "Hellenist." The upper two-thirds are a merging of colors. A top band is wheaten, symbolic of the fundamental importance of agriculture. Below are two triangles of rich blue merging with deep purple – the sea and the mountains. A band composed of slightly larger triangles has vivid yellow blending into brighter orange – the various degrees of sunlight. Slender lines travel through the colors, drawing them together. The whole is supported on the solid base of a Doric capital. The sum of the parts defines the essence of Greece through all time (Plate 1).

The revival of the Olympic Games is symbolic of the acknowledged appreciation of the legacy from ancient Greece, not only within Greece but universally. Without doubt, the force of the legacy from the past is immense in the acknowledged brilliance and abiding influence of intellectual and institutional accomplishments. Particularly expressive of the link are these lines from the poet George Seferis:

> I awoke with this marble head between my hands
> Which tires my elbows out. Where can I put it down?
> It was falling into the dream as I rose from the dream
> And so our lives grew one, hard now to be separated.

May the current conservators of that accomplishment tend it carefully.

Notes

1. Jane Kramer, "Letter from Europe," *The New Yorker*, May 24, 1982, 76.
2. Jeffery R. Hughey, Peristera Paschou, Petros Drineas, Donald Mastropaolo, Dimitra M. Lotakis, Patrik A. Navas, Manolis Michalodimitrakis, John A. Stamatoyannopoulos, and George Stamatoyannopoulos, "A European population in Minoan Bronze Age Crete," *Nature Communications*, May 14, 2013.
3. Plato, *Laws* 901A.
4. The discrepancy reflects the function of *Iliad* as a title and of *Odyssey* as a metaphor for a journey as well as a title.
5. Jacob E. Conner, *National Geographic* XXVII, May 1915, 532.
6. Isocrates, *Panegyricus* 50.

Further Reading

Browning, Robert, ed. 1985. *The Greek World: Classical, Byzantine and Modern*. London: Thames and Hudson.
Major scholars have contributed chapters on Greek history and culture that are richly illustrated.
Hamilakis, Yannis. 2007. *The Nation and Its Ruins: Antiquity, Archaeology, and National Imagination in Greece*. Oxford: Oxford University Press.
Through seven specific examples, the author assesses the role of ancient material culture in defining the national identity of Greece after its independence from Ottoman control.
Kazantzakis, Helen. 1968. *Nikos Kazantzakis: A Biography Based On His Letters, translated by Amy Mims*. New York: Simon and Schuster.

The combination of evidence from letters and personal memories of his sister, Helen, bring the reader closer to the subject of the biography.

Vyronis, S., ed. 1978. *The "Past" in Medieval and Modern Greek Culture*. Malibu, CA: Undena Publications.

His article (pp. 23–56) examines "Recent scholarship on continuity and discontinuity of culture: Classical Greeks, Byzantines, Modern Greeks."

Zacharia, Katerina, ed. 2008. *Hellenisms: Culture, Identity, and Ethnicity from Antiquity to Modernity*. Aldershot and Burlington, VT: Ashgate Publishing.

This volume explores the nature of Hellenism from the Archaic Age to the Modern culture of Greece from the perspectives of distinguished scholars in their respective areas of specialization. In the words of the editor, it treats "a vastly complex subject matter in a large diachronic sweep" with the intent "to open up the issue of Greek ethnicity and culture to inquiry through a number of diverse disciplines" that will "contribute to an ongoing dialogue" (17).

Chronology
Major Ages of Greek History

Paleolithic Age in Europe: Migratory patterns; limited human presence in Greece	750,000–10,500 years ago
Mesolithic Age: Temporary settlements	10,500–7,000 BCE
Neolithic Age: Settled villages and food production	7,000–3,000
Bronze Age Mycenaean Age of Heroes	3,000–1,200 1,500–1,200
Dark Age: Collapse of Bronze Age civilization	1,150–800
Archaic Period: Slow reshaping of complexity	800–500
Classical Period: Second age of heroes	500–323
Hellenistic Period: Incorporation into a larger state	323 BCE–30 CE

Greece: A Short History of a Long Story, 7,000 BCE to the Present, First Edition.
Carol G. Thomas.
© 2014 John Wiley & Sons, Inc. Published 2014 by John Wiley & Sons, Inc.

Graecia Capta: Incorporation into Roman Empire	30–476
Byzantine rule: Power returns to Greece	324–1453
Ottoman rule: Conquest by Ottoman Turks	1453–1821
Freedom from Ottoman control: Building a Greek state	1821–1935
Greece in the modern world	1935 to present
Before the Common Era – synonymous with BC	BCE
Common Era – synonymous with AD	CE

Index

Greece: A Short History of a Long Story, 7,000 BCE to the Present, First Edition.
Carol G. Thomas.
© 2014 John Wiley & Sons, Inc. Published 2014 by John Wiley & Sons, Inc.